The Trial of Edward Gibbon Wakefield, William Wakefield, and Frances Wakefield, Indicted with One Edward Thevenot, A Servant, for A Conspiracy, and for The Abduction of Miss Ellen Turner, The Only Child and Heiress of William Turner, Esq., of Shrigley...

Anonymous

The Trial of Edward Gibbon Wakefield, William Wakefield, and Frances Wakefield, Indicted with One Edward Thevenot, A Servant, for A Conspiracy, and for The Abduction of Miss Ellen Turner, The Only Child and Heiress of William Turner, Esq., of Shrigley Par

Trial of The Wakefields for the Abduction of Miss Turner
HTR01216
Monograph
Yale Law Library
London: John Murray, Albemarle-Street. 1827

The Making of Modern Law collection of legal archives constitutes a genuine revolution in historical legal research because it opens up a wealth of rare and previously inaccessible sources in legal, constitutional, administrative, political, cultural, intellectual, and social history. This unique collection consists of three extensive archives that provide insight into more than 300 years of American and British history. These collections include:

Legal Treatises, 1800-1926: over 20,000 legal treatises provide a comprehensive collection in legal history, business and economics, politics and government.

Trials, 1600-1926: nearly 10,000 titles reveal the drama of famous, infamous, and obscure courtroom cases in America and the British Empire across three centuries.

Primary Sources, 1620-1926: includes reports, statutes and regulations in American history, including early state codes, municipal ordinances, constitutional conventions and compilations, and law dictionaries.

These archives provide a unique research tool for tracking the development of our modern legal system and how it has affected our culture, government, business – nearly every aspect of our everyday life. For the first time, these high-quality digital scans of original works are available via print-on-demand, making them readily accessible to libraries, students, independent scholars, and readers of all ages.

The BiblioLife Network

This project was made possible in part by the BiblioLife Network (BLN), a project aimed at addressing some of the huge challenges facing book preservationists around the world. The BLN includes libraries, library networks, archives, subject matter experts, online communities and library service providers. We believe every book ever published should be available as a high-quality print reproduction; printed on-demand anywhere in the world. This insures the ongoing accessibility of the content and helps generate sustainable revenue for the libraries and organizations that work to preserve these important materials.

The following book is in the "public domain" and represents an authentic reproduction of the text as printed by the original publisher. While we have attempted to accurately maintain the integrity of the original work, there are sometimes problems with the original work or the micro-film from which the books were digitized. This can result in minor errors in reproduction. Possible imperfections include missing and blurred pages, poor pictures, markings and other reproduction issues beyond our control. Because this work is culturally important, we have made it available as part of our commitment to protecting, preserving, and promoting the world's literature.

GUIDE TO FOLD-OUTS MAPS and OVERSIZED IMAGES

The book you are reading was digitized from microfilm captured over the past thirty to forty years. Years after the creation of the original microfilm, the book was converted to digital files and made available in an online database.

In an online database, page images do not need to conform to the size restrictions found in a printed book. When converting these images back into a printed bound book, the page sizes are standardized in ways that maintain the detail of the original. For large images, such as fold-out maps, the original page image is split into two or more pages

Guidelines used to determine how to split the page image follows:

• Some images are split vertically; large images require vertical and horizontal splits.
• For horizontal splits, the content is split left to right.
• For vertical splits, the content is split from top to bottom.
• For both vertical and horizontal splits, the image is processed from top left to bottom right.

TRIAL OF THE WAKEFIELDS.

THE TRIAL

OF

EDWARD GIBBON WAKEFIELD,

WILLIAM WAKEFIELD,

AND

FRANCES WAKEFIELD,

INDICTED WITH ONE

EDWARD THEVENOT, *A SERVANT*,

FOR

A CONSPIRACY,

AND FOR THE

ABDUCTION

OF

MISS ELLEN TURNER,

THE

ONLY CHILD AND HEIRESS OF WILLIAM TURNER, ESQ, OF SHRIGLEY PARK, IN THE COUNTY OF CHESTER

———

LONDON

JOHN MURRAY, ALBEMARLE-STREET.

———

MDCCCXXVII

LONDON
Printed by WILLIAM CLOWES,
Stamford Street

PREFACE

THE following pages contain the only authentic and correct Report of this interesting Trial

The singularity of the case—the extraordinary circumstances of forgery, fraud, and deception, which it discloses—the cunning and depravity displayed in the formation of the plot—and the artful wickedness developed in its execution, have excited the most intense interest

It is, in truth, matter of wonder that, at this day, in this country, there should be persons hardy enough (and persons, too, said to have moved in good society) to embark in so atrocious an adventure—to sit down in cool deliberation, and, for the sake of lucre, to form a plot for stealing an innocent, an only child, the heiress to a large fortune!

This trial furnishes an instance of crime which, happily, is but of rare occurrence in England, but which, if suffered to be passed over, even in one instance, would strike deeply at the peace of society in general—it is a case that comes home to every family, and much praise has, very deservedly, been given to Mr Turner for the firmness which he has displayed, in the midst of his affliction, in steadily pursuing the offenders to justice.

In it, too, are involved many important considerations, as regards the present defective state of the law applicable to the crime of abduction It was stated by *Mr Sergeant Cross,* in his opening speech, that the only circumstance which had screened two of the offenders from a charge of felony, was the single fact, that the ceremony of marriage had taken place on the Scotch side of the Tweed—in other words, because the whole offence (the taking and the marriage) had not been committed on *English ground.*

This position of the *learned Sergeant* has created, as it was naturally calculated to do, much surprise in the public mind ; and the great importance of the question induces us to bring it under public notice, in the hope that a speedy remedy may be supplied by the legislature To this end it would seem necessary to state briefly the substance of the statute, and of the cases which have arisen upon it, and then to show their application to this particular case

The statute of the 3d of Henry VII. chap 2. enacts, " That whereas women having sub-" stances, or being heirs apparent, &c., for " the lucre of such substances, have been " oftentimes taken by misdoers, contrary to " their will, and after married to such mis-" doers, or to other, by their assent, or de-" filed—what person or persons, from hence-" forth, that taketh any woman *so against her* " *will unlawfully,* such taking, procuring, or

" abetting to the same, and also receiving,
" wittingly, the same woman so taken against
" her will, knowing the same, shall be fe-
" lony, &c."

By the statute of the 39th Eliz chap. 9 it
was made a capital felony; and it so remained till the passing of the 1st Geo IV.
chap 115, which enacts, that the offenders
shall be punishable with transportation for
life, or not less than seven years, or imprisonment and hard labour.

Now, in order to constitute an offence
within the statute, there must be not only a
taking, but a marriage or defilement—Full-
wood's Case, Cro. Car 485, but it is sufficient if the original taking or the marriage
was against consent, for, if the woman went
with the offender in the first instance, and afterwards was forced to continue with him against
her will; or if she was originally taken by
force, and afterwards consented to the marriage, the offence will be complete. See
also Swendsen's Case, 5 State Trials, 450

1 Hawkins's Pl. Cr. c. 41. 7. 8   1 Hales P. C. 660. , and it has been also held, that procuring a woman to be *inveigled* away by confederates, and then detaining her, is a taking within the statute—Rex v Browne, 1 Ventris, 243   In this case one Lucy Ramsay was inveigled into a coach in Hyde Park—Browne afterwards got possession of her person, and she consented to marry him, upon his telling her, that, if she refused, he would take her to France —He was brought to trial and executed   In Swendsen's case, his confederates had caused one Pleasant Rawlins to be arrested for debt   Swendsen was her suitor, and this step was taken to secure and hasten a marriage   He went to her when in custody, and told her that the only thing that would prevent her from being taken to Newgate, was her consenting to marry him—she consented—the marriage took place, and Swendsen was afterwards tried and executed.

In these two cases the consent was induced

through *fear* In the first, the lady consented for fear of being conveyed to France; and in the latter, for fear of being taken to Newgate So in the case of Miss Turner —her consent was induced through *fear*, not of personal danger to herself, but proceeding from an equally powerful cause,—by the *fear* that, if she refused, her *parent* would be seized by sheriff's officers, conveyed to a prison, and ruined for ever

From the evidence disclosed on this trial, it is quite clear that Miss Turner had never seen or been seen by these offenders ,— that she was, in the first instance, stolen and carried away by means of forgery, deceit, and stratagem, (which in law, as applicable to burglary and felony, is called *constructive force* ,)—that she was afterwards inveigled away on a long journey, under the pretence that these offenders were taking her to her father by his command ;—that she was hurried away, under this persuasion, for a distance of more than one hundred miles,

travelling night and day, in the custody of
the men who had stolen her,—that then the
most artful frauds, misrepresentations and
deceptions were practised, and her fears and
affections for her parent worked upon by these
men, with the most singular cunning and
address,—that she refused to fall into their
plans, or to give any answer till she saw her
father, and yet—that she was still detained—
still carried forward, and ultimately conveyed
to Carlisle;—that at Carlisle her dejected appearance attracted the notice of Mrs Holmes,
the landlady, who went to the carriage to ask
her to alight; that this was prevented by the
principal offender, who put his hand to the
carriage door, and said "No,"—that her appearance also called forth the sympathy of a
respectable lady there of the name of Miss
Curwen, who describes this young creature
as being " the picture of despair,"—that
then a new story was invented by the ab-
ducers —Again were her fears worked upon
in a still more powerful degree The sup-

posed perilous situation of her parent was
represented to her in the most horrifying
colours, they told her that he was concealed
in a back room of the inn, surrounded by
sheriff's officers,—unable to cross the border
into Scotland,—and nothing could save him
but her becoming the wife of one of the offenders ;—nay, she was told further, that her
father had said that, if she ever loved him,
he entreated she would not hesitate !

Can it then be said that these circumstances do not constitute a taking and a marriage " against her will unlawfully ? " these
are the words of the statute   It would be
absurd to contend, that her consent was
not *extorted* by working upon her *fears,*
and her affections for her parent   Was it
not then a marriage, if it can be so called,
against the will—the natural will of this
young lady ? was it not a new will—a consent—induced by fear and alarm,—by fear,
brought upon her innocent and unsuspecting
mind, by acts of intimidation, menaces, and

threats, resorted to by the offenders ' Of this there does not appear to be a shadow of doubt .—and this we conceive is, to all intents and purposes, *force.*

It would, therefore, seem to be quite clear that both the taking, upon the established doctrine of constructive force, and the marriage, were a forcible taking and marriage within the meaning of the act of Henry VII.

But the difficulty to which public attention is more especially directed, and the only difficulty, arose upon a question of venue and jurisdiction. The whole offence was not committed on *English ground*, the ceremony took place north of the Tweed, in Scotland, and, as the law stands, neither the county of Lancaster, nor any of the other counties through which the offenders travelled with their prize, had jurisdiction to try them for felony, merely because the act that *completed* the offence was not done in any of them, but in a foreign state! And on this single ground it was, that the offenders were not indicted for felony, so that, in the present imperfect state of the law, any young female of substance, or being an heiress, might be seized in England, carried forcibly into a foreign state, and there married against her will; and yet the offenders could not be convicted of the crime of felony[1]

Various acts of parliament have been passed, the first in the reign of Edward VI, for remedying the defects which have been found to exist in the law of venue, and it is believed that those defects have been cured, as regards every description of felony, *except the crime of stealing an heiress,* which, from its unfrequency in this country, appears to have been wholly lost sight of

It will be observed, too, that a grave attempt was made on the trial, to establish, upon the authority of the Scotch law, the proceedings at Gretna as a legal contract of marriage. Strange, indeed, would it be, if, under such circumstances, the man who had dared to steal the person of this unfortunate young lady, should, by any branch of law of this United Kingdom, have a title to his booty—to the innocent victim of his crime!

The very able cross-examination of the Scotch Advocate, by *Mr. Brougham*, upon this part of the case, suggests considerations of the most vital importance, and will be read with the deepest interest

But the whole subject seems to require the serious and early attention of the legislature, and it is to be hoped that it will be taken up by some one competent to the task of digesting and bringing to maturity, a measure that will effectually meet the evils, and cure the defects which so glaringly present themselves in this case

THE TRIAL

OF

THE WAKEFIELDS,

&c

At the early hour of seven in the morning all the avenues to the Court were crowded to excess by persons anxious to gain admittance. Numbers of persons of distinction had come from a great distance to be present at the trial, and such was the anxiety and excitement manifested by the great concourse of people assembled, that the instant the doors were opened, the spacious Shire Hall was filled to an overflow. The hour appointed for the trial to begin was nine o'clock, but Mr. Baron HULLOCK took his seat on the bench soon after eight, intending to take a short cause in the interval. The cause list was called over, but the counsel engaged in the different causes had all excuses to make, and nothing was done, except an arrangement for sending a few causes into the other court for trial before Mr. Justice BAYLEY.

B

At half-past eight, Mr TURNER, the prose-
cutor, came into Court, attended by his Soli-
citors, and took his seat next to Mr Sergeant
CROSS   Shortly after, the defendant, EDWARD
GIBBON WAKEFIELD, accompanied by Mr. ED-
WARD WAKEFIELD, his father, Mr. DANIEL
WAKEFIELD (the Chancery barrister), his uncle,
and the Solicitors for the defence, entered the
Court

Counsel for the Prosecution

Mr SERGEANT CROSS,
Mr JOHN WILLIAMS,
Mr. BROUGHAM,
Mr. STARKIE

Attorneys.—Messrs GRIMSDITCH and HOPES,
Macclesfield

Counsel for the Defence.

Mr SCARLETT,
Mr COLTMAN,
Mr PARK,
Mr PATTISON

Attorneys —Messrs DUCKWORTH, DENNISON, and HUM-
PHREYS, Manchester, and
Messrs ELLIS, SONS, WALMSLEY, and GORTON, Lon-
don.

The Prothonotary (WILLIAM CROSS, Esq)
called over the Special Jury Pannel, when the

following gentlemen answered to their names, and were sworn:

SAMUEL MATTHEWS, of Moseley-street, Manchester, merchant

WILLIAM FAIRCLOUGH, of St Vincent-street, Liverpool, merchant.

JOHN LYNCH, of Rose-place, Liverpool, merchant

LEONARD SLATER, of Garston, Esq

HENRY HAMMOND, of Piccadilly, Manchester, merchant

WILLIAM BROWN, of High-street, Garstang, merchant.

ROBERT J. J NORREIS, of Barton-upon-Irwell, Esq

JOSEPH LYON, of Rathbone-street, Liverpool, merchant

RICHARD EDWARD ALLISON, of Croston, Esq

THOMAS WILSON, of Rodney-street, Liverpool, merchant.

RICHARD WALKER RUSHFORTH, of Broughton View Pandleton, merchant.

NICHOLAS DISTILL, of Caznau-street, Liverpool, merchant

After the Jury had been sworn, Mr. Baron HULLOCK ordered the defendants to be called on their recognizances, when Edward Gibbon Wakefield, on his name being called, answered, but William Wakefield was not in Court.

Mr. Pattison-said—Your Lordship knows the circumstances under which Mr William Wakefield is not in court

Mr Baron Hullock —He ought to be in court.

Mr. Pattison —Will your Lordship have the goodness to make an order for that purpose? Your Lordship knows that he has been arrested in a civil action for debt since he came to this place

Mr Baron Hullock —You move for an order to bring him into court?

Mr. Pattison —Yes, my Lord.

An order was made, and he was shortly brought into court in the custody of Mr Higgin, the gaoler of the Castle.

The other two defendants were then called, when it was stated, that Thevenot had fled the kingdom, and that Mrs Wakefield was not under recognizances to appear at the trial

Mr Baron Hullock —Mrs. Frances Wakefield is not bound to appear at the trial, is she?

Mr Pattison —No, my Lord

Mr Baron Hullock. —Very well you may go on, Brother Cross.

Mr STARKIE rose, and opened the Indictment, of which the following is a copy .—

Lanca-shire. { The Jurors for our Lord the King, upon their oath, present, that, before and at the time of the committing of the offences in this and in the second count of this indictment mentioned, Margaret Daulby, Phœbe Daulby, Elizabeth Daulby, Anne Daulby, and Catharine Daulby, by lawful means, that is to say, by the consent, direction,

and appointment of William Turner, esquire, the father of Ellen Turner, a maid and unmarried, had the
order, keeping, education, and governance of the said
Ellen Turner And the Jurors aforesaid, upon their
oath aforesaid, do further present, That, on the seventh
day of March, in the year of our Lord one thousand
eight hundred and twenty-six, at Manchester, in the
county of Lancaster, Edward Gibbon Wakefield, late
of Manchester aforesaid, in the county aforesaid,
gentleman, then and there being a person above the
age of fourteen years; William Wakefield, late of the
same place, gentleman, then and there being a person
above the age of fourteen years; Edward Thevenot,
late of the same place, labourer, then and there being
a person above the age of fourteen years, and Frances,
the wife of Edward Wakefield, late of the same place,
gentleman, then and there being a person above the
age of fourteen years, not having any right or authority whatever to take and convey the said Ellen
Turner out of or from the possession, and against the
will of the said Margaret Daulby, Phœbe Daulby,
Elizabeth Daulby, Anne Daulby, and Catharine
Daulby, unlawfully, wickedly, and injuriously, and
for the sake of lucre and gain, did conspire, combine,
confederate, and agree together, and with divers other
persons, whose names to the jurors aforesaid are unknown, by divers subtle stratagems and contrivances,
and by false representations, unlawfully to take and
, convey, and to cause and procure to be taken and conveyed, the said Ellen Turner, then and there being a
maid unmarried, and within the age of sixteen years,
to wit, of the age of fifteen years, from and out of
the possession of, and against the will of, the said
Margaret Daulby, Phœbe Daulby, Elizabeth Daulby,

Anne Daulby, and Catharine Daulby, then and there having, by such lawful means as aforesaid, the order, keeping, education, and governance of the said Ellen Turner, and unlawfully to cause the said Ellen Turner, so then and there being a maid unmarried, and within the age of sixteen years as aforesaid, to contract matrimony with the said Edward Gibbon Wakefield, unknowing of and to the said William Turner, then and there being the father of the said Ellen Turner, and in life, to the great disparagement of the said Ellen Turner, to the utter heaviness and discomfiture of the said William Turner, and against the peace of our lord the king, his crown and dignity

And the jurors aforesaid, upon their oath aforesaid, do further present, that the said Edward Gibbon Wakefield, the said William Wakefield, the said Edward Thevenot and Frances Wakefield, being such persons as aforesaid, and not having any right or authority whatever to take and convey the said Ellen Turner out of or from the possession, and against the will of the said Margaret Daulby, Phœbe Daulby, Elizabeth Daulby, Anne Daulby and Catharine Daulby, afterwards, to wit on the same day, and in the year aforesaid, at Manchester aforesaid, in the county aforesaid, unlawfully, wickedly and injuriously, and for the sake of lucre and gain, did conspire, combine, confederate and agree together, and with divers other persons whose names to the jurors aforesaid are unknown, by divers subtle stratagems and contrivances, and by false representations unlawfully to take and convey, and to cause and procure to be taken and conveyed, the said Ellen Turner, then and there being a maid, unmarried and within the age of sixteen years, as aforesaid, from, and out of the possession and against the will of the said Margaret Daulby, Phœbe Daulby, Elizabeth Daulby, Anne Daulby and Catharine Daulby, they the said Margaret Daulby, Phœbe Daulby, Elizabeth Daulby, Anne Daulby and Catharine Daulby, then and there having by such lawful means as aforesaid, the order, keeping, education and governance of the said Ellen Turner, to the great disparagement of the said Ellen Turner, to the utter heaviness and discomfort of the said William Turner, and against the peace of our lord the king, his crown and dignity.

And the jurors aforesaid, upon their oath aforesaid do further present, that before, and at the time of committing the offence hereinafter mentioned, the said Ellen Turner was within the age of sixteen years, and a maid, and was the only child and heir-apparent unto William Turner, esquire, he the said William Turner then having substance in lands and tenements, to the value of five thousand pounds by the year, to wit, at Manchester aforesaid, in the county aforesaid · And the jurors aforesaid, upon their oath aforesaid, do further present that the said Edward Gibbon Wakefield, the said William Wakefield, the said Edward Thevenot, and the said Frances Wakefield, well knowing the premises on the day and in the year aforesaid, at Manchester aforesaid, in the county aforesaid, unlawfully, wickedly and injuriously, and for lucre, and for the sake of the said substance of the said William Turner, did conspire, combine, confederate and agree together, and with divers other persons, whose names to the jurors aforesaid are unknown, by divers subtle stratagems and contrivances and by false representations, unlawfully, feloniously, violently and against the will of her

the said Ellen Turner, to take, force and convey away
the said Ellen Turner, and by the aid, procurement,
and abetment of the said William Wakefield, Edward
Thevenot and Frances Wakefield, feloniously and for
lucre, and for the sake of the said substance and
against the will of the said Ellen Turner, to marry
the said Ellen Turner to the said Edward Gibbon
Wakefield, to the great disparagement of the said
Ellen Turner, to the utter heaviness and discomfort
of her friends, and against the peace of our lord the
king, his crown and dignity

And the jurors aforesaid, upon their oath aforesaid,
do further present, that on the same day, and in the
year aforesaid, the said William Turner was seised
of, and lawfully entitled to divers lands and tenements, situate in the county palatine of Chester, and
lawfully possessed of, and entitled to, divers monies,
goods and chattels, to wit, at Manchester, in the said
county of Lancaster, and that the said Ellen Turner
on the same day, and in the year aforesaid, was, and
still is, the only daughter and child of the said William
Turner, and then was an infant, and under the age
of sixteen years, that is to say, of the age of fifteen
years, to wit, at Manchester in the said county of Lancaster And the jurors aforesaid, upon their oath aforesaid, do further present, that the said Edward Gibbon
Wakefield, the said William Wakefield, the said Edward Thevenot, and the said Frances Wakefield, together with divers other evil-disposed persons to the
jurors aforesaid as yet unknown, on the same day,
and in the year aforesaid, at Manchester, in the said
county of Lancaster, unlawfully, wickedly and maliciously, did conspire, confederate and agree together,
by divers false and deceitful artifices, stratagems,

pretences and devices, to cause and procure the said
Ellen Turner, then and there being such infant as
aforesaid, to marry the said Edward Gibbon Wakefield, without the knowledge or consent of the said
William Turner, her said father, he the said William
Turner then (to wit, at the time of the said last mentioned conspiracy) and there being alive, with intent
thereby to obtain and procure for the said Edward
Gibbon Wakefield, divers lands, monies and goods of
him the said William Turner, to the great damage of
the said William Turner, to the evil example of all
others in the like case offending, and against the
peace of our said lord the king, his crown and dignity

And the jurors aforesaid, upon their oath aforesaid,
do further present, that on the same day, and in the
year aforesaid, the said William Turner was seised of,
and lawfully entitled to divers lands and tenements,
situate in the county palatine of Chester, and lawfully
possessed of, and entitled to divers monies, goods,
and chattels, to wit, at Manchester, in the said
county of Lancaster, and that the said Ellen Turner,
on the same day, and in the year aforesaid, was, and
still is, the only daughter and child of the said William
Turner, and then was an infant and under the age of
sixteen years, that is to say, of the age of fifteen years,
to wit, at Manchester, in the said county of Lancaster.
And the jurors aforesaid, upon their oath aforesaid,
do further present that the said Edward Gibbon Wakefield, the said William Wakefield, the said Edward
Thevenot, and the said Frances Wakefield, together
with divers other evil-disposed persons to the jurors
aforesaid as yet unknown, on the same day and in the
year aforesaid, at Manchester, in the said county of

Lancaster, unlawfully, wickedly, and maliciously, did conspire, combine, confederate, and agree *together by* divers false and deceitful artifices, stratagems, pretences and devices, to cause and procure the said Ellen Turner, *then and there being such infant as aforesaid,* to marry the said Edward Gibbon Wakefield, without the knowledge or consent of the said William Turner, *her said father,* he the said William Turner, then (to wit, at the time of the said last-mentioned conspiracy) and there being alive, *to the great disparagement of the said Ellen Turner,* to the utter heaviness and discomfort of the said William Turner; to the evil example of all others in like case offending, and against the peace of our said lord the king, his crown and dignity.

Mr SERGEANT CROSS then rose and addressed the Court and Jury on the part of the prosecution, as follows —

May it please your Lordship,

Gentlemen of the Jury,

His Majesty having been pleased to call his late Attorney-General to a high judicial situation, the duty of conducting this singular prosecution has devolved (I fear unhappily) upon the individual who has now the honour of addressing you, but although that circumstance is a circumstance that is to be lamented, as regards the present proceeding, I cannot help congratulating the public on the elevation of one who has always possessed too commanding an intellect (unawed by political or party feelings) to be the creature of either party, for he is too proud to possess any qualification of that description In that state of manly and dignified independence, I have long had the happiness to know and esteem him , and it is with great pleasure that I witnessed his recent advancement to that high station, which will afford him a full opportunity of serving his country to the utmost advantage, both as a legislator and a judge.

Gentlemen, by the statute law of England, carrying away a young female under the age of sixteen, whether with her own consent or not, from the custody of her parents or instructors, and afterwards marrying her, whether with her own consent or not, is a high misdemeanour, that subjects the offender to five years' imprisonment, and a fine at the discretion of the court, and subjects the female herself, if she consents to such a marriage, to the forfeiture of her inheritance as long as the husband whom she has chosen shall live

Gentlemen, by another statute, stealing away an heiress against her own consent, and afterwards marrying her, whether with her consent or not, is a capital felony , and if that offence had been committed on English ground, two, at least, of these defendants, would, in the due course of justice, have been condemned to an ignominious death, and been executed upon the walls of this Castle twelve months ago! * But, gentlemen, you may be aware, that although England and Scotland form but one kingdom, under one government, they are, for all the purposes of municipal law, still two separate kingdoms, and, therefore, a crime may be begun in England and completed in Scotland, and if so, the law will not completely reach the delinquents. These defendants, therefore, are not now upon their trial before you for a breach of either of those statutes, but they are brought before you, to-day, upon a charge of a conspiracy to commit a violation of both those statutes, and the crime of conspiracy is completed, though the intended purpose should not be executed at all.   The defendants, therefore, stand charged before you, first, with conspiring together, to carry away a young female under the age of sixteen, from the custody of her parents and instructors, and afterwards to marry her to one of the offenders, and they are, secondly, charged with a conspiracy to commit the capital felony to which I have alluded, namely, the taking away an heiress against her will, and afterwards marrying one of the offenders to her.

* The learned Sergeant afterwards said that the capital part had been taken away by Sir James Mackintosh's Act, 1 Geo. IV , but that it was still a felony under the statute

This is the crime for which the defendants are now on their trial before you

Having stated to you the nature of the charge, I will now beg leave to apprise you who are the parties to this prosecution —The prosecutor is a gentleman of the name of Turner, who has, by long and successful pursuits in commercial business in this county, acquired an ample fortune, and some years ago purchased an estate in the county of Chester, where he has resided, and in the course of last year, he filled the high and honourable office of high-sheriff of that county.

Gentlemen, he is the parent of an only child, and his daughter, that only child, is the subject of this proceeding She, at the time this offence was committed, had just passed the age of fifteen—in the month of February, in the last year She was then, I understand, a delicate child She is certainly much grown, as you will see when she comes into court, since that period, and the sixteenth year, you know, is generally an age at which persons of both sexes do grow very fast to maturity.

Gentlemen, one of these defendants is a lady of the name of Wakefield, and this lady, you will find, was the contriver of all this wicked enterprise—the principal contriver of the whole She

had, about three years ago, the chance, I will not
say the misfortune, but she had the chance to go
to Paris in company with a lady of great respect-
ability, a neighbour and acquaintance of her's, re-
siding at Macclesfield. These two ladies went
together to Paris, they stayed some time there,
and returned home   Mrs. Wakefield was then
Miss Davies—at least when she went, but she returned Mrs Wakefield, although that was a circumstance never known to the lady who accompanied her to Paris, or to her neighbours at the
town of Macclesfield, nor, I believe, to the lady's
own father, till after this transaction had become
known   Some time previous to Christmas in the
last year, Miss Davies, who resided at the town of
Macclesfield with her father—a respectable old
gentleman a clergyman and a schoolmaster, persuaded him to take a journey with her to Paris,
and they went there together, and at Paris, it
seems, they met with these two other defendants,
Edward and William Wakefield. She was, in
fact, at that time, their step-mother, although she
was still known only by the name of Miss Davies.
Edward Wakefield and William Wakefield,
though Englishmen by birth, are inhabitants of
the city of Paris, and have their domicile and residence there   Edward Wakefield, the elder of
the two, is a widower, with a family of his own.

William Wakefield, his younger brother, a ba-
chelor, who has been since married, I believe, at
Paris. They formed a sort of society, it seems,
there, which they were pleased to call " the first
society in Europe " In fact, I believe it was a
little *coterie* of ladies and gentlemen acquainted
with each other, who, it seems, designated themselves by this description, and among others was
a lady of the name of Bathurst, who calls herself
a daughter-in-law of the venerable Bishop of
Norwich And this lady, although I don't mean
to say she was actually an accomplice in the criminal conduct of these defendants, has made herself too busy in the transaction both before and
after it was completed. This lady said, in a letter
to one of the defendants, William Wakefield,
" Little did I think when we laughed with Miss
Davies about Miss Turner, and I desired her to
get her for you or him, that Edward would, in
two or three days' time, woo, wed, and carry her
off "

Gentlemen, this conspiracy was hatched in this
little coterie at Paris—there it was that the thing
was first propounded. I don't mean to say that at
Paris they had conceived the foul design of carrying off the young lady by force, or committing
all the frauds that they have practised since, but
there the plot was first hatched. In the course of

a little while, Doctor Davies and his daughter
(still Miss Davies) returned home to Macclesfield.   And then Miss Davies began her operations at Shrigley, where Mr Turner resides.
Mr Turner had resided there, I understand, for
about eight years   The first thing that Miss
Davies did, was to call upon a lady in the neighbourhood, who was a common acquaintance of
both—both of herself and of the family of the
Turners, and she was particularly urgent to have
an introduction to the family at Shrigley.   She
proposed to this lady, that the first time she made
a visit there, she might have the pleasure of accompanying her in her carriage.   The lady as-
sented to this, and the visit was made at Shrigley.
When the ladies got there, they saw Mrs Turner,
the mother of the young lady.   Miss Davies made
many inquiries about Miss Turner, whom, I believe, she had never seen, and of whom she knew
nothing, except that she was an heiress to a large
fortune.   She said, she should be particularly
happy to have the pleasure of her acquaintance
she lamented that, as she was returned to school
the day before, she must wait some time before
she could have that pleasure , but begged, as soon
as ever Miss Turner returned into the neighbourhood, she might have the pleasure of seeing her.
This was her first step.   Then, gentlemen, her

two friends, the two travelled gentlemen, arrived
from Paris at the house of Dr Davies, at Macclesfield. Now you will hardly suppose that two
such persons would be very likely to quit the gay
circles of Paris—" the first society in Europe,"
—for the pleasure of spending a few days with
a country schoolmaster in Cheshire, taking a journey of four hundred miles to get there, and four
hundred to get back. You will, no doubt, perceive they had some more important business to
transact in this country, on their arrival at Macclesfield. Their demeanour left no doubt that
they had taken this long journey for a very different object There they did arrive, however, I
think about the 1st of March in the last year,
and then they began their operations They lived
there as gentlemen Doctor Davies, and his
daughter too (Miss Davies), were highly respected
in the neighbourhood, and they had the opportunity of introducing these two strangers to the respectable families of that town. They rode about
the country for a few days. They rode about the
grounds at Shrigley, and made themselves acquainted with the house and domain they also
visited the residences of the neighbouring families,
and got acquainted with their history. Well,
but it was not an immaterial circumstance that
they should know the person of a gentleman who

C

has had a good deal of concern in bringing these offenders to justice,—the respectable solicitor who conducts this prosecution, and who has for some years transacted the law business of Mr. Turner. Miss Davies and her two friends took an opportunity, one morning, of calling at the office of this gentleman, in the town of Macclesfield She had an excuse to bring him to the door. Mr Grimsditch, the gentleman to whom I allude, came out, and Miss Davies then had an opportunity of showing him She made many inquiries about the Turners, and other neighbouring families in fact, it would seem she wanted also to get from him all the information she could on that subject At another time, she threw herself in the way of Mr. Grimsditch, a few days after this, and asked him further questions about Mr Turner's family. And from him she learnt, at that interview, (this being about Friday, I think, or Saturday,) that he, Mr Grimsditch, would depart for London on the Monday following, and that Mr. Turner, the father, would do the same. That was some important information very material to the purpose now under consideration. She then inquired of Mr. Grimsditch about the state of health of Mrs Turner, the mother. Mr. Grimsditch told her that Mrs Turner had been much indisposed, that she had had an unpleasant

affection of the head (a determination of blood),
but he said, " Between ourselves, in my opinion,
it is a paralytic affection " Now this was an opinion Mr. Grimsditch had communicated to this
lady, and not mentioned (at least, as that gentleman recollects) generally among his friends, but
he did mention that circumstance to her, which
you will find is very material afterwards

In this way they went on from day to day, pick-
ing up all the information they could relative to
Mr Turner's family, and particularly to Miss
Turner herself. On the Sunday, when they had
been there four or five days, Mr Turner being
about to set off for London the following evening,
they took their departure from the Doctor's house
But before they did so the supplies were wanting
—the supplies were wanting, they were urgent
It had not occurred at that time, or probably it
had not occurred that the time was come when the
enterprize could be achieved to the greatest advantage, in consequence of the departure of Mr.
Turner for London on the following evening.
Where was the money to be had ? The stepmother,
Miss Davies, was applied to. She was able to
raise the means on the Sunday morning, and
accordingly, she sent to one of the bankers of that
place, and hoped it would be convenient to him
to transact a little business on the Sunday ; that

she wanted 150*l* for a very pressing occasion ;
that a cousin of her's was arrested and in gaol for
debt, and she did not wish to lose a moment in
finding the means for his liberation   For such a
charitable purpose this gentleman felt it to be
his duty instantly to advance the money Accordingly he took to Miss Davies, and gave her, in
the presence of her two friends, the sum of 150*l* ;
and that money, you will find, was actually ex-
pended in the accomplishment of this wicked
purpose.

In order that I may possess you at once with
what relates to that lady, I will apprize you now
that we shall be able to shew, not only that she
was acting in this business down to the very moment of their departure, but that on the Sunday
evening another of these defendants, a Frenchman,
who cuts a considerable figure in this transaction,
though he is not now upon his trial They having
left Doctor Davies's house on the Sunday evening,
when they had got one stage from Macclesfield,
they sent him back, in order to have some further
communication with Miss Davies   What was the
subject of that communication we are not in a
condition to prove, but you may infer.   On the
Monday morning they proceeded to Manchester,
which is about twenty miles from Macclesfield ,
they had made a circuitous course by way of

Congleton, for some purpose or other, which is
not material to the present inquiry, arrived at
Manchester, Edward Wakefield, William Wakefield, and a Frenchman of the name of Thevenot,
who acted the part of their servant They arrived
at the Albion Inn, in that town, at an early hour
in the morning   One of these defendants, Edward
Wakefield, was introduced there by the name of
Captain Wilson.   They had breakfast, and then
they proceeded to purchase a carriage, they went
to a coachmaker's, and there they met with an old
second-hand green carriage, with a barouche-box
to it, and they purchased it, I think, for the sum
of about 40*l*.   In this carriage they all three set
out together from Manchester for Liverpool, at
two o'clock on the morning of Tuesday.   But
before that I should state to you, that they had,
the preceding evening, again sent the Frenchman
to travel post in a chaise all the way from Manchester to Macclesfield, to have another interview
with Miss Davies.   He accordingly went there,
and remained in consultation with her for a considerable length of time, and then returned in the
same manner that he went, at a very considerable
expense, you will perceive, and therefore for some
very urgent and important purpose.   Now, it was
of the last importance at that critical time, that
they should have the latest intelligence of the state

of the family at Shrigley ; that they should ascertain, for a certainty, that Mr Turner was gone off to London, and that he should be disposed of so as not to be able to interfere to prevent their wicked purpose. The Frenchman came back to Manchester at an hour past midnight, and as soon as he arrived they prepared for their departure. A letter was framed, addressed to the mistress of the school where Miss Turner was, purporting to come from a physician, who was then attending Mrs Turner on a dangerous and sudden illness

Gentlemen, one cannot doubt that the preparation of that wicked fabrication was one, if not the principal, object of the Frenchman's visit to Macclesfield that evening The letter is in these terms · " Shrigley, Monday night, half-past 12, March 6th," addressed to MissDaulby (that is, the schoolmistress.)

" Madam,

" I write to you by the desire of Mrs. Turner, of Shrigley, who has been seized with a sudden and dangerous attack of paralysis (that was what Mr Grimsditch had supposed and suggested to Miss Davies) Mr. Turner is unfortunately from home, but has been sent for, and Mrs. Turner wishes to see her daughter immediately. A steady servant will take this letter and my carriage to you to fetch Miss Turner, and I beg that no time may be lost in her departure, as, though I do not think Mrs Turner is in immediate danger, it is probable she may soon become incapable of recognizing any one Mrs Turner particularly wishes that her daughter should not be informed of the extent of her danger, as, without this precaution, Miss Turner might be very anxious on the journey, and this house is so crowded, and in such confusion and alarm, that Mrs Turner does not wish any one to accompany her daughter.

" The servant is instructed not to let the boys drive too fast, as Miss Turner is rather fearful in a carriage.

" I am, Madam,

" Your obedient servant,

" JOHN AINSWORTH, M.D."

" The best thing to be said to Miss Turner is, that Mrs. Turner wishes to have her home rather sooner, for the approaching removal to the new house, and his servant is instructed to give no other reason, in case Miss Turner should ask him any questions Mrs. Turner is anxious that her daughter should not be frightened, and trusts to your judgment to prevent it She also desires me to add, that her sister, or niece, or myself, should she continue unable, will not fail to write to you by the post."

Gentlemen, I need not tell you this was an infamous fabrication from the beginning to the end. There was no such person as a physician of the name of Ainsworth. There was no such sickness as required the attendance of the daughter; but there was just as much truth as they could pick up, in order to give an air of probability to the story. Miss Turner had had a previous indisposition, and Mr. Turner was actually gone to town about the time that Thevenot, the other of the conspirators, was in attendance at Macclesfield, in consultation with Miss Davies.

Gentlemen, from Manchester, at the early hour of two o'clock, that letter bearing date half-past 12—at the early hour of two o'clock on the Tuesday morning, the three parties set out together—namely, the two Wakefields and the Frenchman. They set out in their newly-purchased carriage, and made the best of their way to Liverpool. William Wakefield was left behind half way from Manchester, at Warrington: the other two proceeded on to Liverpool, immediately to the school; Edward Wakefield, however, getting out of the carriage shortly before it came in sight of the school, and the servant, sitting upon the box, went with the empty carriage to the door of the school. The letter was sent into the house—the letter, such as you have just now heard,—well calculated to impose upon any one The servant was called into the house. They asked him questions, and he stated that he was Mr. Turner's own servant; that he had only been lately hired by him, and therefore he was a stranger to them, that the carriage was not her father's carriage, but that it belonged to the Doctor, who wrote the letter, and that on his way to Shrigley he was to take up a physician, a Dr Hull, at Manchester. All this seemed fair and plausible. No doubt came across the mind of any one of the Miss Daulbys about the truth or reality of this proceeding They are persons of experience. Their first object is, to take peculiar care of the persons of the young ladies that are entrusted to them And you will not for a moment suppose, that if they had had the least idea of the guilty purpose for which that letter was written, that they would have parted with their innocent charge They were persons of experience, I say; and now the matter is over, every body wonders how they could suffer themselves to be so imposed upon

Gentlemen, the poet has well expressed the situation of persons in that condition —

" For oft when Wisdom wakes,
　Suspicion sleeps at Wisdom's gate,
　And to Simplicity resigns her charge,
　Thinking no wrong where no wrong seems."

Under such impressions as these, it was that the Miss Daulbys, who have ever since been plunged in the deepest affliction for the misfortune that then befel them, resigned their charge to a set of swindlers

Gentlemen, the Frenchman set off with his prize Edward Wakefield, perhaps by some unaccountable blundering, I don't know why, but he missed them, and had to pursue the expedition by himself till he got to Warrington At Warrington, I have told you, William Wakefield was left behind. There he was waiting in great anxiety the result of this enterprize. And he waited till the carriage arrived at the door of the inn to change horses. He there saw that the prize was carried off He there held a consultation with the Frenchman privately. He was at a loss to know what had become of his brother ; he was very anxious for his arrival, and he thought the best way would be to proceed towards Liverpool in search of him. But before he did so, he sat down and wrote a letter addressed to his brother, and left it at the inn, in order that he might receive it, in case he arrived there first ; and then he set off towards Liverpool to meet him They did meet, but it happened they did not return to the same inn, and so the letter was left behind, and they have

never called for it since, and here it is This
is addressed, I should tell you, to Capt Wilson,
that is the name which, for this purpose,—I don't
know whether for any other,—the defendant,
Edw. Wakefield, had assumed. He purchased
his carriage in that name, he appeared at Manchester under that name; and he is addressed by
the name of Capt Wilson by his brother upon
this occasion " Go immediately to where we
dined yesterday." Then there is a short French
expression " She must be made to expect her
father, she is to wait for her father She has
just left this place at 11 o'clock " That was the
time when they changed horses He had not
gone far towards Liverpool when the two brothers
met, and they immediately made the best of their
way to Manchester, the Frenchman having arrived with the young lady some time before At
Warrington, William Wakefield had a good deal
of conversation with his confederate, the Frenchman, and it was arranged between them how
they should wile away their time at Manchester
until the two Wakefields came up. That you see
is the purpose. The Frenchman was to tell the
young lady she was to wait until her father
should come to see her He was to meet her
there Her mother, she was given to understand, was ill, though they took care not to alarm

her by telling her it was a dangerous illness.
She wished to go out to see an uncle of her's,
who lived hard by That would have defeated
the whole; but the Frenchman had the dexterity
to throw in with great readiness, "You will miss
your father, if you do, for I expect him here
every minute;" he personating the servant of
her father. "Don't go (he said), your father will
be here directly."

Now, gentlemen, down to that moment the
young lady had never seen or heard of either
Edward or William Wakefield—never! She
was shown into a parlour at the inn, and she
was left sitting alone. And the Frenchman, when
the waiter happened to go into the room, said,
"You need not trouble yourself to attend upon
my young mistress, or the young lady, or something of that kind, I will attend upon her myself." She, wholly unsuspecting, stayed there,
waiting the arrival of her father Then, for the
first time, Edward Wakefield presented himself
—a man of some fashion of appearance, I understand, and of some address—a consummate master,
as you will find in the sequel, of all the arts
of dissimulation and treachery, which he is able
to practice in the highest perfection. Miss
Turner had heard something of the tremendous
convulsions that had happened in the commercial

world about that time, and it is a singular co-
incidence, of no importance at the time it happened, but that had a good deal of influence over
her mind Now she recollected that a short
time before, when her father had taken her to
school, he had not money enough to settle Miss
Daulby's account She had been talking with
her father about different failures in the country,
and Mr Turner said, finding his money ran short,
" Why," says he, " I think I shall have to stop
payment next, and take you from school." There
was another young lady at that school to whom
the same misfortune had actually happened.
She was saying, such a young lady had left school
because her father had failed, and, " I think,"
said Mr Turner, " I shall fail too " This was
said in jest to the young lady ; and, not attaching
much importance to that observation when it was
made, she never had taken much notice of it till
the time I am now adverting to She was a
young lady, I understand, of a remarkable confiding and ingenuous disposition. The person
who addressed her is such a person as I have
described to you. He said, " I am sorry your
father is not come yet I wish he had been here
to introduce me to you, but I hope I shall soon
have the opportunity of being properly introduced. Your father has sent me to tell you that

it was not really your mother's illness which occasioned your being sent for from school, but
the embarrassed state of his affairs." Now this
happened to coincide exactly with what had be-
fallen her friend, the other young lady, at the
same school. She was shocked, as you may
suppose, at this intelligence, and he then went
on to tell her. that he was sent by her father to
conduct her into his presence He was a man of
the appearance I have described to you, and
possessed of all the requisite information of the
neighbourhood, the friends, and acquaintances,
to show he was intimate with the family, she
never doubting or distrusting the truth of that
story. And when he told her it was necessary to
go and meet her father,—it was his particular
desire—he was then at Blackburn, but she was to
meet him at some place in Yorkshire—she stepped
into the carriage and went with him—for what
purpose? For the purpose of meeting her father,
and no other purpose Did she consent to go
away with them into Scotland, in order to be
married? or was she taken with her consent only
to go to her father at that time? Did the
Miss Daulbys consent to part with their charge
because they were deluded by that forged letter?
What did they consent to do? They consented
that the young lady should go home to visit her

mother, and under the care of her father's servant, that is all they consented to Can it be said, either in the one case or the other, that this was a consent to do the thing that was afterwards done? It might as well be said, if a man was attacked on the highway, and a pistol put to his head, accompanied by a threat, " I will blow your brains out unless you give me your money ," and the man puts his hand into his pocket and pulls out his purse, and delivers it under the threat, that it is his own voluntary act —he does not consent, of his own free will, to part with his money to the thief. This is the sort of consent, and the only consent that was ever given, to these proceedings, either by the Miss Daulbys or by Miss Turner

Gentlemen, having got the young lady away from Manchester, they had gained their second step—they took her through Yorkshire, a circuitous route towards Kendal, kept on travelling all night, and they arrived at Kendal about six o'clock the next morning And when they got there, she was told, " Your father is not here, I will go to the post-office to see if there be a letter," and then, pretending to have received a letter —(the two brothers affect to read it at the window)—that was to draw and inveigle her a little further. They set off again northward, and so

she was carried on step by step. But, on the
road from Kendal to Carlisle, they then began
to take another course They had then had her,
you will observe, in their power twenty-four
hours she had been harassed by a long journey,
and had had no rest all night, and they then
began to detail to her the circumstance of her
father's misfortunes, to deplore that he did not
meet her there as he promised, that they might
not be the bearers of the dreadful news. They
began thus : they said, " Here (at Kendal) is a
rich banker of the name of Wakefield, he is our
uncle the Macclesfield bank has failed, and the
Blackburn bank has failed." She knew her father
had accounts with one or both of these banks ;
and that circumstance gave an air of reality
to the whole fiction. " But our uncle here, at
Kendal, is a noble and generous-minded man.
I (says Edward Wakefield) am your father's
dearest and nearest friend, and I have pre-
vailed upon my uncle to lend your father
60,000*l* ! In consequence of the failure of the
Macclesfield and Blackburn banks, your father
is plunged into irretrievable difficulties and ruin.
An expedient has been suggested for relieving
himself and all your family from this distress,
by Mr Grimsditch, your father's confidential adviser, from whom I have received a letter ; and

what do you think it is? Why, that you should
marry me! and then my uncle, if you do, will
settle matters between you and me, and it will
save your father from being turned out of doors,
and all your family from destruction." The young
lady, exhausted as she was with fatigue, as you
may suppose, was perfectly astounded with this
proposal After she had been pressed about it a
considerable time, she said, " I must see my papa
first before I can answer upon such a matter as
that " " Well, well, (he said) Carlisle is not
far off, you will have an opportunity of seeing
him there ' They proceeded to Carlisle, they
arrived at an inn at Carlisle, and stopped there
to change horses, they travelled with four horses,
and, as is generally the case, you know, about an
inn door, when a carriage arrives with four
horses, there is a crowd of people gathered together to look on The two defendants stepped
out of the carriage, and left the young lady
there The landlady would have offered the usual
courtesies of attending the young lady into the
house, but they said, " Oh, no, never mind,
she will prefer staying in the carriage." They
then disappeared for a few minutes, and came
back to her, got into the carriage, and went on,
saying they would explain matters when they got
out of the town, and then they said this—(Mr.

D

Turner, you will observe, being at that moment in London, 300 miles off, and Mr Grimsditch there also) " I have been into the house, I have seen your father, and I have seen Mr. Grimsditch they are concealed in a back room in the house, and those persons whom you saw standing about the inn door are bailiffs lying in wait to apprehend him It is impossible therefore that you should have an opportunity of seeing him ; but he entreats that you will not lose a single moment in proceeding over the borders of England, and get a certificate of your marriage, which if you bring back, your beloved father will be immediately liberated from custody, and from all his miseries "

Gentlemen, did the young lady believe this story, or did she disbelieve it ? Will you suppose that she saw through the whole of it, and that it was a fiction, and that she freely and voluntarily went on ? or did she believe it ? Can you doubt that she was drawn away by these threats and intimidations of the utter ruin and destruction of her family if she refused compliance ? And by way of giving a still better air of sincerity to the whole transaction, one of them adds, " Mr Grimsditch (pretending to read a letter from Mr. Grimsditch) desires that you will show the same fortitude that has been shown by your excellent parent on this occasion " They carried her off into Scotland, and under the influence of terror at the impending destruction of her family, and their fortunes, if she refused compliance, and, in the hope that she might be the saviour of them all, she gave her hand to Edward Wakefield, in a pretended contract of marriage in Scotland, in the presence of a drunken blacksmith, the landlord of a public-house, and a post-boy

Gentlemen, this being over, they proceeded to return, and the young lady, still never doubting that she had saved her father from destruction, expected, when she returned to Carlisle, that she was going to throw herself into her father's arms, and to congratulate him on the salvation that she had bestowed upon him There was then another excuse " Oh, (he says) he is gone on before—he is at liberty , the post-boys carried him the intelligence , we have nothing to do but to go on after your father ; we shall find him either at Shrigley or in London, business may have carried him on to London " She felt she had rendered a service to her family beyond what she had ever hoped she could have an opportunity of doing, and appeared somewhat cheerful after she had done it She was gratified at the event, not having any doubt that she had rescued him from impending ruin They got to

Penrith in the evening, and there beds were ordered for the whole party—three separate beds, and there they slept that night No misfortune happened upon that occasion, for if any violation had occurred, then the defendants would have been within the reach of the law, and would have been tried for a capital felony. They hurried her away, (I won't detail to you all the circumstances,) they hurried her away finally to London They arrived at the Brunswick Hotel, Hanover-square, or that neighbourhood, about 11 o'clock at night on Friday She was taken away on Tuesday from school, on Wednesday she was taken into Scotland, she was made to travel all Thursday and all Thursday night, and Friday, and it was not till 10 or 11 o'clock at night that they arrived at the hotel in London, on Friday; Edward Wakefield then being in company with the young lady, and William Wakefield having been gone to see and confer with Miss Davies, on this subject, at Macclesfield. When they got to London, a friend of Edward Wakefield met him at the inn, and he said, " I have come from your father with a message. He desires that you won't remain in London a single hour, for that you are liable to be apprehended and brought to justice " He immediately ordered a carriage and horses, made some

other excuse, and hurried the young lady away,
saying, that he had received information from
that gentleman that her father was gone on to
Calais in France, on some urgent business, and
that she must follow in pursuit of her father
thither, and away he hurried her off immediately into France. They arrived at Calais on the
Saturday evening, having made this poor young
creature travel a journey of six or seven hundred
miles in a state of the deepest anxiety and affliction on account of her father, and her disap-
pointment in not seeing him

Gentlemen, before I state any thing that occurred at Calais, I will bring your attention
back to Macclesfield The day after they had
been in Scotland, William Wakefield was de-
spatched to Macclesfield, in order to obtain some
information respecting the family at Shrigley,
for there was then a hope that they had done
something irretrievable, and that the family at
Shrigley would be obliged to make the best of it.
The object of this proceeding was not, as you
may suppose, any love for the young lady. The
sole object of his affection was the money of her
father, and the object and meaning of these proceedings was, by the hand of the daughter, to
pick the father's pocket William 'Wakefield
went then to Macclesfield ; he conferred with

Miss Davies, and in order to show you that Miss Davies was not only acting in this business, in contriving it, but that she knew of it when it was over, and was still carrying on her operations, I will show you a letter which she wrote (which has fortunately fallen into the hands for which it was not intended) on the Sunday following. At that time, although she had been carried away from school at Liverpool on the Tuesday morning, the family at Shrigley were never apprised of what had become of her, or the manner of her departure, until the Sunday following, nay, indeed I believe, until, by the contrivance of these defendants, the marriage had been formally announced in the usual way in the London newspapers

On the Sunday evening, and not till then, Miss Daulby set off to Shrigley with the forged letter that had induced her to part with her charge, and then, for the first time, she communicated to the afflicted family at Shrigley the manner in which they had lost their daughter Miss Davies was very busy on that day, and before Miss Daulby arrived to communicate the intelligence, it is quite clear, from this letter, that Miss Davies knew all that had happened—for she writes to him, " Dear William," (that is, one of the defendants, William Wakefield,) " Mr. Turner did not come down the

night you left, it was a mistake. My father
(that is, Dr Davies) saw Mrs. Critchley (a relation of the family) yesterday, who seems very
kindly disposed, but she did not know what her
brother's feelings would be. Perhaps Edward
(that is, the other defendant, who had gone off)
ought to write to her, *touching tender chords*
The old uncles have been written to by her wish
Miss Daulby has not yet written to Shrigley—"
—(Miss Daulby has not yet written to Shrigley !
Who is Miss Daulby ? What does she know about
Miss Daulby ? The Miss Daulby to whom that
letter was given has not yet written to Shrigley
to acquaint the family of what has passed at her
school, and the manner in which the child was
taken away from her custody)——" Miss Daulby
has not yet written to Shrigley, but Miss Turner
(the niece) wrote to her yesterday This is all Mrs.
Critchley's information to my father. You must
not let a foolish account of the affair get into the
papers—it would much annoy Turner, I am sure "

Gentlemen, this fatal intelligence was no sooner
made known at Shrigley, to Mr and Mrs Turner,
—for Mr. Turner, singularly enough, had left London on the Friday evening, to go home, within a
few hours of the time when his daughter arrived
in London, and they probably might have passed
each other on the road, on the first or second stage

from town she going to London, and he coming
down into the country—immediately, without a
moment's delay, the friends of Mr Turner, and
I believe himself, set off immediately in quest of
his daughter. They proceeded as far as London,
Mr. Turner was unable to proceed any further,
and his brother and Mr Grimsditch, and another
gentleman, proceeded to Calais, and there, on
the Pier, they saw Miss Turner and the defendant,
Edward Wakefield They took the necessary
steps, which I need not detail to you, to recover
the person of the young lady He then began to
insist upon his superior right to her person, beyond the right of her own father. He said he
had a right to detain her—she was his wife !
Upon this pretence they found some difficulty in
getting the young lady away, but as soon as the
veil was drawn, and the delusion cleared away,
the young lady was struck with the utmost abhorrence and detestation of the wicked author of
all the misery that had been occasioned to herself
and her family, and she shrunk away into the
arms of her uncle, and when she heard this man
audaciously claiming her as his own property, she
expressed her abhorrence and detestation in terms
you will hear from the witnesses, but still he for
some time insisted on his right, till they went before a magistrate at Calais, and the magistrate

heard the young lady's account of the manner in which she had been carried off, and he immediately ordered that she should be delivered to her uncles, and she was brought home

Gentlemen, the magistrate in that foreign country, on hearing her story, was of opinion, and I should think the same opinion that all civilised beings must have, that by such a course of fraud, forgery, falsehood, and treachery, if a man could acquire a right in the person of his booty, it would be one of the most horrible rules that could possibly be established in society.

Gentlemen, after the young lady had gone from him, Edward Wakefield wrote a letter to his confederate William Wakefield, and there (if any where) one may expect to find a little truth—that when he wrote a confidential letter to his brother, that letter would contain the whole truth, little expecting that the communication of that letter would, by a piece of good fortune, fall into the hands of the prosecutor, and through his hands come before the public. It is a letter addressed, " William Wakefield, Esq.," Calais, Thursday (This was immediately after the young lady was recovered.) " My dear William, I write in haste to save the post, only to give you news, and nothing else:—Mr Robert Turner, Mr Critchley, and Grimsditch arrived by the packet to-day,

with warrants, &c.   I soon knew what they were
come for, but would not attempt to avoid the
question Shortly after I saw them, and found that,
with Ellen's consent, they could take her away
They insisted on seeing her; I could not object,
she told all, and was very anxious to leave me
when she knew all I expected as much, and therefore made a merit of necessity, and let her go.
They tried to take me, but for that they were on
the wrong side of the water, as I well knew.
However, I offered to go with them, but begged
Mr. Critchley to believe that I would be in
England to answer any charge as soon as I had
seen my children, and settled my affairs. Nothing
could be more hostile than the whole spirit of
their proceedings   I could readily have escaped
with Ellen—but their account of Mrs and Mr.
Turner's state made such a step impossible "
(Why, observed the learned Sergeant, did it
make it impossible?   Why because he should
break the hearts of the afflicted parents, and
should never get any thing out of their pockets)—
" I made and gave in a solemn declaration that
she and I have been as brother and sister.   How
this may affect the validity of the marriage, I
know not, nor could I raise the question.   I was
bound, and it was wise, to give some comfort to
Mr. Turner. I am now in a stew about *you*, and

wish that you were safe   There can be no doubt
that the law can punish us   For myself, I will
meet it, come what may , but if you are able, get
away as soon as possible.   I do not care a straw
for myself   The grand question now is, is the
marriage legal?   They all said no, and quoted
William and Mary upon me till I was tired of their
Majesty's names " (He had had this quoted upon
him when he arrived at the Brunswick, by his friend,
who told him to be off)   " Pray let me know
that, but I write to Nunky." (Nunky, I understand, could tell them whether or not it was legal.
But I think, gentlemen, he must have had a hint
from this Nunky at the Brunswick Hotel, when he
hurried her away with so much expedition on the
Friday night, into a foreign country)   " Do not
stay, you can do no good   I shall be in England
as soon as possible   Upon this you may depend I
shall not write again till I hear from you, for fear
of accidents.   Percy came with the two, and has
witnessed the row. We start early in the morning.
Pray write, but say nothing to any body.   I am
the person to speak "   He mentions here the name
of a Mr. Percy, a gentleman of rank and respect-
ability, I understand, who had some employment
under the Secretary for Foreign Affairs, to whom
application had been made, in order to assist Mr.
Turner in the recovery of his daughter in France,

and it is only to be hoped that that respectable
gentleman did not lend any facilities to the escape
of the defendant Edward Wakefield, or to the
detention of Mr Turner's daughter. What he
seems to rely upon is, that, in the perpetration of
this atrocious crime, he had acquired a property
in the young lady, and made her his lawful wife.
And I am told that there is a gentleman of the
profession of the law come to Lancaster, in order
to defeat this prosecution, if he can, by giving
you evidence of the custom of Scotland upon
this subject.   And he is to tell you, I understand,
that, by the custom of Scotland, if a man gets
possession of a young lady by means of forgery,
and carries her off, and persuades her to go away
by menaces and intimidation, assuring her that it
is by the particular desire of her own father, and
nothing else can save her, her father, and the whole
of the family from destruction, but making a
contract of marriage with the robber ,—that gentleman, I understand, is come here to tell you that,
according to the law and custom of Scotland, that
is a legal marriage ' They have caught one man in
all Scotland, I understand, of that opinion. How
they came by him I don't know, I have not the
honour of knowing the gentleman, neither by his
name nor by person, but I think that if any gentleman, bearing the name of a lawyer, shall exhibit

himself in a court of justice to prove such a thing
as that, he will never hear the last of it as long
as he lives, and particularly if he shall come spon-
taneously to do this, entirely of his own accord,
and entirely to defeat the purpose of justice, to
prove that this young lady is, by the custom of
Scotland, the legal wife of the defendant Edward
Gibbon Wakefield, and therefore an incompetent
witness to tell her story to-day See what this
comes to,—it is a capital felony, if committed on
English ground—no, the capital part has been
recently taken away,—it is, on English ground,
a felony. Then it is a felony on one side of the
Tweed, and a meritorious action on the other!
That is a singular state of things It is the
custom of Scotland, this gentleman is to tell us,
to reward the thief with his booty, and to consign the wretched party who has been injured to
eternal misery! And not only that, but to stop
her mouth for ever from making any complaint in
a court of justice! This is what 1 understand,
indeed it has been circulated in all the newspapers,
is to be done to-day, and this is to be the defence
They are to object to the competency of this
young lady as a witness, because—what ? Because the law of England does not allow a wife
to be a witness against her husband ? And why?
Lest it should occasion implacable animosity be-

tween them. So this gentleman is to make out that the young lady is not to be heard as a witness to-day, lest it should provoke implacable animosity between her and Mr. Edward Wakefield !

Gentlemen, if there be any country on the face of the earth where such a transaction as this could be legal—where, as I said, the thief was to be rewarded with his prize, and the injured party was to be punished in the way one has read of—where, in ancient times, the tyrant punished the victims of his resentment by tying them to a dead carcase, and plunged them to perish in that contact—if such a doctrine as that was to be applied to a case like the present, the consequence would be, that this wretched victim of delusion would be plunged into the deepest affliction. for what can be more intolerable than that, after coming here for justice for this atrocious outrage, dragged on a public stage to tell her afflicting story, she is to be told that she is bound for the remainder of her life to be the companion of the wicked wretch who stole her away ? and it would be to consign her afflicted father and mother to misery and wretchedness for the remainder of their days !

Gentlemen, I have the highest opinion of the discretion of my learned friend, Mr. Scarlett, the

Attorney-general for this County Palatine, who defends two or more of these defendants—all these defendants, and I cannot bring myself to believe that he will be guilty of so gross an outrage to common sense, and to all the principles of law and justice, as to make that attempt, which, it has been bruited about the country, is to be made to-day, of disabling Miss Turner from giving evidence in this cause, because, according to the account of this curious gentleman from Scotland, it is a legal marriage.

Gentlemen, this is the nature of the case which it has been my duty to state to you somewhat more in detail, from the importance of the subject, than is usual, and this, I believe, is the nature of the defence that is to be made on the other side.

WILLIAM TURNER, Esq, *sworn Examined by* Mr Williams.

Mr Sergeant Cross —I believe, my Lord, I was mistaken in saying it was a capital felony The recent act of Parliament has taken away the capital offence.

Mr Baron Hullock.—It is still a felony

Mr Williams (to the witness)—What is your daughter's name ?—Ellen.

Have you any other child ?—No.

What is her age, Mr Turner ?—It was fifteen, on the 12th of February, 1826.

Is her mother living, Mr Turner ?—She is.

Is she at Lancaster?—Her mother ?

Yes.—She is not

What is the reason of that ?—She is unwell.

Is she able to undertake the journey ?—She is not

I am now going to ask you some questions for form's sake, you will excuse my putting them to you. Are you in possession of any landed property in the county of Chester ?—I am

I don't at all wish to know the particulars ; you wont so understand me Is that property considerable ?—It is

Now, besides furniture—I am not speaking of particulars—but besides the furniture belonging to your house, are you in possession of personal property ?—I am

Well, again, I don't go to particulars at all, and you will so understand me ,—is that considerable ?—It is

You, I believe, have been high sheriff of the county of Chester ?—I have

The last year, was it not ?—The last year.

Well, sir, I wish to know whether, in the month of March, 1826, your daughter was living with you under your care, or whether she was at school any where?—She was at school at Miss Daulby's.

She was at school at Miss Daulby's, a school in Liverpool, I believe?—In Liverpool

Well, sir, of course, I need not ask whether that was with your assent —I took her there

Now, sir, how recently before the month of March had she been at home with you—Miss Turner?—I cannot tell to a few days; she had been a few weeks before.

Mr Baron Hullock —Before what time?

Mr. Williams —Before the month of March, 1826, my lord

How long had she been with you on that occasion?—During the vacation

But about what time?—From December

Well, then, as much as two months, or thereabouts?—From December to February.

I wish to know whether you had observed any alteration in her manner as to gaiety or seriousness, or in any other respect during that time?—None, whatever.

Now, before the month of March, 1826, did you know the person of Mr. Edward Wakefield?—No

Then I need hardly ask you whether you had ever seen him, on any occasion, at Shrigley, which

E

is the name of your residence, I believe, or that neighbourhood —I never had.

Did you know there was such a person at all?—I did not

Had you ever seen the other defendant, Mr. William Wakefield?—Never

Nor knew there was such a person?—No, sir.

So far as you knew, was your daughter in any degree of acquaintance with him?—No, she was not

To your knowledge?—Not to my knowledge.

Mr. Williams—Not to your knowledge as far as you knew?—No.

Were any of your family, to your knowledge, acquainted with either of them?—No, sir, not to my knowledge.

Now, except being at Miss Daulby's, had your daughter been in the care of any other person except yourself and Mrs. Turner?—No, sir.

I just wish to know how long had she been at that school?—Oh, she had been there four or five years

And never at any other?—And never at any other

Cross-examined by Mr. Scarlett.

Mr. Turner, will you permit me to ask you, you were appointed sheriff at the last assizes?—Yes.

Had you been resident some time at Shrigley?
—Seven or eight years.

Constantly there?—Constantly.

I suppose from your being appointed sheriff, a good many gentlemen in the neighbourhood paid their respects to you?—They did, sir.

Called upon you?—Yes—I beg your pardon, none called, that I know of, before the time of my going to Chester.

MISS ELIZABETH DAULBY *sworn* *Examined by*
Mr Brougham

Elizabeth Daulby is your name?—Yes

Now will you speak out, Miss Daulby, I am afraid you are unwell, but I must trouble you to speak so that those gentlemen may hear you (*pointing to the jury*) Do you keep a boarding-school in Liverpool, Miss Daulby?—Yes, sir

Did you in March, last year?—Yes

Was Miss Ellen Turner under your care?—
She was, sir

By whom was she entrusted to your care?—By
Mr Turner

Mr Turner, the gentleman sitting here?—Yes.

How long had she been with you, previous to March, 1826?—Between five and six years

Did she go home at the Christmas holidays?—
She did.

E 2

Immediately preceding ?—She did

Who fetched her ?—Mr Turner.

Mr Turner himself ?—I think so.

Do you recollect, at that time, a young lady also under your care of the name of Miss Greenway ?—Yes, sir.

Was she a companion of Miss Turner's ?—She was, sir

Had she been under your care for some time, madam?—Several years.

Was she taken away from under your care?—She was

By whom, madam ?—By her father.

On what occasion are you aware was she so taken away ?—On account of his circumstances

Had he become unfortunate in his business ?—He had.

Which made him take her away ?—Yes

Was that known at your school ?—No, not generally

But you say Miss Turner was intimate with Miss Greenway ?—Yes.

Now, when Mr Turner took away his daughter at the Christmas immediately preceding the month of March, 1826; when she was taken away, do you recollect any incident of his leaving any part of the account unsettled ?—Yes.

He was short of money I believe ?—Yes.

Was this known to Miss Turner?—I don't know.

Oh! you don't know. Well, now, madam, do you recollect one morning in March, after Miss Turner had come back to you, after the Christmas holidays, do you recollect, one morning in March, a servant arriving at your house?—Yes.

In what conveyance did he come?—A carriage.

Was it a private carriage?—It appeared to be.

It appeared to be a private carriage and pair?—Yes

Did you see the person who came? did you see the man?—Yes I did

Did he deliver you a letter?—Yes.

Will you look at that (*handing a letter to the witness,*) and see if that is the letter he delivered to you?—Yes, this is the letter.

Did you make an indorsement upon it at the time, after you read it?—Not at that time.

Well, but did you afterwards?—Yes

Well, look and see if you recognise your writing?—Yes, this is my hand-writing.

Did you happen to read that letter, Miss Daulby?—I did

What did the person who brought you that letter say, at the time he delivered it to you?—He said that he came from Shrigley, he was sent for Miss Turner, that Mrs. Turner was very ill.

And gave you the letter?—Yes.

Did he mention, madam, at the time any particulars respecting Mis Turner's illness?—Yes, sir.

What did he say?—I asked him when she was taken ill

Was that after you had read the letter?—Yes.

You read the letter, and then asked him when she was taken ill?—Yes

What said he?—He said the night before, whilst at supper.

Did he mention any particulars of her seizure?—He said the knife and fork dropped from her hand

Did you ask him any thing respecting who he was himself?—Yes.

What did you say?—I asked him if Miss Turner would know him

What said he?—He said she would not. He had been lately engaged by Mr Turner.

Did you say anything about the carriage, or did he? the carriage he came in?—No

Did he say in what way he had been engaged by Mr. Turner,—for what purpose?—To go to the new house

Did he say who he had lived with before?—Yes, he said he had lived with Mr Legh, of Lyme.

You were aware, I believe, that Mr. Turner was about to remove to a new house?—Yes, I was

Now just let me ask you, did he speak like an Englishman or a foreigner ?—His accent was rather foreign

But he spoke as if he understood English ?—Oh ! perfectly

Now, in consequence of the letter you read, and the conversation you had with this man, he did not tell you his name, I believe ?—He did not.

In consequence of that did you go to Miss Turner ?—Yes

Did you make any communication to her ?—Yes.

For what purpose, ma'am ?—I told her Mrs. Turner had sent for her, and wished her to go home; she was not so well as usual. Mr Turner was absent, and she wished her to go home sooner than was intended. She was expecting to go home.

She was expecting to go home, but was to go, in consequence of that, sooner than was intended ?—Yes.

Did Miss Turner then make any preparation for going ?—Yes

I believe you did not show her the letter, madam ?—No, I did not, I was desired not to tell her the state of Mrs Turner's health

While Miss Turner was getting ready, did you ask the servant anything respecting travelling ?—Yes

What did you ask him?—I asked him if she was to travel alone.

What said the man?—He said she was not, they were to take up Dr. Hull at Manchester

There is a physician at Manchester of that name, I believe?—Yes.

Had he any refreshment?—He had a little brandy.

Did he say anything why he preferred brandy?—He said he had travelled all night, and had got a bad head-ache.

Did Miss Turner get into the carriage?—She did.

Did she remark anything about the carriage?—Yes, she said it was not her papa's carriage.

Did the man hear her say so?—He must have heard her

Did he say anything in consequence of that?—He said it was the Doctor's.

Did he say what Doctor's?—No.

By Mr Scarlett—You heard him say that?—Yes.

Did she leave your house in the carriage?—Yes.

Did the man go in with her?—Not in

She was in the inside, and he on the barouche box?—Yes

Now, madam, while Miss Turner was under your care—during the time she was under your care, did she, to your knowledge, ever see either of the Mr. Wakefields?—No, sir

Did you know anything of them, or ever see them?—I never saw them.

Now, madam, I understand that that letter is signed by Dr. Ainsworth, the letter which you read?—Yes

Do you know any person of the name of Ainsworth, a physician?—I do not

Mr. Brougham—I will just ask Mr. Turner that question Mr. Turner, do you know any person of the name of Ainsworth, a physician?

Mr. Turner—No, I do not

Mr Brougham—You never employed any such person, nor heard of any such?

Mr Turner.—No, sir.

Now, Miss Daulby, one question more If that letter had not been delivered, and but for the statement contained in it, if you had known that Mr Wakefield desired to take away Miss Turner, should you have given your consent to her going? —Certainly not

Now, Miss Daulby, I beg your pardon, another question. You have sisters, I believe?—Three sisters

Who keep the establishment with you?—Yes

What are their names? There is your mother and two sisters, I believe?—Three sisters.

What is your mother's name?—Margaret

And your sister's names?—Phœbe, Ann, and Catherine

You have said that you never saw nor knew anything about the Wakefields, and that, to the best of your knowledge, no more did Miss Turner had you observed previous to that day in March when she went away—had you observed any alteration in Miss Turner's manner or appearance?—None whatever.

When did you first hear, madam, of what had been done—of this not being as it was represented to you, respecting Miss Turner?—On the 12th—it was on the 12th of March.

On going over to Shrigley, I suppose?—We had a letter

I understand you to say you received a letter from Shrigley?—Yes

Did you go there?—Yes

What day?—On the 13th, on a Monday

What time of the day?—About 9 or 10 o'clock in the morning

When did you set off?—We set off on the Sunday.

And went to Macclesfield, I believe, on the Sunday evening?—Yes.

And went to Shrigley the next morning?—Yes

Then I understand you to say that was the

first communication you had on the subject —
Yes

Was it the first communication you made to the
family on the subject ?—Yes, it was

Cross-examined by Mr Scarlett

Miss Daulby, Miss Turner had been with you
four or five years, had she not ?—Yes.

At your school are there a considerable number
of pupils ?—No

You take but a few pupils ?—Yes

She was very well educated (Miss Turner) was
not she ? I don't mean it as a compliment to you,
but as a fact ?—She had been well grounded as
far as her education had proceeded.

But she had capacity ?—Certainly she had

Rather clever, was not she ?—Yes

A very clever girl, was not she ?—She had very
excellent talents.

And very great quickness ?—Yes.

And sagacity ?—Yes

Very quick at learning, was not she, always ?
—Yes, very.

And a very good temper and disposition ?—
Yes

Re-examined by Mr. Brougham.

My friend has asked you about Miss Turner's

tempei and disposition What was hei disposition as well as her talents ?—Hei disposition was veiy good.

Now was she of a suspicious, oi of an easy, confiding disposition ?—Oh! iemarkably confiding, sii

Not suspicious ?—Not in the least.

Was she of an open and ingenuous tempei ?—Yes.

And remaikably confiding ?—Yes.

Do you mean that she was distinguished among hei companions foi being remarkably confiding? —Yes, she was.

Mr Brougham (to *Mi Cross*, the piothonotaiy) —Now, iead that lettei.

Mr Cross.—This letter is dated Shrigley, Monday night, half past 12, Maich 6th It is signed John Ainswoith, M D, and addiessed to Mrs. Daulby. "Madam, I wiite to you by the desire of Mrs Tuinei of Shrigley, who has been seized with a sudden and dangeious attack of paralysis Mis Tuinei wishes to see hei daughtei immediately. A steady servant will take this lettei, and my cariiage to you, to fetch Miss Turner; and I beg that no time may be lost in hei depaiture, as, though I do not think Mrs Tuiner is in immediate dangei, it is piobable she

may soon become incapable of recognizing any
one Mrs Turner particularly wishes that her
daughter should not be informed of the extent
of her danger, as without this precaution Miss
Turner might be very anxious on the journey, and
this house is so crowded, and in such confusion
and alarm, that Mrs Turner does not wish any
one to accompany her daughter The servant is
instructed not to let the boys drive too fast, as
Miss Turner is rather fearful in a carriage —Postscript The best thing to be said to Miss Turner,
is, that Mrs Turner wishes to have her home
rather sooner for the approaching removal to the
new house, and the servant is instructed to give
no other reason in case Miss Turner should ask
him any questions Mrs Turner is very anxious
that her daughter should not be frightened, and
trusts to your judgment to prevent it. She also
desires me to add, that her sister, or niece, or myself, should she continue unable, will not fail to
write to you by the post."

Mrs ANNE BROCKLEHURST *sworn.* *Examined
by* Mr. Starkie.

Mrs. Brocklehurst, do you reside at Macclesfield, or in the neighbourhood?—In the neighbourhood.

Previous to January, 1826, were you acquainted

with Miss Davies,—Mrs Frances Wakefield, that is now ?—Yes

Do you know of her going from home about the time I mentioned, January, 1826 ?—I was aware that she went to Paris.

Did you know from her whether she was going to Paris ?—It was generally known.

Was she to purchase anything for you ?—Yes, she was

At Paris ?—At Paris.

Now, do you know about what time she went, madam ?—It was during the Christmas vacation, I believe.

When did she return, madam,—about what time ?—When the school recommenced—when her father's school recommenced

About what time would that be,—in January or February ?—I suppose, about the end of January, or the beginning of February.

Now, do you know, madam, whether, previous to that time, she had visited Mrs. Turner's family at Shrigley ?—I believe she had not.

But after her return did anything pass between you and her as to her going to Shrigley—to call there ?—She called upon me, on her return from Paris ; and, during the conversation, Mr Turner and his family were spoken of

Do you happen to recollect, madam, who first

made mention in that conversation of Mr. Turner and his family?—I do not know, I am sure, which it was that first mentioned the subject. it was spoken of in general conversation

Well, but the subject being mentioned, what did Miss Davies say on the subject?—I was induced to believe from what she said, that she wished for an introduction to Mrs Turner.

Well, when she wished for an introduction, what further passed?—I proposed her accompanying me, if it was agreeable to her, for that purpose

Well, why was she to go with you?—I don't know what particular motive she had

Did she say anything about it?—She said she never had called, and she regretted not having done so.

Do you know how long Mr Turner then had lived at Shrigley?—Several years

Well, when you proposed to take her, what did she say to that?—She seemed very agreeable to do so.

Well, did you see her afterwards upon the subject?—Yes, sir, I called upon her shortly afterwards.

Had any day been fixed during the conversation you have been speaking of?—No, there had not.

There had not been a day fixed, but you called upon her a few days afterwards?—Yes

Well, did you and she go together to Shrigley?—We did

Which of the family did you see there?—Mrs Turner and Mrs Critchley

That is, Mr. Turner's sister, I believe?—Yes

Well, did she make enquiry as to any other member of the family?—She enquired particularly after Miss Turner.

Mr. Baron Hullock—By her, she means Miss Davies, I suppose

Do you mean Miss Davies?—Yes

Well, what passed respecting Miss Turner?—She regretted that she had not then an opportunity of seeing her

Miss Davies, do you mean?—Miss Davies

Very well, did anything more pass?—The conversation was rather long—various subjects were talked about.

Do you recollect how long it was after Miss Davies's return from Paris that you had this conversation with her about her going to Shrigley?—Very soon after

Well, I wish you would recollect what passed respecting Miss Turner—what was said about her at the time?—It was mentioned that Miss Turner had returned to school.

Cross-examined by Mr. Scarlett.

Mis. Brocklehurst, allow me to put a few questions to you —Have you been long intimate with Mr. Turner's family?—Yes, sir, I have been several years acquainted with them.

You were in the habit of visiting them very much, were you?—Occasionally, not very frequently.

When was it announced that Mr. Turner was made high-sheriff?—It was known some time before that

It was a matter of general conversation, was it not, in the neighbourhood?—It was

Had you known Miss Davies long?—Yes.

Were you intimate with her?—Not on terms of very great intimacy

That you say?—I was not on terms of very great intimacy with Miss Davies

Were you in the habit of visiting her?—She visited at my house occasionally, I did not often go to see her.

How long had you known her?—Twelve or thirteen years

Will you allow me to ask you—You say she was to buy something for you at Paris?—Yes.

Who proposed that?—I did, I requested that she would do so.

F

You did not disdain to ask that kindness of her?—Oh dear, no! I was sufficiently known to her to make so free as to do that

You proposed to call upon her, to introduce her to Mrs Turner?—She called on me.

But you proposed afterwards to call upon her?—Yes, during the conversation, I did so

When you called at Shrigley, you took her in your carriage, probably?—I did

At first, I believe, there was some demur about the family being at home, and she proposed to leave cards, and go away?—No, nothing of that kind took place.

Pray, did not you ask after Miss Turner too?—Yes, I did

Did you do so extraordinary a thing as to ask after Miss Turner?—I did not consider it extraordinary.

Very well did you ask after her?—Yes.

And you stayed some time?—Yes, we stayed some time

Do you remember asking Miss Davies, when she was going abroad, to call upon your brother at Versailles?—Yes.

You requested that particularly, did not you?—Not particularly. I think I gave her a letter to take—I am not certain

(*Here the witness turned round to some per-*

*son who was behind her, and said, " Did
I, Mary ?"*)

Who keeps your memory in reserve for you ?—
I quite forgot it myself, I was asking my sister,
who sits behind me

I dare say, that at many of the visits you make
in a morning, a good deal of gossip takes place
that you forget ?—Very probably

But is it not certain ?—Quite certain

Unless there is somebody present who remembers it, you don't keep these things in your memory ?—No, I would not attempt it.

Re examined by Mr Starkie

Up to that time you knew her only as Miss
Davies ?—I did

Who was it first proposed your going to Shrigley ?—From Miss Davies's conversation I was induced to believe that she wished to go

Mr. Thomas Grimsditch *sworn   Examined by*
Mr Serjeant Cross

Mr Grimsditch, I believe you have been for
some years solicitor to Mr. Turner ?—I have, sir.

You reside at Macclesfield ?—I do, sir.

Did you know Miss Davies ?—Yes

Early in the last year ?—I did.

You have known her, perhaps, for some time ?
—For many years I have known her.

Did you see her any time at the beginning of March in the last year?—I did.

On what day was that, sir?—I believe it was on Wednesday the 1st of March, or Thursday the 2nd, I cannot charge my memory with it, but it was one of those days

How came you to see her on that day?—In consequence of a message I received, I went into the street to speak to her.

Did you find her there?—I did

Any body with her?—She was on horseback, and the two Mr Wakefields were also on horseback with her.

Had they an opportunity of seeing you at that time—the Wakefields?—Certainly, I had never seen them before, to my knowledge.

Did they stop and hold any conversation with you?—Miss Davies did, they did not say anything

I need not trouble you with the particulars of the conversation, but was anything said about Mr Turner or his family at Shrigley?—Not at that time, with this exception,—she asked if she might ride round the grounds at Adlington-hall; that—

Nothing was said about Shrigley?—For that they were going to Shrigley and Lyme, and thought of returning by way of Adlington.

Well, sir, on any other day did you see Miss Davies shortly after?—I did.

When was that, sir?—It was on the Saturday morning.

Was that the 2nd or 3rd of March?—That, I think, would be the 4th of March

On the Saturday morning?—On the Saturday morning.

How did you happen to see her that morning?—I was walking up the street where Dr. Davies lives

Well, sir?—And I had passed his house about one hundred yards, when Miss Davies met me in the street, and she told me that she and her two friends had been to Shrigley and Lyme, and had rode into the grounds at Adlington, but that they had not seen me there.

Go on, sir.—She then began to speak of Mr. Turner's appointment as the high-sheriff, and said she supposed he was from home, as they had not seen him in their ride to Shrigley, or any of the family.

Mr. Scarlett —Let him relate the whole of the conversation

Mr. Serjeant Cross.—You are desired to relate the whole

Mr. Scarlett.—Relate the whole of the conversation—give us all about Adlington and Lyme, as well as about Shrigley too.

Mr Grimsditch Very well   I told her that Mr Turner had been very much from home of late, in consequence of the death of his eldest brother at Blackburn, but that he had returned home the night before, when I had had an interview with him on business—that I had seen him.

Do you recollect how the conversation began about Mr Turner?—It began about his being appointed the high-sheriff of the county

Do you recollect how the conversation began about his being at home or not?—That they had not seen him, or any of his family, in their ride

Well, go on.—Upon that she said, " I believe Mrs. Turner is very ill " I told her that she was very ill ; and then she asked me what was the nature of her complaint, I told her that it was said by the doctors to be a determination of blood to the head, but that from her appearance I thought it had been an attack of paralysis—that I had made that remark to Mr Turner, who thought otherwise.

Did she say anything about London ?—She then began to talk about preparations making for Mr Turner's going to the assizes as sheriff   I told her I had heard but little about it, he had been so much from home.

Well ?—And that he was very shortly going from home again , in a day or two, I believed, he was going to London

That was on the Saturday, you say?—It was on the Saturday morning

Well?—She then said, " I think you are a great deal in London, you are probably going with him." I told her I was going to London on the Monday night, but not with Mr Turner, but I thought he was going the same evening—I was not certain.

I believe nothing more passed at that time, Mr. Grimsditch?—No.

Mr Sergeant Cross.—I shall call Mr. Grimsditch again before my learned friend's cross-examination. He may either cross-examine him now or hereafter

Mr. Scarlett.—I shall cross-examine him on this part of the case now.

Cross-examined by Mr. Scarlett.

Mr. Grimsditch, the first interview you have been speaking of with Miss Davies was on horseback, and the two gentlemen were on horseback also, were they not?—They were.

She asked you if they might ride through Adlington-park?—Yes.

Are you the agent of Mr. Cross Legh?—I am the agent, the place is under my care during his absence

They were going to Shrigley and Lyme, and proposed to return through Adlington, and wished to ride through the park?—Yes.

Do you recollect whether you said they might, and you would meet them there?—I told her I expected to be there about one o'clock, and if I was there I would desire the housekeeper to shew them the house.

And when you saw Miss Davies a day or two afterwards in the street, she told you she had not met you at Adlington as she expected, did she not?—She did

And probably she told you that somebody there refused them permission to see the house?—No, she did not.

Well, declined shewing it?—I believe the servant did not come in time; they were gone away before she got round to the door. I had been there, but was gone away, I was too early, and could not wait, because I had to meet a tenant of Mr. Legh's on business.

However, the object of their seeing the park was frustrated by somebody, I am not saying by you?—They saw the grounds, but not the house

What distance is Shrigley from Macclesfield?—Five miles

What distance is Adlington?—That is five miles in a westerly direction from Shrigley.

And Lyme?—About seven miles and a half; that is, two miles and a half from Shrigley.

Do you remember any conversation in the neighbourhood, about Mr and Mrs Turner going to give fêtes when he was appointed high sheriff ?—I do not

Were you his under-sheriff ?—I was

When was the appointment known ?—He was sworn into office as high-sheriff on the 6th of February, I believe

And from that time, I suppose, it was known in the county ?—Yes

Well, though there was no conversation, was there no expectation that there would be some entertainment given at Shrigley, by Mr Turner, on his appointment as high-sheriff ?—Oh, certainly. The former sheriff had given a public breakfast, and he was expected to do the same I had not heard any thing at all from him about it, or any of the family, not having seen him much, on account of his absence from home.

I ask you whether there was not an expectation that he would do the same as the former sheriff ?—Yes.

And that a public breakfast would be given, which was to be attended by ladies and gentlemen ?—I was not aware there would be ladies at that time.

Who had been the former sheriff ?—Mr. Daintry.

Mr. Turner being known to be a man of fortune, was there not an expectation that he would be as magnificent as the former sheriff had been ?—No doubt there was.

Did he give them a breakfast ?—Yes

Was it soon after that?—It was in April, the 1st of April

Was it very much attended ?—Yes

You were there, probably?—I was

Any ladies ?—There were ladies, friends of the family ; various friends of the family.

Was not that breakfast very much attended by persons who had not been in the habit of visiting Mr Turner before ?—There was a great crowd of persons, the same as there always is on those occasions

Rather ambitious to be invited ?—Some came without inviting

Mr. Scarlett.—He says, my lord, some came without inviting.

Mr Baron Hullock —I dare say they did

Re-examined by Mr Sergeant Cross.

Were there any ladies at the breakfast ?—There were some ladies in the drawing-room

Was any company expected to be invited from Paris at that breakfast ?—Certainly not.

Was that the time he was about to set off for Chester, or some time before that ?—It was the morning of his departure

By Mr. Baron Hullock.—To the assizes ?—Yes, attended by his tenants

By Mr. Baron Hullock —What day of the month ?—I think it was the 1st he set off, the 1st of April the assizes commenced on the third

By Mr. Baron Hullock.—He set off from his own house ?—Yes, my lord.

Mr ROBERT BAGSHAW *sworn* *Examined by* Mr. Williams

You, I believe, sir, are in the firm of Brocklehurst and Co , bankers, at Macclesfield ?—Yes

Now, are you acquainted with Miss Davies, as she was called in March, 1826 ?—Yes

And was so before ?—Yes.

Do you remember, at any time in the spring of that year, 1826, being sent for by her ?—I do

When was it, sir ?—On Sunday the 5th of March

Well, sir, did you see her ?—I did.

Where did she send for you to ?—To her father's house

Did you see her ?—I did

Where ?—At her father's house

What was her business with you ?—She wanted a little business doing.

She said so ?—Yes

What else did she say ?—She wanted a little

money, if I could conveniently assist her with it

What answer did you make to that?—I told her I could, and wished to know what kind of money she wanted.

Well, sir, what did she say?—She said she wanted two 50*l.* Bank of England notes, and the rest in 5*l* or 10*l.* to the amount of 150*l.* or 160*l*

Did she mention at that time what she wanted it for?—Yes

What did she say she wanted it for?—To pay on Doctor John's account, meaning Dr. John Davies's account.

Did you understand who she meant by that?—Yes

Was that an uncle?—A cousin.

That you understood from her?—Yes

Well, sir, accordingly, did you go to get the money?—I did

Did she go with you?—No.

And you got it?—Yes

Did you take an account of the notes that you furnished to her?—Yes.

Now tell us, if you please, what was the money you gave her?—I gave her a 50*l.* Bank of England note

You took the number, I take for granted?—Yes

What was it?—The number in our book was 11,075, the number in the bank-note was 14,272.

Now, was there a bank post-bill?—Yes.

What was the number of that?—That was marked B. 1429.

By Mr. Baron Hullock.—What was the value of it?—60*l.*

Now take those in your hand, will you (*handing the two to the witness*) —do you know whether or nor that bank post-bill, and that bank-note, were two of the notes that you gave to her?— They were

What other notes did you give her?—Eight 5*l.* bank-notes.

Making together 150*l.*?—Yes.

By Mr. Baron Hullock.—County bank-notes or Bank of England notes?—Bank of England

Now when you gave her the money, do you remember being about to write something?— Yes

What was it?—An order upon the Manchester Savings' Bank.

What was that for?—To receive this money back again.

Which she was to sign for you?—Yes.

How did that happen?—She had a sum of money in that bank.

Did she say so?—She produced the bank-book.

This was an order in your favour to that extent?—For more than that extent—for all that she had in the bank.

For the whole amount in your favour?—Yes

Where was this order written?—In her father's parlour.

Now, while you were engaged in writing that, do you remember either of the Wakefields coming in?—There came in two gentlemen

Do you know them again now?—Yes.

Look and see if you can see them?—That is one (*pointing to Edward Gibbon Wakefield*), and that I think is the other (*pointing to William Wakefield*). I had never seen them before. Mr Gibbon Wakefield I am certain of, but I am not certain of William.

You believe him to be the person?—Yes, but I am not certain.

Well, while you were doing it, do you remember either of them coming up to Miss Davies?—No

Well, saying anything?—They came into the room, and Mr. Gibbon Wakefield went to the side of the fire, and entered into conversation with Miss Davies.

Did you hear him say anything about what you were writing?—When I handed over the order to Miss Davies to sign, Mr Gibbon Wakefield asked whether she was signing her will.

Now, sir, how long is it ago since you were served with a subpœna to come here as a witness? —The first subpœna was on the 4th of August last.

Do you know whether Miss Davies knew you were coming as a witness?—On being served with the subpœna, I went to inform her.

Well, what did she say to you upon that occasion?—I told her I did not know what I had to do about the business except the money transaction, that was all that I knew of.

What did she say on that occasion?—She said she did not deny having advanced some of the money to them, because they had some French bills, and could not part with them there

What else passed between you?—That was most that passed at that time —no, I asked her whether she had informed her father of that money transaction, and she said she had not I recommended her to do so, and she said she would.

Now I wish to know whether or not, upon the first occasion, when the money was advanced, anything was said about French bills?—Not a word

Did you see any?—None

Either then or afterwards ?—No.

Did she bank with you regularly ?—No, she did not   I have accommodated her a time or two with a little exchange of notes, exchanging local notes for Bank of England notes.

Did she bank with anybody else ?—Not that I know of.

Cross-examined by Mr. Coltman.

Mr. Bagshaw, I presume you would not have had any difficulty in making the advance of money to her, even though she had not assigned any reason to you ?—Not at all.

Were you aware that she had lodged a sum of money in the saving-bank at Manchester, to answer a liability she had incurred respecting this cousin, Doctor John Davies?—Not before that Sunday morning

And then she stated she had placed a sum of money there to answer a liability she had incurred respecting Doctor John Davies, and I believe she produced an order on the bank to show it was so ?—She produced the bank-book, and said she had placed money there

Exactly so; and she gave you an order to receive that money ?—Yes.

And left the book with you, I believe ?—Yes

Mr. WILLIAM CARR *sworn. Examined by* Mr. Brougham.

Mr. Carr, what are you?—A coachmaker.

Where at?—At Manchester.

Do you recollect two gentlemen coming to your shop on the 6th of March, on a Monday morning?—Yes.

Who were they? Do you see them now—do you see the gentlemen?—Yes

Mr. Edward Wakefield?—Yes

Did Mr William Wakefield come with him?—Yes.

By Mr. Baron Hullock —Monday morning: what day of the month was it?—The 6th of March

Now, did Mr. Edward Wakefield say any thing to you?—Yes

What did he say?—He said he wanted to purchase a second-hand carriage

What time of the day was it?—A little after ten in the morning.

Mr. Edward Wakefield said he wanted to purchase a second-hand carriage?—Yes

Did he ask you if you had got one?—Yes.

Did you show him one?—Yes.

Now, what colour was it?—Green.

Dark-green, or light-green?—A darkish green.

G

How much did you ask him for it ?—40*l*

Did he object to the price ?—No, sir.

Did it want any repairs?—It did

Did he give any directions about doing it ?—Yes, he told me to get it repaired

Did he give any directions within what time you were to get it repaired—what time he wished it done ?—Yes, by six o'clock in the evening

Did he say it must be done by six o'clock in the evening ?—Yes

If it was not done at that time did he say any thing ?—He said it would be of no use if it was not done by six o'clock

Where were you to send it to ?—To the Albion Hotel

To whom—to what address?—Capt. Wilson.

Did he mention the name of Wakefield at all ?—No

Did either of them ?—No.

Did he pay anything at that time on account ?—2*l* I believe

Did you promise to get it done by six o'clock ?—Yes.

Did he come to you before six ?—Yes; he came to me again about three o'clock.

What did he say then ?—He asked if it was going on, whether it would be ready, or not

What time did you send it ?—A little before 7.

Did you go yourself with it?—Yes.

Who did you see there?—At the Albion?

Yes who did you see?—Mr Edward Wake-field

The gentleman who had made the bargain with you?—Yes

Did he come to look at it?—Yes, sir.

Did he pay you for it?—Yes.

Now stop. in what money did he pay you, Mr. Carr?—He gave me a 60l bank post-bill

Now, sir, you say it was a 60l bank post-bill? —Yes.

Should you know it again if you saw it?—Yes

Do you recollect the name on the face of it to whom it was payable?—Not now, I do not

Now, what is your belief, Mr Carr, respecting that being, or not being, the bill he gave you (*handing a bill to the witness*)?—I believe that is it.

Does the name upon it of the payee draw it to your recollection?—I believe that to be it

By Mr. Scarlett.—Did you indorse it yourself?—No, sir

Did you give him change for it?—Yes

What change did you give him?—I gave him a 20l. note.

Then, there had been 2l. paid before?—I returned that

Mr Scarlett —I have nothing to ask him.

JAMES HOULGRAVE *sworn. Examined by*
Mr Starkie.

Mr Houlgrave, were you in March last a waiter at the Albion Hotel, Manchester ?—I was

Do you recollect two gentlemen coming there on the Monday morning ?—I do

What Monday was that ?—Monday the 6th of March

What time did they arrive ?—About half-past seven

In the morning?—Yes, in the morning.

Did you observe how they came ?—In a Wilmslow chaise.

Wilmslow, I believe, is on a road to London— not through Macclesfield ?—No.

Do you see those persons here now ?—I see one of them, sir.

Which is that one ?—Mr. Edward Wakefield.

What name did he go by ?—Capt Wilson

Well, do you see the other gentleman here ?— I do

Do you know who that person is ?—Mr. William Wakefield.

Did they breakfast there ?—They did, sir.

And dined and supped there, I believe ?— Dined and teaed.

Do you happen to recollect what they had for dinner ?—No, I do not.

Now, do you know Mr. Carr, the coachmaker?
—I do, sir.

Did he come in while those gentlemen were
there?—He did, sir

What time did he come in?—It was between
six and seven. I believe, in the evening.

Well, what did he come about?—He asked to
see Capt Wilson.

Very well did you show him in?—I did.

To Mr. Wakefield?—To Mr Edward Wakefield

Did you hear what business he came about?—
He came about selling a carriage to Mr. Wakefield

Did you hear him talk about it?—I heard Mr
Carr say that the carriage was brought into the
yard

Now you saw those two gentlemen come in the
morning, did any other person come with them?
—Yes.

What did he appear to be—the other person?
—The servant.

Well, what became of that person in the course
of the day that came with them?—He was there,
sir, until the evening about six o'clock.

Well, and then what became of him?—A post-
chaise was ordered to take him the first stage to
Macclesfield.

Do you know who ordered that?—I do not.

Did you hear the servant's name mentioned?—Thevenot

Do you know whether he was an Englishman or a foreigner, from hearing what he said?—I did not know from his discourse. He spoke very good English.

Well, did he go in the chaise towards Macclesfield?—He did.

By himself, or was any one with him?—By himself.

Did you see the carriage which came from Mr Cair?—I did.

What coloured carriage was it?—Green

Now, the next morning were those gentlemen there?—They were not

Did the man you call Thevenot come again that day?—No, I did not see him.

The day after?—He did.

By Mr Baron Hullock.—When did he come?—About half-past twelve.

That was on the Tuesday?—On the Tuesday.

By what conveyance did he come?—A carriage—a green carriage.

Do you know whether that was the same carriage, or not, that you had seen the day before?—I could not tell.

Well, who came with Thevenot?—A lady, sir.

A young lady ?—A young lady.

Well, did you see the carriage arrive ?—I did.

Well, was he outside or inside ?—He was outside, on the box.

And the lady inside ?—Yes.

Well, now, what became of the lady ?—She was shown into a room, sir.

Now, after she was shown into a room, did Thevenot say who was to wait upon her ?—He mentioned to me that if the bell rang, he wished to answer it himself.

Very well did you leave it to him to attend upon her ?—I did, sir

Did you see any thing of the two gentlemen again ?—I did

What time did you see them ?—It was about an hour afterwards, or about half an hour.

That was after the lady came ?—Yes.

How did they come ?—In a chaise and four horses.

Did you see the horses ?—Yes

Did they appear to have gone quickly or slowly ?—Quickly

Well, what did they, or either of them, say after they got out of the chaise ?—They spoke to one of my fellow-servants , not to me.

Did you hear what they said ?—No, I did not.

What became of them—what room did they go into?—Mr. Edward Wakefield was shown in,—to the lady

Do you know whether any order was given for horses after they came?—Yes, there was.

How long after they came?—About five minutes.

Did you hear the order given?—I did.

What was the order for the horses?—Four horses to Delph.

Well, when were they wanted?—Immediately.

Well, were the four horses put to the carriage? —They were

What carriage was that?—The same carriage that came up with the lady

The green carriage?—Yes.

Very well, was that done quickly?—It was

Did you go into the room where the lady was? —Yes, sir; the bell rang

And you went in?—Yes

Did you see them get into the carriage?—I did

Were any of the blinds up at that time?— Two of the blinds were up.

Mr Baron Hullock.—Who are " they"—you say " they?"

Who do you mean by " they"—who did you see get into the carriage?—Miss Turner and Mr. Edward Wakefield.

Well, what became of Mr William Wakefield?
—He went on the box, sir.

Well, you say two of the blinds were up?—
They were

Did you attempt to take them down?—I did

Did you put the blinds down?—I did not.

What prevented you?—Mr Edward Wakefield said " Never mind them, he would put them down himself "

Well, was Thevenot, the servant, there at that time?—He was

Did he go along with them?—He went on the box.

They then drove off?—Yes

By Mr. Baron Hullock.—They drove off, you say—where to?—To Delph.

Cross-examined by Mr Scarlett.

When the lady came with the servant, was she shown into a room that looks out two ways?—She was.

A corner-room, I think?—Yes.

One looks opposite the Infirmary?—Yes

And the other looks into the road that goes towards Oldham?—Yes

Did you carry anything to her when she was in the room?—I did not

Was anything handed to her?—Yes

What was it?—A tart and a custard.

Was that by one of your fellow-servants?—By the housekeeper.

By the housekeeper you mean a female?—Yes

She took a tart and a custard to her?—Yes.

No spirits nor wine?—No.

Had you occasion to go into the room while she was sitting there, before Mr. Wakefield came?—Yes

Where was she sitting or standing then?—She was sitting opposite the window that fronts to Piccadilly

That is opposite the Infirmary?—Yes.

Was she sitting near the window, or in the centre of the room?—In the centre of the room, near the table

Did she make any remark to you?—No.

Was that the only time that you went into the room when she was there alone?—No, I was in the room afterwards, when Mr Wakefield came

I said, when she was alone. When Mr. Wakefield came, how soon did you go into the room after he was introduced to her?—Two or three minutes after

Did you find her in the same place?—Yes.

Where was he?—He was standing by her.

Did you observe anything particular?—No, sir.

How long did you stay in the room?—About half a minute—I was asked for a glass of Madeira

Did he ask you for a glass of Madeira?—He did

And I suppose you brought it?—I did.

Very well you were not a moment bringing it?—I was not long.

When you brought it, did he drink the glass of Madeira?—Not while I was there

Did you come again there?—I did

You returned a third time?—Yes

Was that to tell him the horses were ready?—It was

Had he ordered the horses of you?—No, not of me

You did not hear the order given?—Yes, I was in the passage.

Well, when you returned he paid you, I suppose, for the glass of wine?—Yes, sir.

Well, did you observe anything remarkable at that time?—I did not

You had never seen the lady before?—Never

What age did she appear to you to be?—As near as I could judge—Indeed, I have no idea, I took so little notice of her.

Was she tall?—I did not perceive that

Well, when the horses were ready, were they

placed with their heads towards Oldham?—They were

Did Mr. Wakefield hand her out to the carriage?—He did.

How long had they been there altogether, before they went away, to the best of your judgment?—About ten minutes, perhaps a little more

Do you remember when Mr. Wakefield was in the room with the lady, he asked you any question about a sitting-room and a bed-room in that house?—He did

What was the question he asked you?—He asked me, if he came back in six weeks, whether he could have a bed-room and sitting-room adjoining up-stairs

You answered him, 'Yes,' I suppose?—I did.

Do you know Mr Robert Turner?—I cannot say I know the gentleman by name.

Re-examined by Mr Starkie.

You say the horses' heads were turned towards Oldham · that is the road to Delph, is it not?—Yes

JOSEPH BLACKSHAW *sworn* *Examined by* Mr Sergeant Cross.

Joseph, I believe this time last year you were ostler at the hotel at Macclesfield?—I was.

Do you remember seeing two gentlemen, who were at Dr. Davies's about that time?—Yes, sir.

Was there a man there as their servant ?—Yes,
sir

Do you recollect his coming in a chaise one
evening to your house ?—Yes, sir.

What evening was that ?—On the 6th of
March

Was that Sunday or Monday ?—Monday, sir.

About what time did he arrive ?—Between six
and seven I suppose it might have been

By Mr. Baron Hullock —Morning or evening?
—In the evening

Well, how did he come ?—In a chaise

A chaise, from whence ?—From Bullocksmithy.

Is that the stage between Manchester and Macclesfield ?—Yes, sir, one of them.

Well, what became of him upon his arrival ?—
As soon as he got out of the chaise, he inquired
the road to the Park-house

How far is that from Macclesfield ?—Near
upon a mile

Who lives there ?—Mr Ryle.

The banker ?—Yes.

Did you see what became of him, or which way
he went ?—He turned to the right, to Doctor
Davies's.

Was that the way to Park-house ?—No, sir.

Well, when you saw him go that way, did you
say any thing to him ?—No, sir.

Did anybody, that you heard ?—No, I did not hear any person say anything more to him

Well, had you told him which was the way to Park-house ?—No, I did not myself, but I heard him ask a person

And did you hear whether that person told him the way ?—He shewed him the way, right down the market-place.

And then you say he did not take that course, but went on towards Doctor Davies's ?—Yes

How long was he away ?—About half an hour, as near as may be.

Did you see him come back to the inn ?—Yes, sir

Did he come that way back—the way you had seen him go ?—I did not see which way he came back, but I saw him when he came back in the house, in the lobby.

Well, what did he say then ?—He ordered the chaise out again immediately.

Well, and what did he do then ?—The driver said the horses had not eaten their corn, and were not fit to go out again

Did he appear willing to wait, or very anxious to get away ?—He was very anxious to get away.

Well, how soon after did he go away ?—Perhaps in about a quarter of an hour

In the meanwhile what did he do with himself ?—He got into the chaise

He sat in the chaise without the horses, did he?
—Yes

Was he away long enough to have gone to the place called Park-house?—No, he was not

Nor did you see him go that way? you did not see him go that way?—No

How far was Doctor Davies's from the inn?—He might walk it in about two minutes

And he was away, I think you say, about half an hour?—Half an hour, or better, as near as I can tell

Cross-examined by Mr. Park

You say you saw the two gentlemen there at the Macclesfield Arms?—I saw them pass backwards and forwards

There was a chaise ordered at your house on the Sunday, was there not?—I was not in at that time.

Do you know of a chaise going from your house?—Yes, to Congleton

On the Sunday evening?—Yes

With those two gentlemen?—Yes, with those two gentlemen

Mr Baron Hullock —A chaise, was it?

A hack chaise?—Yes, sir

Do you know of that chaise having been previously ordered to go to Leek?—No, I do not.

Did the two Mr. Wakefields and their servant

go together to Congleton on the Sunday evening?
—They did

In the same chaise?—In the same chaise.

Did you happen to see the servant return that
evening?—No, sir.

Joshua Richards, *sworn   Examined by* Mr
Williams.

You are a post-boy at the Albion Inn, Manchester?—Yes.

Do you remember taking a servant from Manchester to Bullocksmithy?—Yes, sir

When was that?—The 6th of March.

What day of the week?—Monday.

In the course of that night were you called up
to go to Irlam in the way towards Warrington?
—Yes

What time was it?—Two o'clock in the morning.

The next morning, in the night of Monday,
and the morning of Tuesday?—Yes

Accordingly, did you take anybody?—Yes.

Who were they?—Two gentlemen and a servant.

Mr. Baron Hullock —To what place?

Mr. Williams —To Irlam, my lord, in the
way to Warrington.

Now can you tell whether that servant that you

took, was the same that you had taken to Bullocksmithy?—No, sir, I cannot tell

Do you know the two gentlemen again by sight?—No, sir, I know one, sir.

Which is he?—That gentleman there, sir, (*pointing to Mr Edward Gibbon Wakefield*)

Well, there was another with him —Yes

You don't know the other—Mr William, do you—the younger one?—No.

You took them, accordingly, to Irlam, did you? —Yes, sir

JAMES BROWN *sworn.* *Examined by* Mr. Brougham.

You are a post-boy at the Legs of Man, Prescott?—Yes, sir.

Now, do you recollect a green carriage coming there between six and seven in the morning, in the beginning of March last?—Yes, in the morning

Were you the boy in turn?—Yes.

Did you drive it?—Yes

Were you directed to go to Liverpool?—Yes.

Where were you directed to go to at Liverpool?—To inquire for Miss Daulby, Seminary, Liverpool.

Who was in the carriage?—One gentleman and a servant.

H

Had you ever seen the servant before?—No, sir

Did you hear his name?—No, sir.

Did you observe whether he talked with a foreign accent, or not?—No, he talked English.

But I mean as to his accent, was his accent foreign?—No—I don't know.

Did you ever see the gentleman that was with him before?—No, sir

Should you know him if you saw him again ? Yes.

Just look about and see if you can see him?—That is him (*pointing to Edward Gibbon Wakefield*)

Do you mean him with a black handkerchief? —Yes

On the second seat?—Yes

Mr Baron Hullock —That is Mr Edward.

Mr. Brougham —Mr. Edward Wakefield.

Well, did he tell you to drive quick or slow?— He never mentioned anything about driving quick when we were going down.

Well, where did you drive to at Liverpool?— To the Blue Bell

What did he desire you to inquire for when you got there?—Miss Daulby's seminary, Liverpool.

Well, did you go out of the way?—Yes,

How much?—About a mile

Had you to turn round to get back again?—Yes.

What road was that?—The west Derby road.

Was the servant and the gentleman both in the carriage at the same time?—Yes.

Well, what part of Liverpool, then, did you drive to?—I turned back to the high road?

Well, where did you go to then?—Then the gentleman inquired for the school.

Did he get an answer to his question?—Yes.

Where did you go to then?—Into Islington-street

Well, what did he desire you to do when you got to Islington-street?—The servant desired me to pull up at the first public-house I came to.

Did you stop there?—No, sir, there was no public-house, and I pulled up in the street, and opened the door and let the gentleman out

Did the gentleman get out?—The gentleman got out.

Did the gentleman say anything to the servant?—Yes, he thanked the servant for his ride, and said he had given him a great lift.

What did the servant say when he thanked him?—He said you are welcome.

Could you see whether he gave him anything when they parted?—He gave him something, but what it was I cannot tell

Where did you drive to next?—To Miss Daulby's school

Did the man get out there?—Yes

Did he go into the house?—Yes

How long did you stay there?—Fifteen minutes.

Who came out to you there?—A servant lass

By Mr. Baron Hullock.—Did he go with the carriage to Miss Daulby's?—Yes, the man-servant

Where did the servant ride?—On the dickey.

By Mr Baron Hullock—Well, what became of the carriage when the servant was in at Miss Daulby's?—It stopped at the door.

How long did you remain there?—Fifteen minutes.

Did he give you any directions how you were to drive back?—I was to drive back as quick as I possibly could.

Nothing happened till you got back to Prescott?—Nothing at all

Did you land them at Prescott?—Yes

By Mr. Baron Hullock.—The servant desired you to drive back as fast as you could?—Yes

JANE HUGHES *sworn. Examined by* Mr. Starkie.

Mrs. Hughes, are you the landlady of the Nag's Head, at Warrington?—Yes, sir.

Do you recollect a young gentleman coming to your house on Tuesday the 7th of March.—I recollect seeing a gentleman on Tuesday the 7th of March, about seven o'clock in the morning.

How did he come ?—I was informed he came in a chaise

You did not see him come ?—No; he came about four o'clock in the morning

Mr Baron Hullock —She saw him about seven

Had he breakfast there ?—I believe he had

Now, did you see a green carriage come in the course of that day ?—I did

What time of the day was that ?—About ten o'clock

In the forenoon ?—Yes.

Which way did it come,—the Liverpool way, or the other way ?—It came up from Prescott

Did you see who was in the carriage ?—No, sir, there was a servant outside.

Well, did they go on immediately after changing horses ?—As soon as the horses were put too.

Now, was any letter left there by that young gentleman you are speaking of?—There was a letter given to me.

Do you know who gave you that letter ?—In the hurry of business, I cannot recollect who gave it me, but I believe it was the waiter.

But whoever it was that gave you the letter, is

that the letter that was given to you (*Handing a letter to the witness*)?—It is.

WILLIAM EDWARDS *sworn*   *Examined by* Mr Starkie.

Mr Edwards, do you know Mr William Wakefield's handwriting?—I do.

Is that in his handwriting—(*Handing the letter to the witness*)?—Yes, it is.

    Cross-examined by Mr Scarlett.

When did you last see him write, sir?—Not within the last four years, or about that time. It is four years since I left his father's office.

Is it no more than four?—It was four years last January, the 21st or 22nd.

You know his handwriting?—I do

Mr. Starkie.—Very well, put it in

Mr Cross.—This letter is without date, it is addressed to Captain Wilson, but I don't see any date, and it is without signature. "Go you immediately to where we dined yesterday on cod and mutton chops." "She is to wait for her father She has just left this place at eleven o'clock" (This was the prothonotary's translation of the following passage in French "Elle doit y attendre son perè elle est partie d'ici a 11 heures.")—"Write to Mr Wilson, at the same place, from wherever you succeed"

SARAH HOLMES *sworn   Examined by* Mr. Sergeant Cross.

Mrs Holmes, you keep the Bush Inn at Carlisle, I believe?—Yes, sir.

Do you recollect, in the month of March last year, a green carriage arriving at your house?—Yes

Do you remember the day, Mrs. Holmes?—Tuesday, the 8th of March.

Are you clear about that, madam?—I am not clear about it, I believe it was I don't know whether it was Tuesday or Wednesday. it was the 8th of March

Very well that was Wednesday. About what time did the carriage arrive at your house?—I think about eleven—eleven or twelve, some time in the morning, eleven or twelve in the forenoon.

Did you see the company that arrived in that carriage?—I did, sir.

Who did the company consist of?—Two gentlemen and a lady.

Have you ever seen the lady since—have you seen the lady since?—Yes, I have seen her, but not that I should know her again.

Well, when the carriage drove up to the door, what happened?—The gentlemen got out, and the lady remained in the carriage.

Well, madam, and what then ? Did any body
attempt to hand the lady out of the carriage ?—
Our waiter went to the door first, I believe, and
I went myself to ask the lady to alight out of the
carriage , but one of the gentlemen (the taller gentleman) stepped on one side, and put his hand on
the carriage-door, and said " No "

Did he say any thing else, besides " No" ?—
Not to me

Were the blinds up or down ?—Down, sir.

Do you mean all, or was the window open next
to the house ?—Yes, it was quite open

Could you see the lady in the inside of the carriage ?—I could see her very perfectly , I saw
her in the carriage, and that made me go out

Did any thing particular occur to your mind,
to induce you to propose her alighting ?—Certainly

What was that, madam ?—A friend near me
observed that the lady looked very dispirited,
and it was on that account that I went to the
carriage to ask her to alight The lady had been
asked before to alight, and I thought it my duty
to go, which I did myself.

I don't know whether you happen to know the
persons of the parties that arrived at that time ?—
I think I should know the gentlemen—one of the
gentlemen

Well, do you see either of them ?—Yes

Which is that ? — Mr. Wakefield, there—
(*pointing to Edward Gibbon Wakefield.*)

Which of the gentlemen was it that said " No,"
when you proposed to the lady to alight?—That
Mr. Wakefield, the taller gentleman. The other
was not near the carriage, neither did I see that
Mr Wakefield, until I went out

How long did the carriage stop at the door,
before it set off again?—I believe, about fifteen
minutes

Well, did any other remark occur to your mind
at that time, about the situation of the young
lady?

Mr Scarlett —Don't let us get something that
is not evidence, by asking her what she observed.

Mr Sergeant Cross.—Surely I may ask her
what she observed.

Mr. Baron Hullock —You may ask her what
she observed respecting her appearance, but not
what passed in her mind

In about a quarter of an hour they set off again?
—Yes.

Did they return in the course of that day?—
Yes, they did.

About what time?—About six o'clock in the
evening ; I am not very correct as to the time.

Cross-examined by Mr. Scarlett.

They stayed about a quarter of an hour the first time?—Yes

Where were the gentlemen during that quarter of an hour—do you know?—I do not know.

But the lady was by herself in the carriage?—Yes, I believe one of the gentlemen was there the whole time. The latter was near to the carriage when I went

Were you there the whole time?—I was not.

Mr Scarlett.—Nobody believes here what they don't know.

Your waiter had first opened the door, had not he?—I dare say he had

Is that what you represented just now?—I know the company are always asked to come in.

Who opened the door?—I think the waiter

Have you the least doubt of it?—No, not the least.

Is he here?—He is here

What is his name?—Thomas Atkinson

Mr. Scarlett.—Because we shall know whether the lady wished to get out or not.

Now, when they returned, how long did they stop?—About two hours

Now, the carriage was parted with there, was it not?—Yes.

Did they stop two hours at your house?—Yes.

Did you see the lady then?—I did

Where did she stop?—She remained in the parlour, sir

Did you see much of her?—No, sir, very little

Where did the gentlemen remain?—I suppose in the same parlour   I was not there the whole time   The gentlemen went into the parlour where the lady was

Did they dine there?—No, they took tea

Well, did you go into the room during the tea-time?—No, sir, I did not.

And then they went away by the mail, did not they?—No, they left our house in a post-chaise

By Mr Baron Hullock.—What! did they leave their own carriage?—Yes, they left their own carriage.

The carriage was broken, was it not?—It was sent to the coachmaker's

It was unfit for use, and they left your house in a post-chaise?—Yes.

MISS CURWEN *sworn. Examined by* Mr Sergeant Cross.

I will just trouble you, Miss Curwen, with one question   You were living with Mrs. Holmes, I understand, the last witness, at the time when this party arrived at the house?—Yes, sir, I was on a visit there.

Did you see the carriage standing at the door?
—Yes, sir.

Did you see the young lady in the carriage?—
I did.

Had you an opportunity of observing whether
she was cheerful, or otherwise? — I certainly
thought she was very much depressed

Did you observe that at the time?—I did, sir.

Well, how did it strike you at the time—her
appearance?—I said to Mrs. Holmes, the lady
looked the very picture of despair. I thought
so at the time

Cross-examined by Mr Scarlett.

Did not you rush to the door and let her out?—
No, it was not my place to do it.

JAMES HAMILTON *sworn.*   *Examined by*
Mr Williams.

You, I believe, live at Penrith, do you not?—
Yes, sir.

At the inn there—you are a waiter there?—
I am.

Well, now, do you know the Mr Wakefields
by sight?—Yes, sir

Both of them?—Yes, sir

The elder and the younger—you remember
them?—Yes.

Do you remember their coming?—Yes.

From which way?—From Shap—from the Kendal road.

Did they come back?—They did.

When was it they passed downward?—Between 10 and 11 o'clock in the morning.

On what day?—Wednesday the 8th of March

And came back about what time?—About 11 o'clock the same evening

Do you remember a 50*l*. note being changed? —I do, sir

Who changed it?—I got the note, and took it myself for change.

Did you notice it?—I noticed it to be a 50*l* note

Well, was there a lady with them?—Yes

Both going down and coming back?—Yes.

A servant?—No, no servant

Cross-examined by Mr. Park.

You saw them as they went through towards Carlisle?—Yes.

How long did they stop?—Not more than ten minutes.

Had they any refreshment?—None.

No wine, or any thing of that sort?—No

The first time they came you opened the door to them, did you not?—I did.

Did both the gentlemen get out?—They did.

How long did they remain?—While the horses were put to

How long might that be?—Five or ten minutes—ten minutes

Did the lady get out of the carriage?—She did not.

Where did the gentlemen go?—They remained before the door.

Did the lady appear to you to be under any restraint, or any dejection of spirits?—The lady seemed very composed

Now, when they returned, did they stop at your house?—They did

What time of night did they get back?—About 11 o'clock

Did they go into a sitting-room together?—They did

Did you see the lady there?—I did.

Did you hear anything pass between the lady and gentleman?—No

Did there appear to be any uneasiness or restraint on her at that time?—No.

Now, in the morning at breakfast, did they breakfast together?—They did.

Very well; I believe they went off by the mail, did not they?—Yes

Did you see the lady before breakfast—did she come down before them?—Yes,

She was in the bieakfast-ioom befoie they came down ?—Yes

Did you see hei there ?—Yes.

What was she doing ?—Reading.

Reading what ?—A book

Did you ask hei any question ?—I asked hei if she would take breakfast.

What did she say?—She said, " I don't know ; you must enquiie of the gentlemen."

Well, did you enquire of the gentleman ?— I did.

What did he say ?—That I was to get it ready as soon as possible

Did you know they were going by the mail, then ?—I did.

Oh ! they had aiianged to go by the mail the night befoie ?—Yes.

Did you wait upon them at the table during bieakfast ?—Yes, sir.

Did the gentleman appear to be attentive to the lady ?—Yes

You observed nothing iemaikable ?—Nothing remarkable.

Do you remember the chambermaid coming in about the beds ?—I do

Do you iemembei the gentleman saying any-thing about the lady's bed ?—I do.

What did he say?—He said, " I must see where you sleep, my dear."

Did he go up-stairs to see?—He did

By Mr Baron Hullock.—Who said that?—Edward Wakefield

Re-examined by Mr. Williams.

They had separate beds, I believe?—They had

MARGARET DUNWOODE *sworn. Examined by* Mr. Sergeant Cross

Mr Sergeant Cross.—I call this witness, my Lord, in consequence of some questions that were put to the last witness on cross-examination.

You were the chambermaid at Penrith this time twelvemonth, were you not?—I was

Do you remember two gentlemen and a lady arriving one evening?—Yes, sir

Do you remember what evening it was?—I believe it was on Wednesday evening

Did you hear the waiter examined just now, who has just left the box—have you heard what he said?—Yes

Should you know either of the gentlemen if you saw them?—I think I should.

Look before you, and see if you see either of them at this table (*pointing to the table*).

You see a gentleman there, with a paper in his hand?—Yes

Well, was he one of them?—I think so

Did you see the other gentleman there, in the white waistcoat, do you recollect whether he was there?—I cannot exactly say

Was there a lady of the party?—There was

And did they all come together?—Yes

Did they sleep there that night?—Yes, sir, they did

What beds had they?—Three.

The next morning had all the beds been slept in?—Yes, sir, they had.

Did you observe whether more than one person had slept in a bed?—I don't think that more than one person had slept in a bed

Cross-examined by Mr Coltman

What time was it when these parties arrived the second time: you did not see them the first time they arrived?—No, sir, I did not

What time was it when they got there the second time?—Eleven, near eleven.

What directions were given to you?—They rang the bell and ordered three separate beds to be made

Very well; who were the beds ordered by?—Mr. Wakefield

I

By this gentleman? (*pointing to Edward Gibbon Wakefield*)—Yes, sir

Now did you hear the gentleman say, " I must see where you sleep, my dear ?"—Yes, sir, I did.

Did he go up to see the bed-room ?—He saw the bed-room

Now, pray, how did the parties seem to be , did the lady seem under any restraint ?—She did not appear so

Or any dejection of spirits ?—Not at all, that I saw, sir

Nothing of the sort ?—No, sir.

Did you see her in the morning ?—I saw her on the stairs ; but I did not speak to her, nor yet she to me,

What time in the morning was it when she was coming down stairs do you know at all ?—I cannot exactly say ; but I think about eight o'clock in the morning.

How long was it before the gentlemen came down ?—Perhaps a quarter of an hour, or it might be more , I cannot exactly say

I suppose she went into the room where they had been the night before ?—Yes, she did.

Now how did he seem to treat her, and how did they seem to treat each other ?—I saw nothing between them but what was very loving.

On both sides ?—Yes.

By Mr. Baron Hullock —Were the beds in three separate rooms ?—Yes, they were.

JAMES HAMILTON *again called, and examined by*
Mr. Williams

Now do you remember the gentlemen getting up in the morning ?—Yes

Were you in the room of either of them ?—Yes.
Which ?—The tall one.

The elder Mr Wakefield ?—Yes

Well, how did you find him ?—He was undressed

In the room he went into over night ?—I don't know which room he went into

But you found him in a bed-room by himself ?—Yes, by himself

ROBERT JALLEY *sworn   Examined by* Mr
Brougham

Are you the waiter at the Brunswick Hotel, in London ?—I was

You were in March, 1826 ?—Yes.

Do you recollect any of the Wakefields coming to your house in the beginning of March ?—Yes.

Which ?—Edward Gibbon

Was he the one that came first ?—Mr. William Wakefield came first

Which is Mr. William Wakefield ?—He is not here, that I see

Now do you recollect on the Friday any body coming to you before Mr Edward Wakefield and the young lady came ?　On the Friday ?—Two or three of the brothers, and Mr Wakefield

The gentleman that is sitting there, the father ?—Yes.

Now had anybody come before, who was connected with them, to your house ?—Yes, several gentlemen

But had a servant come ?—Thevenot.

Was Thevenot their servant ?—Yes

Did Mr Wakefield, the father, see Thevenot ?—Yes, he did.

Was Thevenot down stairs or up stairs ?—Up stairs a-bed

Was anything the matter with him ? was he ill ?—He said he was

Did he go to bed ?—Yes.

And did he keep his bed as if he was ill ?—Yes, sir, he did

Now what time did young Mr Wakefield, the son, come ?—In the morning part

By Mr Baron Hullock —Which son is that, because you don't mention the names ?—I am talking of Mr. Edward Wakefield's brother.

Did you see that gentleman sitting there ? (*pointing to Edward Gibbon Wakefield*)—Yes

When ?—At eleven o'clock at night.

What night ?—On Friday, the 10th of March.

This was after his father had been with you —Yes.

Did he come with any body or alone?—He came with a lady

A young lady?—A young lady.

Who did he ask for when he came to your house?—He asked if we had any apartments? I said yes, we had.

Did you show him into one?—I told him his brother was up stairs, and he desired me to show him into the room where his brother was.

Now did you show him into the room where his brother was?—I did

Did they talk to one another?—They talked very fast.

Loud or low?—Low

So that you could not hear?—I could not.

Where was the young lady at that time?—She was out of the sitting-room at that time.

Could you see her?—Yes.

What appearance had she?—I saw her in the bed-room, she was crying then

Did you hear them say any thing to her, or propose any thing to her?—In the bed-room, sir?

Yes, or at any time?—They asked her if she would take something

Very well, what did she say?—She said no, and Mr Wakefield said, I think you had better not.

How long did they stop with you?—About an hour and a half, I think.

What did they then do after the hour and a half, did they leave you?—Before that Mr. Wakefield desired me to order a chaise and four.

Did you order it?—I did.

Did it come to the door?—It did.

Where did you order it to go to?—To Dartford, I think

Now did the gentleman who was there, or did Mr Wakefield, pay the bill?—The gentleman.

Now you say the servant who was there said he was ill, and kept his bed, was he there at the time Mr Edward Wakefield was there?—He was.

Did Mr. Edward Wakefield ask to see him?—He did

Did he see him?—Yes.

How long was he with him?—A good bit.

Were they alone?—No, the other Mr. Wakefield was with him.

When Mr. Wakefield paid the bill, did he say any thing about money to Mr. Edward Wakefield?

Mr Baron Hullock—Who is Mr Wakefield?

Mr. Brougham—Another brother, my lord, who is not here

Mr. Baron Hullock—Is he the gentleman he showed him up stairs to?*

Mr. Brougham.—Yes, my lord.

* This Gentleman, who passed with the waiter as Mr. Edward Gibbon Wakefields brother, was a Mr. Mills.

The Witness.—He said I had better pay the bill, in case you should not have enough to carry you, (meaning where he was going to,) at the same time holding a handful of notes to Mr. Edward Gibbon Wakefield

Did he take any of them ?—No, he did not.

Well, did that gentleman stay all night, or go away the same evening ?—He staid all night, and went away the next morning about eight o'clock

Where did he go to ?—He went to the Gloucester Coffee-house, Piccadilly.

Did he say where he was going to when he went away ?—No, he did not—Oh yes he did, he said he was going to Reading

Cross-examined by Mr Scarlett

You say a brother of Mr. Wakefield was there before he came ?—Yes.

What, was it that gentleman ? (*pointing to William Wakefield*)—No, it was not that gentleman

How did you know it was a brother of Mr Wakefield ?—I understood so from him—I believe he told me.

Have not you been desired to make inquiry about him ?—I have not

Have not you been employed by the prosecutor's attorney ?—No, sir.

Have not you served some subpœnas for him ? —Yes, I served some subpœnas. When Mr

Grimsditch was in town, he wrote a letter to me to say he should be glad to see me   he said he had some subpoenas to serve, and I said I would go and serve them

How many did you serve ?—Only one.

Were you paid for that ?—No, I only took it in a friendly way.

How came you to see the lady in the bed-room ? —I was on the landing.

And you peeped into the room ?—No, I did not peep, I could see her quite plain without peeping.

What was it you saw ?—I saw Miss Turner— She went out of the sitting-room into the bed-room.

Did the sitting-room open, by folding doors, into the bed-room ?—Yes.

And so you were arrested by seeing her in tears ?—Yes.

You mean to swear she was in tears ?—I do.

Pray, when Mr Edward Wakefield went away, did he give you his address ?—He did

What was it ?—Mr. and Mrs E. Wakefield, for Paris

Did he give you any money ?—He did.

Was the lady by ?—She was

Did he write it for you himself ?—Yes, he did —I have got the paper now, I believe

He told you first he would not trust to your

memory?—I don't know, sir, I don't recollect that, he might have said so

You have been in three or four places, have not you?—No, I have not.

How many then?—I have been in one

Which one is that?—In Bond-street, at Molloy's Hotel.

You went there from Mr Blake's—Something or other happened there, and you did not return to Mr Blake's service?—I did not

Then you went to Molloy's Hotel, in Bond-street?—Yes

How long did you stay there?—I was there about six months.

Are you there now?—No

What place have you now?—I have none now, I don't want any

You live on your own means?—I am going into business for myself—I am going to take a chop-house

Were you turned away by Mr. Molloy?—No, sir

Are you certain of that?—I am certain of it—I am quite certain it was as much my fault as his that I left.

Did not Mr Molloy make you refund a sum of money before you were turned away?—No, sir

Are you certain of that ?—There was 1*l.* 5*s.*, a difference between him and me.

Well, that is a sum of money ?—There was a dispute between us about that He said the gentleman had paid it to me, and I said he never had

And Mr Molloy made you refund the money ? —He did not make me

Well, you did it voluntarily ?—I told him, if he wrote to the gentleman, and the gentleman wrote word back that he had paid it to me, he should have the money.

And then he discharged you ?—No, he did not

Take care what you say ?—He did not discharge me

Upon your oath, did not Mr Molloy discharge you the very day that he discovered you had received that money ?—Not that day He said, you have told me a lie, for I have written to the gentleman, and he has written back to say, that he did pay you I said then, and I still say, that he never did.

Mr. Molloy said you had told him a lie, however ?—He did say *so*

Did you stop another day in his house ?— Yes, I did, three weeks afterwards

You remained three weeks in his house after ?— I did

Did not he tell you that you should go?—He did. There was a dispute between me and Mrs. Molloy—we had a dispute, and that was the reason of my leaving

Was that about money?—Not about money, it was about things that had been broken she wanted me to pay for them, and I would not. That was all the dispute, and then I told Mr. Molloy I did not want his service

Do you mean to say Mr Molloy did not give you notice to leave him?—I own, on that day, he did. He said I had told him a lie, (that was the word,) and that I must leave him. I said very well we afterwards got friendly again, and I left because I would not pay for the things that were broken

But you paid him the 1*l*. 5*s*?—I did, and I asked him to write to ascertain the truth.

And then he told you the gentleman had written to him, and said he had paid you the money?—Yes, he did, but he never had paid me.

And he told you, you should leave his service?—He did

Then you afterwards agreed?—We afterwards agreed together He did not look out for a servant, and I never looked out for a place.

You required a month's notice, did not you?—No

Upon your oath did not he refuse you a character?—No

Have you applied to him for a character?—No

Re-examined by Mr. Brougham.

Your brother is still in his service, is he not?—Yes

I understood you to say, with respect to the dispute about the 1l. 5s, it was you that suggested to him to write to the gentleman in the country, upon which he wrote?—Yes.

Then you say Mr. Molloy charged you with telling an untruth, will you swear, upon your oath, you had not told him an untruth?—I will

I understood you to say you put it on that issue if he wrote to the gentleman which you desired; and if the gentleman said he had paid you, you would pay the money?—I did

And you did not look out for a place, nor he for a waiter, for three weeks?—No

And then you had a quarrel with your mistress?—Then I had a quarrel with my mistress, and I said I would leave

Mr GRIMSDITCH *again called—examined by* Mr Starkie

Mr Grimsditch, when was it you set out for London?—The 6th of March.

Did you get to London the following evening?
—I did

When did Mr Turner arrive in London?—
Mr Turner arrived in London about two hours
after.

Well, sir, when was it that you first learnt
that anything was amiss as to Miss Turner having been taken away?—By the public newspapers
of the 11th of March I saw the marriage announced on Saturday morning, the 11th of March.

Well, when was it you learnt any particulars
—(I don't ask you what you heard) but when
was it?—I learnt the whole particulars, and the
character of the transaction, on Tuesday the 14th,
at a very early hour in the morning

Well, sir, in consequence of what you learnt,
were steps taken for pursuing the parties, and
taking the Wakefields into custody?—They were;
I waited on the Secretary of State

And you got a warrant from Bow-street, I believe?—I did

Well, sir, without going through the interme-
diate steps, when did you get to Calais?—I got
to Calais about three or four o'clock, as near as
I can recollect, on Wednesday the 15th

Who went with you, sir?—Mr Robert Turner
and Mr Critchley (Miss Turner's two uncles),
Mr Walford, and Ellis, a Bow-street officer.

Did you, after you got to Calais, see either of the Wakefields?—I did

Which of them did you see?—Mr Edward Gibbon Wakefield.

Where did you see him?—I first saw him in the court-yard of Quillac's hotel

Now will you be so good as to state what passed between you on that occasion?—I went up to him, in company with Mr. Robert Turner and Mr. Critchley, and mentioned my name and where I came from, and he appeared to know me.

Well, sir?—He said, " Oh! will you be so good as to walk into my room." I went into his room with Mr Robert Turner; we followed him up stairs, Mr Robert Turner and myself, and went into his room   I told him that we had come there by desire of Mr. Turner, to take back his daughter, whom he had taken away in a very improper manner.   He said, " But I understand you have taken legal proceedings against me."—Then, pointing to Ellis, the Bow-street officer, who had come in rather suddenly, he said, " Who is that man?"   I desired Ellis to withdraw, which he did, and I told him that we insisted upon seeing Miss Turner immediately.   He said, " I wish to know whether you intend to prosecute me?" I told him we did intend to prosecute him;

how could he expect anything else? That he had stolen Miss Turner—and I told him I had a warrant in my pocket, and a despatch from Mr Canning to Lord Granville at Paris He said he knew all about that warrant, and all we had done in London—his friend Percy had come in the same packet Mr. Henry Critchley then entered the room He again asked whether it was really intended to prosecute? and I told him that the strongest measures had been resorted to, and would be—he could expect nothing else. But the first thing I demanded was, to produce the young lady, and I asked him (in a peremptory tone) to give me an answer, Yes or No He then asked, with some agitation, " But is she to be my wife?"—I told him we could not enter into that question—that the act he had been guilty of was a most atrocious one—that he had got possession of Miss Turner, whom he had never seen—a mere child, by means of a forged letter—and that he deserved to be shot.

Upon your observing that, what further passed? —I also added upon that occasion—I said, he had struck a blow at the peace of the family, the effects of which he never could repair, or to that effect—that I thought it would be the death of Mrs. Turner, if she was not dead already, and that we had left Mr. Turner in London broken-hearted, and unable to go another yard after his lost child.

Well, sir ?—He said my animadversions were severe, but that he did not attempt to justify his conduct—that he had a daughter His words were, " I have a daughter, and if any man were to take her off in the same manner, I believe I should send a bullet through his head " Then he added, " But is the marriage legal? If it is, I must keep her—if it is not, I can have no claim to her." I told him it was not only illegal, but that he was liable to severe punishment I told him there was an Act passed in the reign of Philip and Mary, which declared such a marriage void, and also subjected the party to a heavy punishment I said, " It is useless to go into these discussions, we are authorised to take back Miss Turner, and take her we will !" Mr Critchley and Mr Robert Turner both joined in peremptorily demanding to see her—and I told him that I should seek the assistance of the police at Calais if he refused He told me he had more interest with the police than I had.

Was anything said about who should see Miss Turner first—did he say he should see her first, or you ?—He said, if she was to be his wife, it would be desirable that certain questions should not be put to her, and certain facts not disclosed; and desired us not to disclose such particulars as he would point out, nor put such questions as he would mention, for her own sake, if she was to be his wife.

Well, did he say what she would do, or was likely to do, when she saw you?—He again spoke of her being his wife. Mr. Critchley said to him, " I wonder how you can expect that we should enter into such terms!" or words to that effect; and he added, " We must first see her—you may have made some impression upon her ."—those were the expressions of Mr. Critchley.

Well, now, what answer did he make to that? —He said, " Oh, as to that, you will find her perfectly passive. She may think favourably of me, but nothing compared to the unbounded affection that she has for her parents. I dare say she will fly to you, and from me, when she sees you.' He also said, " I should wish to make every reparation," and, again, he said, if she was to be his wife, he was anxious that certain facts should not be disclosed to her—and desired that he might be present at our interview.

Did you agree to that?—No. Mr. Critchley said, " I wonder you can ask it, Mr. Wakefield we must see her without any restraint." He then asked if he might see her after the interview, which we agreed to.

By Mr. Scarlett.—You wrote that immediately

k

after, I suppose (*alluding to the paper Mr. Grims-ditch held in his hand*)?—I did

Well, what did you do then?—He went down stairs and I followed him, and in (I should think) two minutes he brought Miss Turner from a room which was said to be Madame Quillac's room.

That was the landlady's room?—I don't know whether it was or not, but it was said to be her room

By Mr Baron Hullock.—He brought her from the landlady's room?—Yes, it was a room below stairs, my lord.

Well, sir?—I went up stairs before them, and showed her in the room where her relations were, and shut myself and Mr Wakefield out   Upon that he said to me, " Well, Mr. Grimsditch, I assure you, upon my honour, that Miss Turner is the same Miss Turner as she was when I took her away, there has been no consummation of the marriage "   I told him I was very glad to hear him say that   I then went into the room where Miss Turner was with her uncles, and I learnt then the particulars of the falsehoods and frauds which had been practised upon her

You had not heard what passed in the room?—Not what passed previous to my going in   In about twenty minutes, I think, we sent for Mr. Wakefield, according to Mr Critchley's pledge, and when he came in, I said to him, " We find that you have practised upon this poor child the most extraordinary deception and fraud ever heard of." I said that it was a very cruel case, that we should not only take her from him, but that we should put him into the custody of a Bow-street officer He told me I was on the wrong side of the water for that I told him the police would assist, and I again produced the despatch which I had procured from Mr Canning, but he told me that neither that nor the warrant would avail He asked me if I had taken any legal opinions as to the validity of the marriage

Mr Starkie—You need not go into that

Did he claim her after that?—Yes, he said he claimed her as his wife. We had much discussion about it At length Mr Critchley said, " I am quite sure, Mr Wakefield. it is an illegal marriage ," but he still said he claimed her as his wife. And, upon that, Miss Turner spoke for the first time in Mr Wakefield's presence,—upon Miss Turner hearing him say that, she said, " I am not your wife, I never will go near you again —you have deceived me " In saying this, she clasped her uncle, Mr Critchley, round the shoulders in wild agitation.

When she clasped her uncle round the shoulders, what did she say?—She said, " I am not your wife, I never will go near you again—you have deceived me." Mr. Wakefield said to her,

" You must acknowledge I have behaved to you as a gentleman " She said, " Yes, I do acknowledge that, but you have deceived me, and I will never go near you again "

Was there anything said as to the way in which he got her from school?—Yes, there was.

What was that, sir?—He adverted very frequently to the legality or illegality of this marriage; and I said to him, " I am surprised that you can for a moment suppose that this is a legal marriage!" and I told him that he must know as well as I did, that a marriage obtained by force or fraud could not be legal. He said he had not used force. I said, " What do you call it, then? you got possession of her by means of a forged letter—she was wholly in your power," and I added, that he had taken her off in a chaise and four and conveyed her away by deception and fraud from beginning to end

What said he to that?—He said, " I do not attempt to justify my conduct " And he repeated again, if anybody had behaved so to his daughter, he believed he should have shot him, unless reflection at the moment should have restrained his passion.

Cross-examined by Mr. Scarlett.

Did you tell him you had taken the best legal opinions in London?—I believe Mr. Critchley did

That he had taken the best legal opinions in London, and that the marriage was clearly void?—Mr Critchley said we had taken the best opinions, that Sir Richard Birnie, and all the gentlemen he had seen, had said it was an illegal marriage

Did not you say you had taken the best opinions?—No

But you gave him your opinion, that it was clearly void?—Yes

And I believe you mentioned that she was under sixteen, did you not?—That she was only just fifteen

Did not you mention that she was under sixteen years of age?—Yes.

Did you give that as the reason of your opinion—that, being under sixteen it was clearly an illegal marriage, as well as subjected the party to punishment?—Yes, I did, but I was under a mistake at the time, which I can explain   I had got hold of a clause in another Act of Parliament; I had stumbled on a clause in the Marriage Act.

However, you were of opinion at the time, upon the best judgment you had formed, that being under sixteen was a circumstance that made the marriage void, and would make him punishable?—I was under this impression, that he was punishable, under that statute, for taking her away, she being under sixteen, but I also told him there was another act, passed in the reign of Henry VII. which——

Which had made the marriage void?—Yes; I told him the marriage was void

And that was the subject of a great deal of discussion, was it not, before you saw the lady?—There was not so much discussion before we saw the lady

You said there was a good deal before?—But the greatest part of the discussion on that took place afterwards

She was assured, as well as he, that the marriage was void, was not she?—She might, I told him it was, and she heard me say so, I have no doubt

Well, there was an interpreter, was there not —a Monsieur *Duraine*, from the police-office at Calais, who came into the room during the time? —There was a person who went with me to the Mayor of Calais, and afterwards came with the Commissary, for the purpose of assisting in taking her from him if he refused. In the meantime he had agreed to give her up to her uncles.

Pray, did not Mr. Wakefield tell you he had been to Meurice's hotel to look for you, before you saw him?—No, he did not

You had been seeking him some time before you found him, had not you?—No, not a great while.

Did you go to Quillac's in the first instance?—No, we did not go to Quillac's immediately.

But you sent somebody, did not you?—Oh, yes, I sent persons in that direction, whilst I went to the police-office I went there in the first instance

When the Commissary came into the room, did not the commissary say, if the gentleman chose to part with the lady, of course he would do so, but if not, you could not take her away by force?—No, I understood him to say, as far as I could understand it, he asked her whether she would go with him or her uncles, and her reply was, she would go with her uncles

The Commissary asked her which she would do?—Yes.

Did he speak by an interpreter, or in French?—In French.

There was an interpreter there, was there not?—Yes, there was a person with me.

What is his name?—I don't remember his name

Was is it Duraine?—I don't remember his name.

Perhaps you might not exactly agree about the words, as it was spoken in French, did not the Commissary say, if she was his wife, by the law of France, they could not be separated, and that the Mayor of Calais had been spoken to on that subject—did not the Commissary say so?—I did not hear him say so

He spoke in French ?—Yes

Do you understand that language ?—Very im-
perfectly

MR EDWARDS *again called, and examined by
Mr. Williams.*

Mr Edwards —I made a slight error when I
was examined before, I stated I left Mr. Wakefield's last January four years—it was four years
last November.   Perhaps it arose from my going
in January   I left him in November

Do you know Edward Gibbon Wakefield's
hand-writing ?—I do

Now look at that, and tell me if you believe
that to have been written by Edward Gibbon
Wakefield ? (*handing a letter to the witness*)

Mr Scarlett —Who is this?

Mr Williams —He is the person that proved
the hand-writing before

The Witness —I do

MR. GEORGE AYTON, *sworn.   Examined by* MR
Williams

Do you know Miss Davies's, now Mrs Wakefield's, hand-writing ?—I do.

Now, are those letters, according to the best
of your belief, her hand-writing ?—They are

Mr Serjeant Cross —Now read Miss Davies's
letters.

Mr. Cross.—This is the letter, my lord, of Miss Davies, but I don't see any name

Mr Scarlett.—Allow me to look at that letter. (*It was handed to him*) I wish to observe, my lord, that that letter is stated by my learned friend to have been procured somewhere, but he has not shown where. Does the letter appear to be perfect, Mr. Cross?

Mr Cross.—No, there is a part torn off the sheet, containing the address

Mr Baron Hullock.—This is Miss Davies's letter

Mr Scarlett.—It is said to be, my lord

Mr. Baron Hullock.—Well, it had better be read.

Mr Cross read the letter, which was as follows.—" Dear William,—Mr Turner did not come down the night you left it was a mistake.—My father saw Mrs Critchley yesterday, who seems very kindly disposed, but she did not know what her brother's feelings would be perhaps Edward or Madame ought to write to her, touching tender chords The old uncles have been written to by her wish. Miss Daulby has not yet written to Shrigley, but Miss Turner (the niece) wrote to her yesterday This is all Mrs Critchley's information to my father Ever aff your's, F —You must not let a foolish account of the affair get into the papers It would much annoy Turner, I am sure "

Mr. Sergeant Cross —Now read the other letters.

Mr. Cross—This is another letter, my lord, I
believe, of Miss Davies's, addressed to Mr. Randall, 34, Pall-mall   It is without date, my lord.

Mr Scarlett —Mr Randall might prove where
he got it, you know

Mr Cross read the letter as follows.—" Dear
Sir,—I am greatly obliged by your kindness in
sending the paper   I will thank you to send me
a line directed P. O , Buxton, to-morrow, where
I shall be   I wish to know whether William is
in England   I heard yesterday, there would be a
warrant for him, and also a hint that a search
would be made in Pall-mall, for papers, &c   I
know it would have been awkward to you, to
have any which are committed to your care
brought forward, as it might implicate you   If
you received a communication which might surprise you, you will now know the reason. I feel
many obligations to you, and am, dear sir, most
faithfully, your's—W "

Then, my lord, there is another, post-mark
Congleton, the delivery-mark the 21st of March,
1826, addressed to Mr. Randall, 34, Pall-mall —
" Mr. Randall, in whom it is well known confidence can be placed, is requested to take care
that the enclosed is safely delivered, as soon as

possible   A newspaper is also sent to Mr. William Wakefield. If there could be any means of preventing the paragraph inserted in the *Courier*, and also one which may have appeared in the Macclesfield Herald, from finding their way into the public London papers—the paragraph in the *Courier* is, in fact, the only objectionable one Mr Wakefield, himself, would object to any interference with papers, and therefore it is left to Mr. Randall's discretion.—The letter to Mademoiselle Blanc, under Lord B.'s cover, to be forwarded as soon as possible."

Mr Cross.—The next is the letter, my lord, of Mr Edward Gibbon Wakefield, to Mr. William Wakefield

Mr Scarlett.—Is not there the enclosure, because that letter which you have just read mentions an enclosure.

Mr. Cross.—There was none handed to me —This is signed " E. G. W.," and dated " Calais, Thursday To William Wakefield, Esq."

" My Dear William.—I write in haste to save the post, only to give you news, and nothing else. Mr Robert Turner, Mr Critchley and Grimsditch, arrived by the packet to-day, with warrants, &c I soon knew what they were come for, but would not attempt to avoid the question. Shortly, I saw them, and found that, with Ellen's

consent, they could take her away. They insisted
on seeing her. I could not object. She *told all*,
and was anxious to leave me, *when she knew all*.
I expected as much, and therefore made a merit
of necessity, and let her go. They tried to take
me, but for that they were on the wrong side of
the water, as I well knew. However, I offered
to go with them, but begged Mr Critchley to
believe that I would be in England to answer any
charge, as soon as I had seen my children and
settled my affairs. Nothing could be more hostile than the whole spirit of their proceedings. I
could readily have escaped with Ellen, but their
account of Mrs. and Mr. Turner's state, made
such a step impossible. I made and gave in writing a solemn declaration, that she and I have been
as brother and sister. How this may affect the
validity of the marriage, I know not, nor could I
raise the question; I was bound, and it was wise
to give some comfort to Mr Turner. I am now
in a stew about *you*, and wish that you were safe.
There can be no doubt that the law can punish
us. For myself, I will meet it, come what may ;
but, if you are able, get away as soon as possible .
I do not care a straw for myself. The grand
question now is, is the marriage legal ? They all
said no, and quoted William and Mary upon me
till I was tired of their majesties' names. Pray

let me know that. But I write to Nunky. Do not stay—you can do no good. I shall go to England as soon as possible; upon this you may depend. I shall not write again till I hear from you for fear of accidents. Percy came with the trio, and has witnessed the row. We start early in the morning. Pray write, but say nothing to anybody. I am the person to speak.

Your's, ever,

E. G. W."

Mr. Sergeant Cross—I wish to ask one question of Mr. Grimsditch.

Mr. Wakefield says there, he was going to see his children: did he tell you where those children were he was going to see?—Yes, in Paris.

Miss Turner was then brought into court. Before she was sworn, however, Mr. Scarlett rose to object to her evidence; and the young lady retired, and continued absent during the discussion that ensued.

Mr. Scarlett—My lord, I propose to show that this witness is incompetent. My lord, the threat of my learned friend certainly will not deter me from doing what I conceive to be my duty in point of law, when I am called upon to do it. If he thinks it necessary for his case to examine this young lady, of course I must conceive his object in examining her is to affect the criminal party. And therefore I propose to show to your lordship, she is legally married to Mr. Wakefield. I can do that by giving evidence of the marriage, and other circumstances to show it was a legal marriage, and therefore I apprehend she cannot be examined as a witness. I apprehend I have a right to do that without examining her on the *voir dire*.

Mr. Baron Hullock.—I don't know that, Mr Attorney. Supposing the marriage should turn out to be an invalid marriage, that fact must be acquired through the medium of her evidence. But if the marriage should be considered a good marriage,—that is, should be proved to be a good marriage according to the law of that country in which it was performed,—then another question will arise, whether, even if she be the legal wife of this gentleman, she may not still by the law of this country be a competent witness. I have no objection that they should argue it on the other side, on the assumption that she is the legal wife of this gentleman. I have no objection that it should be argued in that way.

Mr. Sergeant Cross.—We cannot consent to that, my lord.

Mr. Scarlett.—If your lordship considers that fact immaterial, and is of opinion that, though she is his legal wife, she may still be examined as a witness against him, then it would be useless in me to give your lordship the trouble of hearing the evidence

Mr Baron Hullock.—I certainly have an opinion upon it, but I should like to hear your argument, of course, before I state what my opinion is.

Mr Scarlett.—I apprehend the rule of law is, that a wife can in no case be a witness against her husband, except for the purpose of proving force, or some criminal matter. And in the various cases that have arisen under the statutes themselves, where no force has been used, the wife's testimony has never been received I believe there is no example of it Where force has been used, of course the wife's testimony has been received

Mr Baron Hullock.—Are you aware of the case of the King and Perry?

Mr. Scarlett —Yes, my Lord

Mr Baron Hullock —Well, there was no force there.

Mr Scarlett —I believe that was a case under the statute of Hen. VII. I apprehend that was a case of force

Mr Baron Hullock —No, the indictment was framed on that statute, but I happen to know that there was no force used in that case. I have

seen a report of that trial   it was tried before
the late Chief-Justice Gibbs, when he was Re-
corder of Bristol.

Mr Scarlett—I apprehend it will turn out
ultimately, in the examination, that there was
no force, but yet, if the charge is force, and the
other side prove there was force, then, I apprehend, she might be examined, to repel the force,
and show there was none   I believe, my lord,
in that case, too, that force was proved, and the
wife was called to negative it.

Mr. Baron Hullock—I am sure no gentleman
who has read that report will say there was
force   Quite the contrary.

Mr Scarlett—Suppose, my lord, a man is
indicted for an assault upon his wife, there is no
doubt she is a competent witness to prove that
assault, or where she comes forward, as a
witness, not to prove force, but to disprove it,
and show there was none, then she is a competent
witness, from the nature of the charge   Now in
this particular case, there is only one of those
counts that has the least relation to force   One
of the counts charges, that he feloniously and by
force conspired to marry her against her consent.
There has been no evidence of that hitherto
The evidence is just the other way, and therefore I may assume, on the evidence at present,

that the only gravamen here is the supposition
(I say the supposition, undoubtedly well-founded
on the evidence now before your lordship) of
what is called fraud or deception, and I apprehend it is perfectly clear, that where there is
deception on the part of a man, by which he
obtains a young lady's free consent to marry, that
would not in the least invalidate the marriage,
and that she could not be a competent witness to
prove that deception. It is not this or that class
of deception that makes the difference in the rule,
for any thing amounting to menace or threat is
force. It is not that that makes her a competent
witness, and that makes the marriage void, though
nobody can say, that a person who is directly
refusing assent, and by force and terror is compelled to assent to that which is a marriage ceremony, would be valid   The marriage itself is
void   But if the marriage takes place, and force
is used afterwards, then the wife is a competent
witness, to prove that force. But in the case
where a marriage takes place with the consent
of the party, even though that arises from some
misconceptions, fraud, or assurance of a fact
which turns out to be untrue, or some persuasion
on the part of the lady, at the instance of the
husband, that certain facts exist which do not, as,
for example, if a person represents that he is

L

worth 10,000*l*, and it turns out that he is not worth ten pence, or, that he will make a handsome settlement upon her, when he has no means of doing it, and it turns out that all this is wholly untrue, although the marriage would be good, yet still she could not be a witness to prove the inducement after the marriage What I am now discussing is, whether, under the circumstances, she can be a witness if there be a marriage. Now, what I propose to show to your lordship is this,—that there is a marriage, and that it took place distinctly by her consent, without the least force whatever. When I come to go into my evidence, I have not the least fear I shall demonstrate that whatever persuasion there may have been (of which I say nothing at present, as that will be matter of further discussion), that she was at perfect liberty to act as she pleased, and that she gave her full and free consent, and that, therefore, a marriage did take place, which, by the law of Scotland, is a good marriage. Under these circumstances, I submit she is not a competent witness in this case but, if your Lordship decides that, notwithstanding this, she is a competent witness, then, of course, her evidence will be received

Mr. Baron Hullock.—I want to know what the law of Scotland is That must be proved as a fact. But the case on the other side don't admit such a marriage took place

Mr Scarlett—That fact I will prove

Mr. Serjeant Cross—The first question to be disposed of is, whether we can go on with the examination of Miss Turner My learned friend, I think, has answered his own objection in his own words he says, if there is any intimidation, that is force; and she may be examined. I have opened a case of force, and there is a count in the indictment for force, and that is the species of case I am going to prove

Mr Baron Hullock—The only difficulty I have is, arriving at the facts before I can give an opinion upon the subject The question is, whether or no a marriage was celebrated in Scotland? (Putting it in the way you yourself suggested, this marriage was performed,) and until I hear what their witness says respecting the law of that country, I cannot give an opinion upon it

Mr Serjeant Cross.—Does your lordship prefer hearing that witness first, before you hear Miss Turner's evidence?

Mr Baron Hullock—I take it in point of law it is not necessary to examine a witness on the *voir dire* to show her incompetency, but you may do that *aliunde* Is not that so? Am I right in that?

Mr Scarlett —Yes, certainly

Mr Sergeant Cross —But the question now before your lordship is, whether Miss Turner can be rejected as a witness under any circumstances, that is, when your lordship shall have heard me ?

Mr Baron Hullock —The question will arise then. I am not deciding that now at all The ground of objection is, that this lady is the wife of one of these defendants, and that, no matter whether that marriage, under which it is alleged she became his wife *de facto*, was or not obtained by fraud or misrepresentation, still that, in point of law, it is a valid marriage, and therefore she is an incompetent witness I understand that to be the question

Mr Sergeant Cross —I understand that to be so stated, but I understand this to be also further stated,—that, even if the witness be a lawful wife, she is a competent witness, to prove that the marriage was by intimidation, and that is what I am calling her to prove, and therefore the objection does not apply to the evidence I am now tendering by that witness

Mr Baron Hullock —They propose to call a witness on the part of the defendant, for the purpose of showing that this marriage (however it was performed) in Scotland was a legal marriage And I apprehend it is quite clear now-a-days, that a marriage must stand or fall according to the law of the country in which it is celebrated, and therefore the question will be, whether this marriage (however it was performed in Scotland) is a legal marriage according to the law of that country I only want to see what the law of Scotland is

Mr Sergeant Cross —I cannot tell to what length my learned friend means' to carry this evidence of his If he confined it to a single witness, as your lordship seemed to suppose, I should not think it worth while to resist it, but I don't know to what length he is going, and therefore I stand on my right to examine Miss Turner, unless my learned friend can satisfy your lordship that I have no right to do so.

Mr. Baron Hullock —If you insist upon it she must be called, and then she will tell you on the *voir dire* the circumstances under which the marriage took place, and then a witness will be called to prove that the marriage is valid. It comes round to the same point.

Mr Sergeant Cross —Will your lordship allow me to state one other proposition ? I stand, I say, on my right to examine Miss Turner My learned friend's argument has conceded that right, for he says, be it that she is the lawful

wife, yet she may be examined, in order to prove
she was carried away by force, and he says, that
intimidation is force. Now, I have opened a
case of intimidation at Carlisle, by menaces and
threats of the ruin of the family. If, then, she
is a competent witness, though she should be the
wife, I submit the question is not ripe for discussion here, whether she is the wife or not. It is
trying a collateral question, which, on that
admission of my learned friend, I humbly submit to your lordship has nothing to do with the
present enquiry, it being admitted, that should
she be the lawful wife, I have a right to examine
her as to intimidation

Mr Scarlett—Surely my learned friend can
hardly misunderstand the matter so much as he
seems to do. I have admitted, if a woman be
legally married to a man, and he afterwards as-
saults her, that she may be a witness to prove
that, but I neither admit he has opened nor
proved a case of intimidation. I say he has done
no such thing. What I mean to show is, that
there was a marriage without intimidation, and I
have a right to do that before the witness is put
into the box   I might examine her on the *voir
dire* to prove that, if I thought fit, but I have
also the option of doing it *aliunde ;* and it was so
stated by my Lord Hardwicke in the House of

Lords, in a case where they offered to call a witness to prove the incompetency, without examining the witness at all Your lordship knows
there are cases in which it has been done Has
my friend read Lord Lovat's case?

Mr Baron Hullock —I don't remember any
case in which it has been so decided I should
say, on principle, there is nothing in the point
—nothing at all , but at the same time, I would
rather have the examination conducted in the
usual manner , and therefore the lady must be
called, and she must be sworn on the *voir dire*
It appears to me it will only come round to the
same point two hours hence

Mr Scarlett —I have an anxiety which is not
ill intended towards this lady or her connexions

Mr Baron Hullock —You must do your
duty.

Mr Scarlett —I conceive we have a right to
show this *aliunde*, and I submit it would be a
more convenient mode of doing it

Mr. Baron Hullock —I have no objection to
your doing it in that way, but it will come to
nothing You propose to prove that the marriage
took place by apparent consent—(I know what you
mean to prove)—that when they arrived at Gretna
Green this lady expressed no reluctance but that
comes to nothing

Mr Scarlett—I mean to show that long before they arrived, from first to last.

Mr Baron Hullock (in a low tone)—Was it before she left Manchester?

Mr Coltman—I would just observe, my lord, that it was expressly decided, in Lord Lovat's case, and ruled in respect to several witnesses, that that was the proper course   The Lord High Steward (Lord Hardwicke) intimated to Lord Lovat that he might take two courses; he might either examine the witness to whose evidence he objected on the *vou dire*, or he might call other witnesses to prove his incompetency

Mr Baron Hullock—I think that may be done in point of law   No authority has been cited against it   I have heard no reason suggested, why the principle which, in my judgment, applies to this case, ought to be departed from.

Mr Brougham—Will your lordship allow me to say a word against the change of practice which this would be introducing   Your lordship is quite aware, and it has been truly stated, that, whether there is this authority or not of Lord Lovat's case, if it was acted upon, which I don't think my friend said it was, my Lord Hardwicke so said to the prisoner on his defence; but, whatever may be the meaning of that case, this is perfectly clear,—that all practice is uniformly, and

most uniformly, against it   Here the objection to
the witness is on account of identity,—that is to
say, that she is his wife.   It is an equal objection,
and of the same kind precisely, to a witness in
any common civil suit, that he is a partner in
trade with the partner producing him as a witness , and would it not be giving rise to the most
interminable confusion of issues, if he was to be
allowed to say, instead of asking if he be a partner, " You may go down, for I have ten witnesses
here who can produce evidence of the partner-
ship " Then there must be ten witnesses on the
other side, if it be necessary, to try the negative
of that question, and to negative those ten who
are for the affirmative ; and then the court, not
the jury, but the judge who tries the cause, assisted in the trial by the jury, is to have his time
consumed in trying this collateral and springing
issue out of the other, which he is first to try and
dispose of   And among other reasons against it,
in all probability it would prevent the party producing that witness from having the benefit of a
reply , because it requires very little address,
much less than presides over the case of the defendants in this instance, in the person of my
learned friend, Mr. Scarlett, to twist in the best
part of the defence, under the colour of giving
evidence on this collateral issue , and then having

done so, in whatever way the objection is disposed
of, he need not call witnesses to his case, which
cuts out the other party from the right to reply.
That is one inconvenience which, I presume,
among a great many others, exists in allowing a
collateral issue to be tried unnecessarily, and it
would have the effect of altering that which has
long been the established practice of the court

Mr Scarlett —Perhaps your lordship will permit me to point out what one daily experiences
with respect to the incompetency of witnesses,
and which very often arises from evidence *aliunde*
In an action upon a bill of exchange, for instance .
suppose now, I call a witness to prove the bill in
question was an accommodation bill, that is one
mode · or suppose I prove a man is a partner before he is called, do my friends mean to say he
must be called on the *voir dire* over again, to
make him a competent witness? It is in the cause
I ask the question, for the purpose of showing he
is incompetent   Now, here is what my learned
friend calls the practice . if the opposite party
raises the question by independent evidence, then
the party by whom the witness is called cannot
be allowed to put a question in order to repel the
objection in point of fact, on the *voir dire*, because the witness ought not to be examined at all,
It forms the subject of an independent issue al-

together, and therefore is a matter that ought to go to the jury I therefore propose to show it in the way I have stated, not to deprive my friend of the reply, for I will give it him

Mr Baron Hullock — I think myself exercising the best discretion I can here As this is a matter of practice, and therefore must depend on my decision, I shall request Miss Turner to be called I think there is a great deal in what has fallen from Mr. Brougham, but I think I see some inconvenience in not permitting her to be called, which will not exist if she is called

Mr. Scarlett —Your lordship will have the goodness to make a note of my objection, that it may find its way into your lordship's notes that I proposed to give this evidence beforehand

Mr Baron Hullock —Certainly.

Miss Turner *sworn* Examined by Mr Sergeant Cross

Miss Turner, I believe you are the daughter of Mr Turner, of Shrigley ?—I am

Did you go to school in the month of March last, in company with your father ?—The latter end of February, or the beginning of March

Do you remember going away in a carriage about that time, one morning ?—On the 7th of March.

Who told you you were to go ?—Miss Elizabeth Daulby

Did you go in consequence of her directions ?—She told me that she had received a letter which gave instructions that I should go home

Well, and you got into the carriage, I believe?—I did

Where did you intend to go, when you got into the carriage ?—I was told that I was to go to Manchester, where I was to meet my papa.

And from thence ?—To Shrigley, I believed

Had you known a young lady—a Miss Greenway, who had left the school shortly before ?—I had

Do you know the reason why she left the school ?—I believe it was on account of her father's difficulties.

Well, you proceeded to Manchester, I believe ?—Yes

And when you got there, did you go into the house ?—Yes

Did any stranger come into the room while you were sitting there ?—Yes

Who was that ?—The person whose name I afterwards found to be Edward Gibbon Wakefield

Had you ever seen that person before ?—Never.

Upon coming into the room, what did he say to you, Miss Turner ?—I was rising to leave the room, and he requested I would not go.

Well, after he had requested you not to go, what was said then?—He said he was commissioned by my papa to take me to him

And any thing else did he say at that time?—I might be sure it was no slight circumstance that prevented my papa from coming for me himself.

And then what did he say?—That it was the state of my papa's affairs which had induced him to send for me home

Well, did he say what state his affairs were in?—He said that he should afterwards explain to me in what state my papa's affairs were

Did he say any thing else at that time, Miss Turner, that you recollect?—I remarked that it was on account of my mamma's illness that I was sent for home

What did he say to that?—He said that the facts stated in the letter to Miss Daulby were not true

Well, what else—any thing else, do you recollect?—He said that that letter had been written because they did not wish Miss Daulby to know why I was sent for

Was any thing said about where your father was?—I don't distinctly remember what he said about the place where my papa was at that time

I think you have said he told you you were to go to your papa?—He did tell me so.

Well, then, did you see any other stranger

shortly after?—He told his servant to tell the other gentleman to come in

You mentioned a servant—was that the person that attended you from Liverpool to Manchester?—I believe it was the same person.

Did the other gentleman come?—He came into the room

When he came in what passed then? was any thing said about your going any where?—I don't remember any thing particular that was said.

Well, soon after that did you get into a carriage?—Yes

Did he introduce that person to you whom he sent for in?—He did not introduce him, he merely spoke of him as his younger brother.

Who did that person turn out afterwards to be?—Mr. William Wakefield.

Had you ever seen him before?—Never.

I believe you stepped into a carriage then, did not you?—Yes

What was the reason for your going into the carriage with them at that time?—I imagined that I was going to meet my papa.

Well, I will not trouble you to mention all the different places you went to, do you know whether you were taken as far as Halifax?—Yes.

You were?—Yes

Did both the Wakefields accompany you thither?—Yes.

And the man-servant also to Halifax?—Yes.

When you got there was any thing said about your going to any other place, or further on?—Mr. Edward Gibbon Wakefield said, that if there was no letter there, and if we did not see my papa there, we must proceed as far as Kendal

And find him there?—We should be sure to find him there

Did you go on to Kendal?—Yes

Had you any other object for going there but to find your papa?—No other

Well, you stopped awhile at Kendal, and then proceeded, I believe, towards Carlisle?—Yes.

Before you arrived at Kendal, was any thing said about any letter at Kendal?—At Kendal, Mr Wakefield read a letter at the window, and his brother looked over it, but I did not see it

Upon that, was any thing said about your father?—He said that my papa was not there, but was gone forward.

Was that as soon as he had read the letter, or before?—I don't remember whether it was before or after

Well, upon that you proceeded forward, I believe?—Yes.

Was any further communication made to you on the next stage, relative to your father's affairs?
—Yes

What was that?—Mr. Wakefield said that he had received a letter from my papa, commissioning him to inform me the state of my papa's affairs

Go on, if you please, Miss Turner, in the order in which you recollect the circumstances   What did he say about your papa's affairs—what did he communicate to you?—He said that a bank had failed at Macclesfield.

Did he name the bank?—Ryle and Daintry's

Any other bank, did he mention—state what further you recollect?—He said that my papa had been almost ruined

Well?—But that that an uncle of his, who was a banker in Kendal, had lent my papa the sum of 60,000*l.*

Well, did he say any thing else at that time?—He said, that had relieved him for the present.

And then?—That afterwards the Blackburn Bank had failed

And then?—And then his affairs were in a worse condition than before

Any thing further at that time do you recollect?—He said, that his uncle then demanded security for the sum which he had lent.

To your father?—Yes

Did he say what the security was to be?—The estate of Shrigley

Any thing else? Did he say what was to become of your father?—He said, and then my papa might be turned out-of-doors any day

Well, upon that, was any thing suggested?—Yes

What was that?—He said that it had been suggested by Mr Grimsditch, I believe, that he, Mr Wakefield, should be my husband.

Did he say what would be the effect of that?—That then the property would be mine

And any thing else?—And that then it would be in my power to turn my papa out-of-doors, if I liked, but, of course, I should not think of doing it

Did you make any reply to this?—Not at that time.

This, I think, passed on the stage from Kendal towards Carlisle?—Yes

Did he advert to the subject again before you got to Carlisle?—He frequently said that he was desirous to know what conclusion I had come to

And did you give him an answer before you got to Carlisle?—He had said that I should see my papa, and then I said I should give the answer to him.

Was it there that you was to give the answer?—He did not name Carlisle.

He said that you should see your papa were

M

you still in quest of your papa at that time ?—
Yes.

Was it said where he was, as you were going to
Carlisle ?—Mr Wakefield said that he was attempting to cross the Border

Did he give any reason why he was attempting
to do so ?—The sheriff's officers were in pursuit
of him

Well, then you arrived at the Bush Inn, at Carlisle, I believe ?—Yes

Well, when the carriage stopped at the inn
door, what was the first thing that happened ?—
Both the Mr. Wakefields left the carriage.

How long do you think they might be away ?—
I do not know how long it was

Was it a few minutes or hours ?—It was not an
hour

You had been travelling, I believe, from the
time that you left school, at eight o'clock in the
morning, till the time you arrived at Carlisle, had
not you ?—Yes.

Up all night ?—Yes.

Well when they came back to the carriage, what
did either of them say ?—Just as we were leaving Carlisle, Mr. William Wakefield, after having
drawn up the carriage windows, said he had
something of importance to communicate to his
brother.

Before you left Carlisle, had any thing been said where your father was gone then?—I did not expect to meet him at Carlisle

Where then?—Across the Border

Then if I understand you right, you were made to expect your father would be across the Border, and you would find him there—was that so?—It was.

What was the communication that William Wakefield made to his brother?—He said he had seen my papa at Carlisle.

And what else?—And that Mr. Grimsditch was with him.

Go on, if you please?—That he was there concealed in a small room at the back of the house.

Go on, if you please?—That he had made two attempts that day to cross the Border, and could not

What Border was that?—The Border between England and Scotland

Did he say any thing more had passed in the room with your father and Mr Grimsditch?—He said the persons whom I had seen round the carriage door were sheriffs' officers.

Sheriffs' officers, about what?—In search of my papa.

Was any thing more said about Mr. Grims-

M 2

ditch?—That Mr. Grimsditch had intreated that Mr. William Wakefield would not stop in the room, or they should be discovered

Well, any thing else?—And that he had taken him by the shoulders and turned him out of the room

Did he bring any message from your father to you?—He said that my papa requested, if I ever loved him, that I would not hesitate

By Mr Baron Hullock.—Hesitate to do what? —To accept Mr Wakefield as a husband

What did you say to that?—I consented

What induced you to consent?—The fear, that if I did not, my papa would be ruined

Did you believe what he had told you upon that subject?—I did

Well, then you got over the Border, I believe, into Scotland?—I am not sure, whether, at that time, we had crossed the Border, or not

No, not that you had at that time, but you did shortly afterwards arrive in Scotland?—Yes.

Well, did you repeat your consent in the presence of any persons who were there?—Yes.

Mr Baron Hullock.—Where?

In Scotland?—Yes

Cross-examined by Mr Scarlett.

Will you allow me to ask you two or three questions I shan't trouble you at any length. You went through a form of ceremony of marriage in Scotland—did not you?—Yes

And you had a ring?—Yes

The ring was too large for you, I believe—was it not?—It was, rather.

Another was bought for you at Calais, afterwards, I believe?—Yes.

You dined in Scotland?—Yes.

And believed yourself the lawful wife of Mr. Wakefield at that time—did you not?—Yes

And you remained in that persuasion until you were otherwise informed at Calais?—Yes.

Did you write a letter to your mother?—Yes.

Did you use the name of Wakefield?—I did.

When you saw your uncle and Mr Grimsditch at Calais, they assured you the marriage was void?—Yes, they did

Re-examined by Mr. Serjeant Cross

You have been asked about a letter which you signed with the name of Wakefield. Who dictated that letter?—Mr Edward Gibbon Wakefield

Mr. Baron Hullock —I have no objection, now, Mr. Attorney, to your calling a witness to prove that the marriage is a valid marriage, and then I think the question will arise more properly than it did before

Mr. Scarlett —As my friend has taken this course, I shall be under the necessity of adding some other facts, and I may as well do it all at once I shall open my case very shortly.

Mr Baron Hullock —Only now the question will arise Then you will not call your witness now ?

Mr Scarlett —I should prefer calling my witness after I have opened my case in the regular way now.

Mr. Baron Hullock —It is the same thing , only if I should be of opinion, hereafter, that this lady is the legal wife of this gentleman, according to the law of Scotland, then I must decide whether the evidence must be struck out, that is all

Mr. Scarlett —It may go further than that

Mr Baron Hullock —I am only suggesting that that point will arise now

Mr Scarlett.—I fancy they have very near done their case, and I may as well make one case of it

HENRY CRITCHLEY, Esq *sworn   Examined by*
Mr Brougham

You are the brother-in-law to Mr. Turner, the prosecutor ?—I am

And uncle, of course, to Miss Turner?—Yes.

Did you accompany Mr. Robert Turner to Calais, with Mr Grimsditch?—I did.

For the purpose of recovering your niece—Yes

I understand there was a period in Mr Grimsditch's absence during which you were in the room with Mr. Robert Turner, and your niece, and Mr Edward Gibbon Wakefield, at Calais?—Yes

When Mr Grimsditch was not in the room?—Yes

Now turn your attention to that do you recollect having any conversation with Mr. Edward Gibbon Wakefield at that time respecting what he had done?—Yes, I had.

Now will you speak out, so that the gentlemen of the jury may hear you, and tell us what the conversation that passed between you was?—Amongst other topics, I asked Mr Gibbon Wakefield how he could commit so flagrant and cruel an act as to carry away a mere child whom he had never seen

Now, sir, what did Mr Wakefield say in reply to that observation?—He admitted that he had never seen her before he got to Manchester, and that he had spent some time before in the family of Dr Davies

Well, sir?—Where she had frequently been

the subject of conversation, that she was represented to him as a very fine girl, and the heiress
to one of the largest fortunes in the county, and
that he was determined to possess himself of her.

Cross-examined by Mr Scarlett

I believe, Mr. Critchley, you joined in the assurance that the marriage was void ?—Probably
I did, sir, it is very likely

And you told her so at Calais ?—I did.

That was almost your first communication to
her, was it not ?—Not the first but in the course
of conversation, I certainly told her that I had
had every reason to believe that it was an illegal
marriage, and she exclaimed, " Thank God for
it ! It is the happiest intelligence that could be
conveyed to me "

Was that in his presence ?—No ; he wished to
be present at our interview, but that I would not
admit of I said he should have an interview
afterwards

Re-examined by Mr. Sergeant Cross.

When she was in his presence did she alter her
opinion or her exclamation ?—Not at all.

Mr. Sergeant Cross.—-That is my case, my lord

THE DEFENCE

Mr. Scarlett —My lord, I am counsel in this case for the three defendants, the Messrs Wakefield and Mrs. Wakefield, and I am exceedingly glad to observe in the progress of the cause, that the evidence against one at least (Mrs Wakefield) is so exceeding slight, that I trust your lordship will be of opinion I may dispense with the trouble of making a case on her behalf

Mr Baron Hullock —I think there is evidence to go to the jury There are circumstances of suspicion respecting Mrs Wakefield, which, I think, I ought to leave to the jury

Mr Scarlett then proceeded to address the jury on the part of the defendants as follows —

Gentlemen of the Jury,

I propose to trouble you very shortly on this occasion I am aware that this cause has excited great public expectation, but certainly, as far as I am concerned, that expectation, upon any thing I have to urge, will be disappointed.

Gentlemen, there is one topic my learned friend introduced in his address to you, which I cannot pass over without some notice He has thought it right to make a studious panegyric upon a right honourable and learned friend of mine, who has been lately elevated, as my learned friend has stated, to a high judicial situation; and my learned friend lamented, that that circumstance, though fortunate for the country, was a serious disadvantage to the interests of the prosecutor, as it had placed him in the situation of opening the case to you. There are two observations connected with that subject, which I cannot help adverting to. I do not at all agree that it is unfortunate for the prosecutor, that the case is placed in the hands of my learned friend, because, although I have the greatest respect for the talents of that right honourable and learned friend of mine, I will say, that, in my opinion, he never yielded in experience or capacity to my learned friend, nor to many of my learned friends on this circuit, and that many of them who are in the habits of conducting business here, are just as capable of conducting this prosecution as my right honourable and learned friend himself, or his substitute, who now makes that apology for himself unnecessarily

Gentlemen, there is another topic of a more general nature, which I shall advert to. Undoubtedly, I shall agree in the eulogium my learned friend has pronounced on that right honourable gentleman, so far as regards his judicial talent, and I sincerely hope and believe he will be of service to the country in the station he is placed, but as a general proposition, I take leave to say to my learned friend, I do not agree that those persons are the most independent that affect an independence of all parties In general, I believe, the members of the profession of the law who affect to be independent of all parties, are those who are most dependent on any party who thinks fit to select them, and without meaning to make an invidious reflection on any of them, I should not think the worse of a man's honesty or independence, because he was attached to a particular party, whether it was this or that How my learned friend meant to apply that to the late Attorney-general, I know not, whether he meant to say that he is attached to this party or that, but as a general proposition, I beg leave to say, that it is no sort of compliment to a professional man to say he is independent of all parties, because the ready inference which the world draws from that observation is, that he is open to all parties

Gentlemen, with that I dismiss the subject, and come now to the case before you Gentlemen, no man shall ever place me in a situation, either in this court, in public, or in private, to vindicate an act of immorality, or an act of injustice My duty, as an advocate, is to give my humble efforts to the administration of the law, such as it is, and it is not my duty to endeavour to prevent it. If, therefore, my learned friend takes an issue with

me, of whether Mr Wakefield or his brother can
at all be justified in the measures they appear to
have been taking, by abstracting this young lady
from the school where she was, undoubtedly, neither this Mr Wakefield, nor that Mr Wakefield,
nor any man in the universe shall call on me to
maintain the affirmative, that is to say, that the
parties who did that are innocent I am, therefore, neither called upon, nor am I desired to do
that Mr Wakefield has himself admitted, as you
have heard from the witnesses who have been
examined to-day, that the transaction was wrong ;
and however the follies and fashions of men may
lead them into that which they cannot justify in a
court of justice, it is impossible for any man to
advance any thing in palliation, much less in justification of that act

Gentlemen, I wish that the act (though I don't
mean to say it was unnatural)—yet I wish it had
not excited any very angry passion on the other
side. but I say it was not unnatural. I assure you
I feel as a man and as a father for the respectable gentleman who is the father of this young
lady, and I can make every sort of excuse and
allowance for any excess of angry feeling in his
mind, I think it is natural, although not laudable
—excusable, although not justifiable. Because,
when men come into a court of justice, they come
for justice and not for vengeance, and therefore I

wish very much that I could have seen less of that
disposition which must have existed in the minds
of those who were instrumental in getting up this
prosecution, which induced them to include a lady
in this prosecution, on testimony that is really so
—I can hardly use the word slight—but so ridi-
culous, that I venture to say there are hardly
six persons in Macclesfield, who might not, with
equal justice, have been included in the indictment, on the same sort of testimony Surely Mrs
Brocklehurst might have been included in the
same way, because she had taken Mrs Wakefield,
and introduced her to Shrigley-hall, and she had
asked after Miss Turner   The sum and substance
of Mrs. Wakefield's offence is this —that she had,
on the occasion of this gentleman's appointment as
high-sheriff, and whose nomination to the shrie-
valty was known about the time of her return,
which was in the beginning of February, from
abroad, from a visit she had made during her
father's vacation,—that she expressed to a lady
her regret that she had not called on Mrs. Turner
before, and at a season when persons were expecting to be full of gaiety, and the high-sheriff
was about to give a public breakfast, or some
public entertainment, she was introduced there
by that lady and surely it is not necessary to
suppose that this lady was desirous of being introduced there in order to make it subservient to

some desperate crime of conspiracy and treason against the family   I dare say you know enough of the female sex to know, that they are desirous of participating in innocent amusements of that sort , and surely it is not necessary to resort to the supposition that this lady was introduced there with any intention to defraud them of their child or their property   Then what was there in Mrs Davies's regretting that she had not been introduced, and there being some expectation of a public entertainment that she should wish to get an invitation ? But then, it is said, she asked after Miss Turner ?—Oh, what a crime ! What, call on a lady, and ask after her daughter !   Why, I will venture to say that no woman ever called on a mother, more especially at the first acquaintance, without asking after her children   And Mrs. Brocklehurst tells you she did the same thing— that she asked after Miss Turner.   What topic of conversation is more natural than that ?   Well, but there is another thing—it seems that she lent the other defendants money, and she avowed she lent them part of the money she obtained from the bankers   Good God ! are you to infer from that, that she lent it for this purpose ?   It is quite plain that she had lent them money, but then are you to suppose they communicated to her their design ? Nothing, in my mind, is more irrational than such a conception. My learned friend opened,

that he should prove the servants coming back,
and having a conference with her, but not a tittle
of evidence has he given on that subject Then
there are letters of her's—what is more natural?
You will please to recollect her connexion with
the family, and though at that time the connexion
was not avowed, it was well known to them she
was married to Mr Wakefield, and what is remarkable, one of those letters which they put in
was contained in an inclosure, and they have not
put in that inclosure The letter is addressed to
Mr Randall, whom they don't call to prove he
received the letter Then why are you not to infer
that that related to an advertisement in the Courier
and Macclesfield papers, of her marriage with
Mr Wakefield? It is too much, I think, on suspicion like this, to introduce this lady into the indictment, who, from the moment it was known
that she was introduced into this indictment, has,
I am informed, been a victim of the greatest sor-
row She feels that no charge could affect her
more deeply, and from that moment to this she
has been in a state of agitation, which, I am afraid
has operated on her as a degree of punishment
more severe than any Mr Turner could wish
to inflict upon her. I trust, then, I have delivered her from the charge that is made against
her, and I shall therefore dismiss from your con-

sideration all further topics regarding those letters, for you must feel the evidence on which she is included in the indictment does not justify her introduction into the indictment, and therefore you will be disposed, without one single further observation from me, to say she is not in the least guilty

Now for the other parties. Gentlemen, if this indictment had confined itself to the charge of simply taking this young lady away, a conspiracy to do so, and had not contained some other counts of an extraordinary nature, I certainly should not have offered his lordship any observation on this occasion. Gentlemen, I will say further, if my learned friend had not called that young lady—if he had not compelled her testimony to be received here, though I conceive he had a right to do so, I should have been very glad to have been relieved from the necessity of making those remarks on her conduct, and on the transaction itself, which it is now my duty to draw your attention to

Gentlemen, I conceive the character of an offence of this sort to be very different, according as the conduct of the parties—of all the parties concerned—may show consent or compulsion. God forbid I should stand up for one moment in any place to offer the slightest apology for a man who uses any thing like menace, intimidation, or threat, for the purpose of procuring a woman to marry him. You observed I did not ask the young lady many questions. My instructions were not to do so I asked her whether she did not, until she received that intimation at Calais, believe herself to be the lawful wife of Mr Wakefield, and she said she certainly did I have not asked her as to any of the particulars to which I must now draw your attention, because I conceive that it makes a most important difference, in the administration of this particular law, whether or not this lady gave a ready and a willing consent to be married to this gentleman Mind, the first part of the transaction I have disposed of I neither attempt to justify nor apologise for it. There she was at Manchester. The question was, what was to be done? Was she to return to her father's house, or return to school, or was she to go off and be married to Mr Wakefield?

Now, gentlemen, I shall be very short in stating my case to you In the first place, I beg to call your attention to Miss Turner's manner and appearance, undoubtedly an appearance very captivating,—and the evidence proves what Miss Daulby said of her, that she was a very clever girl, of quick apprehension and sagacity, and undoubtedly of considerable talents, and you distinctly saw that, from the exhibition she has made here to-day.

N

Now, gentlemen, one other fact. If, indeed, this marriage was illegal—if the marriage was such as not to place either of the parties at any future time, in any situation of difficulty, but it was a clear point that the marriage was illegal, I am quite sure it would be the interest and the duty of Mr Wakefield to say no more about the subject, or rather to confirm everything he has already said. He acted under the apprehension, at the time he saw these gentlemen at Calais, and, as you have heard from Mr. Grimsditch, they assured him the marriage was illegal, and gave a specific reason for it—Mr. Wakefield was not a lawyer, and knew nothing about it—justify his conduct he did not, but he was informed she was under sixteen, and from that circumstance a particular statute made the marriage illegal, she having been taken away without the consent of her father, and upon that he acted

Now, gentlemen, I have to offer this to you I neither express nor feel any satisfaction or pleasure at it—far from it I have no feeling on the subject, one way or the other—but I shall prove to you the marriage is clearly legal. I shall show you that the lady, when she set out from Manchester, knew that the horses' heads were turned to the Oldham road, and not to the Macclesfield road, because the carriage stood at the corner of the street   There are two roads, one of which goes to Delph, and the other to Macclesfield   I will show you that this young lady was well acquainted with Manchester, and that she had two friends living at no great distance from the hotel from which she went.   I do not mean to call all the mass of evidence that is contained in my brief, a great portion of that evidence (which will be examined very shortly) will prove facts that have been proved by two of the persons that have been called by my learned friend, one a waiter, and the other a chambermaid at the inn, proving what passed when they went towards Gretna-Green, and when they returned. Moreover, I believe almost every witness that I shall call has been examined by the other side, though they have not chosen to call them. I will show to you, the very first stage from Manchester, that she was full of gaiety and alacrity—that from that time till the time of her approaching Gretna-Green, she never ceased her expressions of pleasure and satisfaction to all those persons who saw her on the way, and they are numerous—not connected witnesses, but at every stage, who will describe to you that they, who have often seen parties of the same sort, never saw any who appeared to be more full of cheerfulness and joy, not only when they were on the road, but on their arrival at Gretna Green.

I shall prove, that before the marriage she sat on
Mr Wakefield's knee, with an appearance of the
greatest fondness—that the marriage was contracted, not as by a person who was under some
notion that she was making herself a martyr, but
that she went through the ceremony, not only
without reluctance, but with a degree of alacrity
and impatience that is seldom witnessed at that
place —That, after the marriage was celebrated,
there was the same pleasure, the same expression
of joy and apparent fondness for Mr Wakefield, and that that took place, and continued
up to the very period of their separation I don't
go through the details, because the witnesses
will have to do that   I shall prove these facts
for the purpose of showing that she freely gave
her consent. I cannot call Mr Wakefield as a
witness here to show at what time, or at what
particular moment, that consent was given; and,
surely, it does not become me, nor does it become them, to make any observation on that   I
think, addressing myself to gentlemen of your
description, you will feel what a man of honour
is bound to do, if he has had the misfortune to be
several days in the society of a young lady, and
then to learn she is not his lawful wife, and that
he cannot sustain the marriage. I shall make
only one observation upon that—he is bound, in

that case, to do anything he can to heal the breach he has made   But, if she turns out to be his lawful wife, and he is put on his trial, and that is one of the questions that is indirectly put in issue by the trial, and voluntarily put in issue by the prosecutor, not sought for by me, because I wish to exclude her testimony altogether, and let the case rest where it was—he surely may be excused for endeavouring to vindicate himself from the appearance of having acted under certain delusions upon her mind at the time, which was not unnatural.   And for that purpose it is necessary to see what the real state of the facts is

Gentlemen, that you can collect only from circumstances   But I shall show you that, from first to last. there was no indication of dejection, of intimidation, or of violence done to her feelings, or of any circumstance that can, by possibility, lead you to think that her inclination did not go entirely along with the act she was about to do   She is a very intelligent girl, she was well-grounded in her education, she must have known which way the carriage was going, that it was not going to Macclesfield, but that it was going to Delph, and at Delph she had some sandwiches or some refreshment of some sort.   I shall call witnesses to prove these facts   I am instructed I shall be able to prove, not by one or two witnesses, that can leave no doubt in the mind of any man, that such was the feeling of her mind. After the marriage she went to London, and from London to Calais, and, when they arrived at Calais, I shall be able to show you that she was hanging upon Mr Wakefield's arm in the most affectionate manner,—that she was buying things to fit herself out, and expressing great pleasure and satisfaction at his society, and that to several persons who witnessed it ; and that they drew no other conclusion than that they were (as one of the witnesses has described) a very loving couple

Gentlemen, that is the nature of the case I have to prove to you   One of the counts charges that they conspired feloniously, and by force to marry her against her consent ,—surely upon that count they have been acquitted already   But does it not, in some degree, qualify the offence, if I show the other party consented to it

I remember only one case like this, and which, I believe, his Lordship will also recollect, which was a prosecution instituted by a gentleman of the name of Franks   the cases are rather inverted,—he prosecuted the father of the lady, and the friends of the father who had assisted in helping the lady into the carriage, and who had, in short, been conspiring to marry his son to that lady, who was a person of inferior rank,—the son being under the age of twenty-one

Gentlemen, the prosecution was tried at York,

and I well remember this circumstance; it was
proved, in the course of the evidence, that the
son had gone down on his knees to his father to ask
his consent to the marriage,—the father refused,
and the son took his hat and went out of the
room, and joined the post-chaise where the lady
was waiting with her father, and stepped into it
and went off, and got married And as soon as
the fact was ascertained that he was desirous of
the marriage, the learned Judge put an end
to the cause, and said, " Surely you will
not press this any further ?" Mind I don't mean
to justify the conduct of Mr Wakefield, by
which he accomplished the possession of this
young lady's person,—that is quite another question But if it appears that he, at Manchester,
allows her to go back, and she was her own
agent, she was perfectly at liberty to go back,
—" I confess I have done wrong to get you here,
you are ready to do what you please,"—if you
are of opinion he gave her free will and consent
to go at once, it appears to me to qualify very
much the guilt with which he is charged, if not
entirely to remove it, because, as to the conspiracy to marry because she was under the age
of sixteen, that is an offence under the statute,
which this is not alleged to be ;—this is not an
offence under the statute, this is a charge of conspiracy to violate that statute.

Gentlemen, by the law of nature a girl may marry as soon as she is marriageable but, by a particular statute, if a girl is taken away, and married by force against her will, that is made a crime if she is under the age of sixteen—that is the age the statute selects, but every body knows the age of sixteen to one girl is very different from the age of sixteen to another girl The law of nature is the same everywhere—and I shall by no means consider, if a girl has formed an attachment to a man, and a man to her, that to obtain the consent of a person to marry against the father's consent, provided no improper means are used for the purpose—that that, of necessity, is a crime by the law of the land, because the father has no power after the daughter is fourteen, any more than he has after she is twenty-one —she is free to choose by the law of England after she is fourteen, just as much as she is after she is twenty-one If that were not so, there could be no marriage at all where the parties were under age, without a conspiracy—none at all, unless it is to be said that every man is guilty of a conspiracy who marries a girl of the age of fourteen without the consent of her father But it appears to me, that we must look to the circumstances, and see whether she gave her free consent or not, I say Miss Turner did not desire, or wish, to return back to hei father, that aftei she got into the cainage, and befoie she got the first stage, she gave hei full and fiee consent to the mainage, and knew what was going to happen. All these ciicumstances, which I have stated, we have thought it propei to biing witnesses to piove, foi the puipose of making a case, if it should become necessaiy, and which nevei would have been made at all, but for the declaration that the mainage was illegal

Gentlemen, if the mainage is a legal marriage, his Loidship will deteimine how fai hei evidence is admissible I considei that my learned friend has piessed hei evidence into the cause befoie it could be received I shall call a witness to show it was a legal mainage, and shall show that a mainage obtained by means of the ciicumstances I have stated, and by the additional ones I shall piove, by the law of Scotland, and by the law of England too, is a legal mainage

Mr Baron Hullock —That is, a marriage by banns, by the law of England

The Attorney-General —I have now stated what I am instiucted to do, and the iest I shall leave to you undei his Loidship's diiection

Mr Baron Hullock —I am of opinion that the evidence you have opened, except that which goes

to show the validity of a Scotch marriage, is quite
immaterial to the present indictment   I consider
that the offence stated on this record, if it be satisfactorily proved to the jury, was committed
when they were at Manchester, the moment they
left Manchester, and it is no matter what inducement was used afterwards, or however efficient
that inducement was, however prevailing the promise, or whatever may have been used afterwards
to induce her to acquiesce in the marriage, that
that will not alter the nature of the offence.
Whatever was done afterwards may alter the nature of the punishment, may alter the quantity of
punishment, it may be brought forward on that
occasion   I don't mean to say it may not—but I
shall tell the jury it is no issue in this cause, and
ought not to bear at all on this question   What
does it matter what was done in London or at Calais, or in truth, at any place, subsequent to the
time of their departure? I think Miss Turner's
evidence proves pretty decisively, whether from
fraud or imposition, or whatever cause, that she
did consent, did acquiesce, at Gretna Green, to
the proceedings that took place there.   Still that
is not the offence with which these defendants are
charged.   If you feel there is anything in it, Mr
Scarlett, I will hear the evidence

Mr Scarlett —I feel there is a great deal in that evidence, my Lord, particularly at Calais —I feel that it will be material in another stage of this cause, supposing there should be a conviction The witnesses are here for the purpose, and therefore they had better be called It is for the purpose of showing that the original part of the transaction is more probable That is the nature of my evidence which I have opened very shortly, and I shall endeavour to be as short as I can in the proof

Mr Baron Hullock —On the facts as they now stand, it will be my duty to tell the jury, if they believe those facts, that the case is pretty well established The facts which took place in a subsequent stage of the proceeding, are quite a different consideration

Mr Scarlett —One of the counts alleges force.

Mr Brougham —All the rest are without.

Mr Scarlett —There is a count for feloniously carrying her away by force, and marrying her against her consent

Mr Baron Hullock —I think that count is not established I shall take care to make my observations to the jury on that count I think the facts which have been proved in evidence as the case now stands, can hardly warrant the conclusion that this was a conspiracy to carry her away by force

Mr Scarlett —My evidence is to render that impossible

Mr. Baron Hullock —Then you will have to content yourself with an acquittal on that count.

Mr Scarlett —And that is very important

Mr Coltman —I apprehend, my lord, the evidence will have a material bearing on the question of marriage

Mr. Baron Hullock —Not in the least.

Mr Coltman —I understand the doctrine of the Scotch law——

Mr Baron Hullock —The doctrine of the Scotch law will not sustain you —I only mean to suggest, that in my view of the subject, that evidence is not now very material.—I don't, by anything I say, wish to prevent you from exercising your discretion on the subject   Certainly not

Mr. Coltman —We consider it to be very material in several points of view, my lord

Mr Baron Hullock —Very well, I only wish you may make it so.

ROBERT WILSON *sworn — examined by* Mr Coltman.

I believe you are the landlord of the Albion hotel at Manchester ?—Yes, sir

Do you remember the servant Thevenot returning to Manchester in a green body carriage, along with a young lady?—Yes, sir

On Tuesday the 7th of March, I believe it was?—That is the day they arrived

Well, did you show the lady up stairs into a room?—She was shown into a room on the first floor

How long did she remain in your house?—About an hour and three-quarters

How long might she remain there before either of the gentlemen appeared, or both of them?—I suppose nearly that time.

Did you see any appearance of distress about her at that time?—No, when I opened the chaise door, and offered my arm to help her out, she seemed a little confused

Now, during the time she was in that room, was she under any restraint at all, or was she perfectly at liberty to have gone where she pleased?—Certainly, she was, to my knowledge

I don't know whether you are acquainted with her uncle, Mr Robert Turner?—Yes, sir, I am

Does he live in that neighbourhood?—Yes, he does, sir

How far from there?—Perhaps two or three hundred yards from my house

It is in the same street with your house, I believe?—Yes

I suppose, if she had wished to have sent a message to him, there would have been no difficulty in sending it?—No

Now, do you remember their going off?—Yes

In the direction for Delph?—For Delph

And of course, therefore, in a different direction from the one leading from Macclesfield?—Yes

Cross-examined by Mr. Sergeant Cross.

Well, what name did the gentleman pass by at your house—Mr Edward Gibbon Wakefield?—I went up stairs after they had breakfasted, and I saw the servant, and he said good morning

I asked you what name Edward Gibbon Wakefield passed by at your house?—Yes, and I asked his master's name, and he said it was Captain Wilson

Did not the servant man who came with the carriage say, if the bell rang, don't let any of your servants go in, I will answer the bell myself?—Yes, he did

Re-examined by Mr Coltman

Mr. Wilson, is it an unusual thing when a gentleman has a servant at your hotel, for his servant to attend the bell?—Sometimes ladies get their own servants to attend them, I have frequently known that to be the case.

JOHN WILSON *sworn—examined by* Mr Parke

John Wilson, were you a waiter at the Albion hotel in the month of March last ?—Yes

Do you recollect Miss Turner arriving in a carriage ?—Yes I do.

Were you present when she went up stairs ?—I did not see her go up stairs.

Then she went into a room down stairs, was it ?—Yes.

Did you attend her to the room ?—Yes, sir, I showed her into the room

Did you remark anything particular in her manner ?—Nothing, sir

How long did she stay there before Mr Wakefield came ?—From half past twelve till nearly two o'clock

I believe you took her refreshment in the room?—I did not

Did you at no time go with refreshment yourself ?—No

Now, what distance is the servants' room from the room where she sat ?—I think about twenty yards

Might she have left the house at any time, if she pleased ?—Yes

Do you recollect Mr. Wakefield arriving ?—Yes, sir, I do

And his brother ?—Yes.

Did you show either of them into the room?—Yes

Which Mr Wakefield?—Edward.

Did you see the meeting between him and Miss Turner?—Yes

How did she receive him?—I saw nothing particular, as a lady would receive a gentleman

Did they appear to know each other from their manner?—I saw nothing different from that

Did they shake hands?—Yes

Have you been examined by the other side—by Mr Grimsditch?—No, sir.

Well, have you been examined by anybody on behalf of the prosecution?—No, sir, I have not

Mr. Baron Hullock—They are not obliged to call every witness whom they examine, if they don't answer their purpose.

Cross-examined by Mr Sergeant Cross.

They shook hands the first time he entered the room?—Yes

Oh, she shook him heartily the first time he entered the room?—He went forward as a gentleman would do to a lady

And she advanced half way as ladies generally do?—She was sitting against the window

And she got up and took hold of his hand and shook it heartily?—She went forward and took him by the hand and shook it.

And she called him by his name, I suppose,
" Ah, how do you do ?" Did not she say now,
" How are you—how do you do, Captain Wilson ?
I am glad to see you, I have not seen you this
long time ?"—I did not hear her say that

But you are quite sure she seized hold of his
hand and shook it ?—Yes.

Mr Sergeant Cross (to Mr. Scarlett)—I hope
you have plenty more such witnesses.

RICHARD STEELL *sworn   Examined by* Mr
Pattison

Are you a post-boy at Delph ?—Yes, sir

At the Bell ?—Yes, sir

Do you remember a carriage coming there with
a party on the 7th of March, 1826 ?—I remember
one coming   One thousand eight hundred and
twenty-six, the seventh day of the month.

The 7th of March ?

Mr. Sergeant Cross —No ! no !   He does not
say the 7th of March   The seventh of the month
he says, 1826

What month was it ?—March

Now who were the parties—who were they—
how many gentlemen ?—Two gentlemen, and a
lady, and a servant

Did you drive them on from Delph ?—I did

Had they four horses ?—Yes.

o

Was Fairman the other man who drove?—He was, sir.

You drove them to Huddersfield, I believe?—I did.

Did you see the lady?—I did.

Did she appear to be alarmed at all?—Not at all, sir.

Now was she in good spirits or bad spirits?—

Mr Sergeant Cross —Ask him whether he is in good spirits? [*The witness appeared to be tipsy, and his examination excited much laughter*]

Did they appear to be laughing and talking?—She was laughing and talking to the gentlemen in the carriage.

Did you hear that as they went along?—I did, sir; I rode the wheel

Did you stop any where on the road?—Yes, we did.

Where at?—At Marsden.

To water the horses?—Yes

Did you hear anything there?—No, nothing particular, when we got up to the door, some people said, Who have you got there, Richard—have you got some players? I says no, I suppose it has been a wedding. They were laughing and talking in the carriage, that was the reason they said so

Cross-examined by Mr. Sergeant Cross.

There was a coach-box to the carriage, was not there—a barouche box?—There was a dickey.

Well, and so you saw through that and the boot too, that the lady was laughing?—No, we walked up the hills, I heard them laughing as I was walking up the hills, that is the way I heard them laughing.

Mr. Wigney *sworn   Examined by* Mr. Scarlett

Do you live at Huddersfield?—Yes

Do you remember (I believe you know them now by sight) Mr Wakefield and his brother, and a lady and servant coming to your house?—I remember a party coming in a carriage very well, sir

You know the parties, have you seen any of them since?—I have seen them since at Lancaster

Do you know whether this gentleman was one of them? (*pointing to Edward Gibbon Wakefield.*)—I do not recollect; one was taller than the other, I noticed that particularly.

There was a servant outside?—Yes

And a lady?—And a lady

Did they come with four horses?—They did

What time did they arrive at your house?—To the best of my recollection, it was about half-past seven in the evening, or it might be near eight

Was there any thing the matter with the carriage, do you remember?—I was told so   I opened the carriage door, and the moment the gentleman alighted, he wished to have four horses out immediately   The servant said there was something the matter with one of the springs, and it was necessary to be repaired before it could go further

Did they alight then ?—They did

How long did they stay at your house ?—I think they stopped three-quarters of an hour They had tea

Were you in the room with them at tea ?—No, I was not, they were served with tea.

Did you assist the lady yourself to alight from the carriage ?—I did

They were shown into a room together, I suppose ?—They were, I showed them in myself.

Did you observe them return to the carriage ? —I did.

Did the lady take hold of the arm of either of the gentlemen ?—She took hold of the arm of the taller gentleman

Did you make any remark on the appearance of her spirits ?—I did not observe anything particular ; she seemed the same as any other lady. She came out very freely, to all appearance.

Were the post-boys desired to drive to Halifax? —To Halifax.

Did the lady, as far as you observed her, appear

to be quite at her ease ?—She certainly did, as far as I observed her

CHARLES CROFT *sworn*   *Examined by* Mr
Coltman

I believe you are a waiter at Huddersfield, at the George ?—I am

Now, do you remember this party coming up in a carriage and four ?—Yes, sir

Were they shown up stairs by Mr Wigney ?—They were.

Well, did you supply them with anything—any refreshment ?—Tea.

They had nothing but tea ?—Bread and butter, and so on.

Who made the tea ?—I believe Mr Wakefield made the tea

Very well, how did they appear to be—on what terms did they appear to be ?—They appeared to be as agreeable as man and wife, or sister and gentleman

Mr Baron Hullock.—They did not quarrel, I suppose ?

Did you see any appearance of distress about the young lady ?—No.

Was there any restraint upon her ?—No.

None at all ?—No.

Cross-examined by Mr Sergeant Cross

Well, they did not quarrel or fight?—No.

Mary Brock *sworn   Examined by* Mr Park.

Are you chambermaid at the George Inn at Huddersfield?—Yes, sir

Do you remember the two Mr. Wakefields and Miss Turner being there?—Yes, sir

Had they tea?—Yes, sir, they had

Were you sent for to attend Miss Turner?—Yes, I was

Where did you find her?—In the sitting-room

Was she at tea?—I think the tea-things were removed then

Were you with her alone?—Yes, sir

You had an opportunity of seeing her?—Yes, I saw her

Did she appear to be under any restraint?—She did not appear to be under any restraint at all.

What sort of spirits did she appear to be in?—I did not observe anything particular in her spirits.

Well, did you see her come down stairs from the tea-room?—Yes, sir

How did she come down, alone or with anybody?—She came down upon the gentleman's arm

Now do you recollect anything happening as she was going down stairs?—I do not.

Do you recollect her foot slipping?—I do not.

Did you see her get into the carriage?—Yes, sir, I opened the carriage door

Well, do you recollect seeing her laughing during any part of the time?—I cannot say.

Mr Sergeant Cross—You are beginning to prompt, Mr Park But she cannot say what you prompt her with.

WILLIAM LANGSTAFF *sworn   Examined by* Mr
Pattison.

Are you post-boy at the George Inn, Huddersfield?—Yes.

Did you drive the party to Halifax?—Yes.

Four horses, I believe, they had?—Yes.

Now, when they arrived at Halifax, did you see them get out?—Yes, the two gentlemen got out

Now did you observe, when they returned back, when they stopped there, whether there was any talking?—No

Not at Halifax?—No, I did not see any.

Now was the lady under any restraint, as far as you saw?—No

Did you hear any laughing?—Yes, I heard both the gentleman and the lady laughing when they got into the carriage.

Thomas Issott *sworn*   *Examined by* Mr
Scarlett

Are you a waiter at the Inn at Halifax ?—Yes

Do you remember this party coming, the two
gentlemen and lady, and servant, to your house ?
—Yes.

What time of night did they arrive there ?—
A little before nine, to the best of my knowledge

Very well, did the servant stay there ?—Yes,
sir

Did both the gentlemen get out of the carriage,
or only one ?—I saw only one get out.

Now did he go into the bar ?—Yes

The other two remained in the carriage ?—Yes.

The servant, I believe, took the luggage with
him ?—Yes

And you stopped there ?—Yes

By Mr Baron Hullock —The servant stopped,
and the two gentlemen and lady went on ?—
Yes

While one of the gentlemen was in the bar,
were you near the carriage ?—I was within twenty
yards of it

Did you hear anything passing in the carriage?
—Nothing but laughing between the lady and
gentleman

Was the lady laughing ?—Yes

Did you hear the lady laugh as well as the gentleman?—Yes

At the distance of twenty yards?—Yes

How long did they remain there?—About a quarter of an hour

Did the lady get out of the carriage at all?—No, she did not.

Did they appear to be in consultation?—I did not hear the particular words that passed They were talking and laughing in the carriage.

Cross-examined by Mr Serjeant Cross.

What hour of the night was it?—A little before nine

It was dark then, was it not?—No

Oh! at the hour of nine it is not dark at Halifax, in the month of March?—Yes, but we had gas lights.

Mr Scarlett (to Mr Serjeant Cross)—Just allow me to ask him another question.

Examined by Mr Scarlett

Did you ever see the lady before?—Yes

You knew the lady, did you?—I should have done, if I had seen her in the light.

But you had known her before?—Yes, I had seen her before, she had dined at our house before

How long before, do you recollect?—I don't exactly know, perhaps six weeks or two months

You know a lady of that name, and know her

to be the lady that has been examined here to
day ?—Yes

*The Cross-examination by Mr Sergeant Cross
resumed*

Well, the servant was left at your house ?—Yes

Well, what did he say when he left the party ?
—He did not say anything to me at all.

Did not he say " They may go to the devil now,
for I have got rid of them ?"—I did not hear him
say that

So you were twenty yards off the carriage ?—
What, at the time they started ?

Aye ?—No, not when the carriage started I
was not

But you heard them laughing a long time ?—
There was nothing but laughing from the time
the gentleman got out of the carriage and went
into the bar.

Re-examined by Mr. Scarlett

They went from Halifax to Keighley ?—Yes.

HENRY MASON *sworn   Examined by* Mr.
Coltman.

I believe you are a post-boy at the White Lion,
Halifax ?—Yes.

Did you drive this party from the White Lion
to Keighley from Halifax ?—Yes.

What time did you get to Keighley, as near as

you can judge? I don't want you to be particular to half an hour or an hour.—About half-past nine, sir

When you got there, or when you left Halifax?—I think it was about half-past nine when I got to Keighley.

Now, what spirits did the parties seem to be in when they got to Keighley, or on the road?—They seemed to be in very good spirits

What made you judge they were in good spirits?—I heard them laughing in the carriage when I stopped to water

Did you hear the lady's voice at all in laughing or talking?—Yes

Did she appear to be under any restraint at all, or any alarm, or any distress? Did she appear tobe at all distressed?—No, sir

ANN BRADLEY *sworn Examined by* Mr. Park.

I believe you keep the Devonshire Arms at Shipton?—Yes, sir

Do you recollect the two Mr Wakefields and Miss Turner coming to your house?—I recollect two gentlemen and a lady coming

Mr Sergeant Cross (to Mr Parke)—You keep thrusting the names into the mouths of all the witnesses

You say you recollect two gentlemen and a lady coming ?—Yes, sir

Did they come in a carriage-and-four ?—Yes.

What time did they come ?—About ten o'clock in the evening

What day ?—On the 7th of March

Did you see them in the carriage ?—I did see them, by the light of a lantern.

Did you go out ?—I was at the door

Were any horses ordered ?—Four horses were ordered on to Settle

Did you take them any refreshment ?—I ordered my servant-maid to take them some gingerbread

Did you see what became of the gingerbread, where it was placed ?—It was placed upon the lady's lap

Had they any water ?—Two glasses of water.

Now, you had a lantern, you say, with you ?—Yes

Were you able to distinguish the parties in the carriage ?—I saw there were two gentlemen and a lady, but I could not swear to them again.

Was the lantern handed into the inside of the carriage ?—It was.

Did you make any observation to them as they were going away, did you make any request to them ?—I said I should be glad to see them on their return.

What induced you to make that observation?
—I thought it was a runaway match

What did they say?—I don't know; I cannot speak to what they said, they were very cheerful

Did you hear any laughing?—Yes.

Now, was the young lady in good spirits or bad spirits?—In good spirits

Now, what makes you say she was in good spirits?—I heard her laughing in the carriage with the gentleman

Were you in the house when you heard her laughing?—I was in the bar.

And the chaise was at the outside of the house?—Yes

Where did they go to from Shipton?—To Settle

Cross-examined by Mr Sergeant Cross

My friend has asked you every question but, whether the gingerbread was good—was it good?—Very good

Re-examined by Mr. Scarlett.

It seemed to please the lady, did it not?—Yes

Mr HARTLEY *sworn*   *Examined by*
Mr Pattison

You are the landlord, I believe, of the Golden Lion, at Settle?—Yes.

Do you remember a party coming there on the morning of the 8th of March?—Yes.

About what time ?—Half-past one.

Who were the party ?—Two gentlemen and a lady

Did they change horses there ?—Yes.

Four horses ?—Yes

And went on, where ?—To Kirby Lonsdale.

SARAH COLMAN *sworn*   *Examined by*
Mr. Scarlett

Do you live at the Rose and Crown, at Kirby Lonsdale ?—I do

Do you remember, early in the morning of the 8th of March, two gentlemen and a lady coming with a carriage-and-four ?—Yes

What time in the morning did they arrive ?—Between three and four.

Were you called up ?—Yes, sir

In getting up, do you remember any accident happening to you ?—I fell in going out of the door

Was there any remark made upon that ?—There was a loud laugh in the carriage by the ladies and gentlemen

How many ladies did there turn out to be ?—One.

Then, she laughed so loud as to make you believe there were two ?—She laughed very loud.

Now, had it been a wet night before ?—It did not rain very much

Had it cleared up in the morning?—It was rather misty and warm

Do you remember the lady making any observation about the weather?—Yes

What did she say?—She said, " What a beautiful morning it has turned out!—we are quite favoured with the morning "

Well, did the lady appear to you to be in good spirits?—Very

Where did they go to from Kirby Lonsdale?— To Kendal.

Cross-examined by Mr Sergeant Cross.

She appeared to you to be in as good spirits as a young lady would be in going from school to see her parents, did she?—She was in very good spirits; I thought they were brothers and sister.

Did you ever see a girl going from school to see her parents more cheerful than she was?— No, I did not.

Re-examined by Mr Scarlett

Did you ever see a young lady going to be married more cheerful than she was?—When people are going to marry they seldom are cheerful—that's a serious business

EDWARD GARRATT *sworn   Examined by*
Mr Coltman.

You are a post-boy at the Crown, Kirby Lonsdale?—Yes.

Did you drive the party to Kendal ?—Yes, sir

Well, did they get out at Kendal ?—Yes, sir

What time of the day was it when they got to Kendal ?—About half-past five in the morning

Were they shown up into a room, do you know ?—Yes.

Did you go up into the room afterwards, when you were to receive the pay ?—Yes, sir.

Well, did you find them together ?—Yes, one gentleman and lady sitting in the room.

What ! was it the taller gentleman—do you know which of the gentlemen it was ?   You are not able to say, perhaps ?—No.

You don't know which of the gentlemen it was, or do you know ?—No

Well, now you say, the lady and gentleman were there   what were they doing ?—Walking backwards and forwards, alongside one another

Well, how did they appear ?—When I went up, and opened the door, they were talking together   I did not hear what they said   I heard them talking, but I did not know what they said The lady was further from me—she was talking to the gentleman, and smiling at him as she talked

Well, did you see any appearance of distress or unhappiness about her ?—None at all, sir

How did she appear ?—She was walking about very nimbly, indeed, and looked very pleasant.

Cross-examined by Mr. Sergeant Cross

And you actually saw her smile, did you?—
Yes

Mr. Sergeant Cross.—Indeed!

HANNAH SIMPSON *sworn. Examined by* Mr.
Parke.

Were you chambermaid at the King's Arms,
Kendal, in the month of March last?—Yes

Do you recollect two gentleman and a lady
arriving there in a carriage and four?—Yes.

Did they stay any time at your house?—Breakfasted, sir.

Did you attend the lady?—Yes, sir.

Did you see the gentleman and lady together?
—In the sitting-room

Were both the gentlemen there?—Yes.

With the lady?—Yes.

How long did she remain in that room with
them?—Till the breakfast things came out

How long were they there together? was it
twenty minutes, or half an hour, or what?—I
cannot say.

Now, did you observe whether the lady was in
good spirits, or bad spirits?—I did not see anything particular about the lady

Did she stay by herself any time?—In the bed-
room she was.

P

Well, how long was she by herself?—Twenty minutes or a quarter of an hour.

On what footing did the parties appear to be with each other?—I did not see anything particular with them, but that they were agreeable.

Cross-examined by Mr Sergeant Cross

You did not find them disagreeable, did you?—No.

ROBERT DOVER *sworn.* *Examined by* Mr Pattison

You are a post-boy at the King's Arms at Kendal, I believe?—Yes

Do you remember driving a party, a lady and two gentlemen, on the 8th of March, from Kendal to Shap?—Yes

Did you stop anywhere on the road?—Yes.

To water the horses?—Yes

Where?—At H——.

Now, when you stopped to water the horses, did you hear anything in the carriage?—I did not

Did you hear anything on the road?—Yes.

Where?—At H——

Well, who did you hear?—The gentleman and lady.

Well, did you hear the gentleman and lady say anything?—I saw their lips move, I did not know what they said   The window was down, I could not hear them

I don't ask you whether you heard what they said, but was there any talking?—Yes, there was

Could you distinguish anything they were talking?—I could Mr Wakefield, but not the lady?

Did you hear any laughing?—I did not hear it, I saw it.

Did you see the lady?—Yes, I did, sir

Well, how did she appear to be, as to cheerfulness?—She appeared very well; she appeared rather fatigued with her journey—she looked rather pale

But as to cheerfulness, how was she? was she cheerful, or not?—She was pale a little, to look at

Cross-examined by Mr Sergeant Cross

She was very cheerful, for she looked pale and wearied, was that it?—No, she looked pleasant, as a gentleman and lady in a carriage

Re-examined by Mr Scarlett

She looked happy?—Yes

JAMES ANDERSON *sworn Examined by Mr* Scarlett

Anderson, are you a post-boy at Shap?—Yes

Did you drive two gentlemen and a lady from Shap to Penrith?—Yes

On the 8th of March?—Yes, I believe it was the 8th of March

Do you know the gentleman?—Yes.

Have you seen them since ?—Yes

Was this one of them ? (*Pointing to Edward Gibbon Wakefield*)—Yes

It was a young lady, was it not —Yes.

Had you an opportunity, during the time you were driving, while you were on the road, of seeing whether they were in good spirits, or not ?—Yes, they were in very good spirits.

What makes you say that, what did you hear ?—I heard them laughing, and seemingly in good spirits

Did you hear the lady laugh too ?—Yes.

Now, the road is rather hilly, is it not ?—Not that stage.

Now, when they arrived at Penrith, did the gentlemen get out of the carriage ?—Yes

Well, was the lady left in the carriage ?—Yes.

Well, did you see her at any time when she laughed in the carriage ?—Yes.

Did you see him when he got in again to go on with her ?—Yes

Did you take any notice whether she seemed cheerful ?—She seemed very cheerful, and made way for the gentleman when he got in

Had you a notion what sort of a party it was ?—I thought it was a wedding.

Did you drive fast ?—Yes

Were you ordered to drive fast, or did you do that of your own accord ?—They dropped down the carriage-window, and desired me to make the best of my way.

And you did make the best of your way, thinking it was a wedding party ?—Yes.

Did that make you look at the lady the more ?—Yes

Did she look unhappy ?—Not in the least

Cross-examined by Mr Starkie.

What did they pay you ?—Six shillings apiece

Then that made you look rather cheerful too, I suppose, did it not ?—Yes.

EDWARD BAXTER *sworn*   *Examined by* Mr
            Coltman

Are you a post-boy at the Crown inn at Penrith ?—Yes.

Now do you remember, on the 8th of March, taking this party from Penrith to Carlisle ?—Yes

What time did you leave Penrith ?—Half past ten, sir

You had four horses, of course ?—Yes

Who did the party consist of—how many people were there ?—Three, sir

Who were they ?—Two gentlemen and a lady.

Well, how did you go on—did you drive fast ? A fair pace, they did not hurry me.

You drove a fair pace ?—Yes

Now, I suppose there are a good many hills that road ?—Yes, there are.

Pray, how did the company seem inside, in point of spirits?—They were in very good spirits, as far as I saw.

What made you judge they were in good spirits?—I opened the door and let one of the gentlemen in at H———; he was outside halfway, and they seemed to be talking and laughing among themselves.

Did you hear them talking and laughing?—Yes

Which did you hear talking and laughing?—All of them

Well, did you see the young lady several times in the course of the journey?—No, I did not

Oh, only at that place, and at Carlisle?—There, and at Carlisle

THOMAS ATKINSON *sworn. Examined by* Mr. Parke.

I believe you are head-waiter at the Bush inn at Carlisle?—Yes, sir.

Do you recollect a carriage and four coming there?—Yes, sir

Do you know the gentlemen who were in it?—Yes, sir

Who were they?—Two gentlemen and a lady.

Is this gentleman one of them? (*pointing to Edward Gibbon Wakefield.*)—Yes, sir.

Did you go to the carriage when it stopped ?—
Yes, sir.

Did you see who was in the inside of the carriage ?—Yes, sir.

Could you form an opinion what expedition
they were upon ?—I thought it was a wedding

Did you ask where they wanted horses to, or
what was the question you asked ?—I asked if
they wanted horses to Gretna

Was that in the hearing of the young lady ?—
I have no doubt of it

By Mr. Sergeant Cross —No doubt. But was
it, sir ?—Yes

Did you see anything pass between the young
lady and Mr Wakefield there ? What answer
did you get—what answer was given ?—He asked
for horses to Gretna

Did you see anything pass between Mr Wakefield and Miss Turner before that order was
given ; and he say anything to her, or look at her
before he said he wanted horses to Gretna ?—Mr
Wakefield looked at Miss Turner

Well, did the young lady say anything ?—No,
sir.

You did not hear the young lady say anything,
but he looked at Miss Turner ?—Yes.

Well, what did Mr Wakefield say when he
looked at Miss Turner ?—I don't know

What was the answer Mr. Wakefield gave you, were the horses to go to Gretna or not?—To Gretna

Well, did you get any answer to that question from Mr. Wakefield, when you asked him whether you were to order horses to Gretna?—To order horses to Gretna.

Was the young lady present; did she hear what he said?—Yes.

By Mr. Sergeant Cross.—You know that?—Yes.

Did the two Messrs. Wakefields get out of the carriage?—Yes

Where did they go to?—About two hundred yards from the door

In which direction?—Towards the court-house.

Did you see them return to the carriage?—Yes, sir

Were you standing by the carriage during that time?—Yes, sir

Did you ask Miss Turner if she would get out? —I did after they went away.

Did she wish to get out?—No, sir.

Did you see the gentlemen return to the carriage?—Yes, sir.

Did you see how they were received by Miss Turner, how did she receive them?—(*No answer.*)

Well, did you observe any appearance of dejection about her?—Nothing but pleasantness

Did you observe any bad spirits in her appearance, or dejection?—No, sir.

You say you staid by the carriage the whole time they were away?—Not the whole time, I went into the house for a ticket.

With the exception of that, you staid against the carriage and saw her, and had an opportunity of observing how she appeared?—Yes.

Did you see the party when they returned from Gretna?—Yes, sir.

How long did they remain at your house upon their return?—About three hours.

Had they tea?—Yes

Who made tea, do you recollect?—No; I did not take the tea-things up.

Now, how did she and Mr. Wakefield seem to treat each other?—Very kindly

Did she appear in good or bad spirits?—Good spirits.

Did you see Mr. Wakefield write any letter?—He did

Now, what was she doing in the meantime?—She was playing at draughts with Mr William Wakefield.

Did you hear any laughing?—Yes, sir.

Who was laughing?—Miss Turner and Mr
William Wakefield.

Cross-examined by Mr Williams.

Mrs Holmes, the landlady, that has been examined, is your mistress?—She is.

The lady that has been examined here to-day?
—She is

WILLIAM GRAHAM *sworn. Examined by* Mr
Scarlett

I believe you are a postilion at the Bush Inn,
Carlisle?—Yes.

Did you drive Mr. Wakefield, and the lady
with him, and his brother to Gretna Green?—I
did

They went with four horses I understand?—
Yes

Did you take any notice, while you were going
along, whether the parties were in good spirits or
not?—No, I did not take particular notice until
we got two or three miles on the road, then one
of the gentlemen asked, where are you going?—I
said, Gretna Green.

Well, what happened then?—He said very
well

Did one of the gentlemen get out on the dickey?
—Yes

Did you hear anything pass between the lady

and gentleman in the carriage?—I heard the lady and gentleman laughing.

Did you drive them to Gretna Green then?—Yes.

Well, did you say anything when you stopped at Gretna, did you stop at the usual place?——Yes.

Well, what did you say?—I got off my horse, and went to the carriage door, and the gentlemen asked me if the old parson lived there, and I said no, it was a place where marriages were made

You knew the place to take them to?—Yes

You had been accustomed to it, had you not?—Yes

You knew it was a place where marriages were made, and, therefore, you took them to Mr. Linton's Did Mr. Wakefield say anything else to you?—He asked me how long the parson would be coming.

Well, what did you say to that?—I said twenty minutes, or half an hour

Did they get out?—Yes

Mr. Linton in the mean time, came to the door?—Yes.

Well, did the lady get out?—Yes.

Did you hear her talk or laugh as she got out of the carriage?—I did not exactly observe that.

But did the parson come at last?—Yes.

Very well, how long was it before the parson came ?—I dare say it was about half an hour, there, or thereabouts

But was it some time ?—Yes, sir, it was some time, but I could not say how long.

Very well, what was the parson's name ?—David Laing.

Well, when David Laing came, were you sent for to be present at the ceremony ?—Yes.

Now, have you been present at such things before ?—Yes, I have, a good many.

Now, how did the lady appear at the ceremony? —I did not see anything particular in the lady, more than she behaved like other ladies in the same situation.

Well, did the parson perform the ceremony you have been accustomed to hear there ?—Yes

Was a ring put upon her finger ?—Yes.

Did she make answer to the questions that the parson put to her ?—Yes, and spoke very loud and distinct

Now, when the ceremony was over, did the parson say anything ?—Yes

What is the usual ceremony ?—The usual ceremony is to desire the bridegroom to embrace the bride

Did the parson say that to Mr Wakefield ?—Yes.

Did Mr. Wakefield do that ?—Yes.

How did the lady receive the embrace ?—Why much the same as other ladies,—she turned round as if partly to meet him with a kind of kiss, as may be.

Well, was there a certificate made of it ?—Yes

And did you put your name to it ?—I did

Is that it ? (*handing it to the witness*)—Yes, it is, sir

Very well; did you see the parson put his name ?—Yes, I did

They dined there, did they not ?—They dined at Gretna-hall before they went back

Mr. Linton was the landlord, was not he ?—Yes.

Did you hear him ask the lady for anything ?—I did not hear Mr Linton, but I heard the parson ask for something for gloves

Well, you took them back to Carlisle ?—Yes.

When you got back to Carlisle, did you hear Mr Wakefield say anything to the lady when you were going to open the carriage-door ?—No, I did not open the carriage-door at Carlisle

Did you hear him say anything at any time ?—I had no conversation with him till I went into the room to take my pay   I took them to Penrith the same evening

After they had waited some time at Carlisle?—Yes

Did you see them there after they arrived?—Yes.

Did you hear him say anything to the lady there?—Yes

What was it?—He said, " This, my dear, is our old acquaintance;" and she said, " So I observe."

JOHN LINTON *sworn. Examined by* Mr Pattison

Are you the landlord of the inn at Gretna?—Yes, sir

Do you remember Mr. Wakefield and Miss Turner coming there?—Yes

Did you show them into a room?—The servant showed them into a room, I did not show them into the room

Well, they were shown into the house?—Yes

Well, what became of the gentleman?—The gentlemen went into a small room, I went up stairs immediately after, and desired a fire to be immediately lighted in a better room—in the drawing-room

Well, what then?—I understood from Graham, the last witness——

Never mind what you understood—but did the gentlemen go out or stay in the room?—They went out.

And the lady was left alone?—Yes.

Did you see her while she was left alone?—I did not in the first room—in the second.

Now, how did she appear to you to be—how did her spirits appear to you to be?—Not depressed in any way

Did Laing come afterwards?—He did

Were you sent for then?—I was

And you went into the room?—Yes.

And found them there?—Yes.

And was the usual ceremony performed?—Yes.

In your presence?—Yes.

I take for granted you have been present at many of these ceremonies?—Yes.

Were the usual questions asked the lady and gentleman?—Yes

And did they answer?—Yes.

Did she answer?—Yes.

Distinctly or not?—Very distinctly

Well, now, at that time was she dejected at all?—Not at all

Well, now, when the ceremony was over, did Laing say anything to him?—He said, "Embrace the bride"—and she was very willing, and met Mr. Wakefield very pleasantly

And he did salute her, I suppose?—Yes

Did you attest that? (*handing the certificate to the witness*)—I did

That is your signature ?—Yes.

Did they dine there afterwards ?—Yes

Did you wait upon them at dinner ?—I did.

After the ceremony ?—Yes.

Well, how was the lady ?—Quite agreeable, I thought

Was she cheerful, or not ?—Quite cheerful.

How did they behave to each other ?—Very affectionately and very agreeable, as though they had been perfectly acquainted with each other

Did they behave as people generally behave on such occasions?—I did not see anything different.

Mr. Baron Hullock.—There is a usage at Gretna-green, is there !

Did she give anything to Mr. Laing?—He told me so afterwards

Never mind that, I am not asking you what he told you, did you see her give him anything ?—No

Did she tell you?—No.

Frances Linton *sworn   Examined by* Mr. Coltman.

Miss Linton, you are the daughter of Mr Linton, who has just been examined, I believe ?—A sister

Do you remember the carriage coming up?—Yes, sir.

That brought the two Mr Wakefields and the young lady ?—Yes, sir.

Well, where were they shown into first of all ?—Into a small parlour

I believe you were directed to light a fire in a better room for them ?—Yes, sir , I went to light the fire myself.

What, in the drawing-room, was it ?—Yes, sir

Well, when the fire was lighted, did Mr Wakefield and the young lady come up-stairs into the room ?—They did

How did they come up?—I met them on the stairs · the young lady was linked in his arm

Well, did they go into the room ?—They did, sir

Well, now after they had gone in, and were in the drawing-room, did you go into that room ?—I did

What carried you into the room ?—To put some sticks on the fire

That was whilst Mr Wakefield and the young lady were in the room ?—Yes

Waiting for the clergyman ?—Yes

The parson, or whatever you call him ?—Yes

Mr. Sergeant Cross.—The blacksmith, you mean

Very well, that was before Laing had got there ?—Yes

Q

Now, when you went into the room, how did you find them sitting?—They were upon the sofa, and the lady was sitting on the gentleman's knee

How was her arm?—I cannot tell as to that.

How did she appear—what was her manner towards him before that?—I had not seen them together before that, only coming up-stairs

Then you made no particular observation as to her manner, until you went into the drawing-room, and saw them sitting in that way?—No

Well, how did they appear at that time—their manner towards each other?—I took no notice.

You took no notice, but left the room?—Yes

Did you see them again after dinner?—I did, sir.

Well, now, in what state did the young lady appear to be in point of spirits?—When I saw them again they were standing at the door. The gentleman had hold of the lady's hand; he was talking to her, and they were laughing at something that was said

Now, what was his manner towards her?—Very affectionate.

And how did she appear towards him?—The same.

DAVID LAING *sworn. Examined by* Mr. Parke.

Mr. Laing, I believe you reside at Springfield?
—Yes, I do.

Near Gretna-Hall?—Yes

Do you recollect being sent for to marry a couple on the 8th of March last?—I do

Did you go to Mr Linton's house, at Gretna-Hall?—I did

Who did you find there?—I found two gentlemen, as it may be, and a lady—one lady

Do you know the gentleman again?—Why, no, I cannot say I do

What did the gentleman say to you?—Su— what did the gentleman treat me with?

No When you got to the inn, you say you found two gentlemen and a lady there?—Yes

What did the gentleman want you to do?—He wanted me to do what I had done to many a one before

Was that to marry him?—To join them together—to join hands, and so on.

Did you make a bargain with the gentleman to marry him?—Yes, I did

Was that bargain made in the presence of the lady?—Yes

Did she seem agreeable to it?—Yes, perfectly; she had no objection.

Did you give a certificate of the marriage?—I gave the lady a certificate

Did you get it filled up?—Yes.

Is that your writing?—(*handing the certificate to the witness*)—That is my handwriting, sir

Is that the signature of the gentleman and lady at the bottom?—Yes

Where did you get the lady's address from?—I got the lady's address from the gentleman, and the lady gave consent to it—and where they came from, and who the lady belonged to, and all the whole of the particulars, and so and so.

Who wrote down the lady's address—the lady or the gentleman?—The gentleman, but the lady gave way to it

Did you marry them in the usual form in Scotland?—In the Scotch form

Was there a ring produced?—There was, sir

Was it put on the lady's finger?—It was.

By whom—by the gentleman?—By myself

Now, how did the ceremony conclude?—They seemed both agreeable to join hands, and take one another for man and wife.

Well, what was the end of the ceremony?—Why, I wished them well, and shook hands with them, and so on.

Well, was there a salute?—Yes, they both embraced one another, and seemed to be very agreeable, apparently

Did you ask the lady for any thing?—I told the lady that I generally had a present from them, as it may be, of such a thing as money, to buy a pair of gloves

Well, did you get any from her?—I did, sir; she gave it me with her own hand, but where the lady got it from I cannot say for that, you know.

What was it you got?—A 20s. Bank of England note

Well, did they sit down together afterwards?—Mr Wakefield asked me what sort of wines there were in the house, and I told him there were three or four different sorts of wine, with the best of *shumpine*; he asked me which I would take, and I said *shumpine*, and we had a bottle of *shumpine* —they were going to dine

Did you get any champaigne?—Oh, yes, sir.

Well, did you dine with them?—No, I did not

Did you stay and drink the wine?—I went down stairs while they dined, after dinner I returned, and we finished the wine, and I bid them good day, and off I came

Were they in good spirits after dinner?—Yes, they were in the very best comfortable spirits

Both the lady and the gentleman?—Yes.

Cross-examined by Mr Brougham.

You got some money, as well as champaigne, for this job, did not you?—I did.

How much?—Perhaps 20*l*. or 30*l*

Perhaps 40*l*?—May be, I cannot say to a few pounds

Mr. Scarlett.—Now, read that certificate, Mr. Cross.

Mr Cross.—It is dated the 8th of March, 1826, signed David Laing

Mr Baron Hullock—I don't permit this to be read as a certificate, but as a paper signed between the parties.

Mr. Scarlett—Signed by the lady herself.

Mr. Cross read the paper, which purported to certify Edward Gibbon Wakefield and Ellen Turner had been duly married by David Laing, according to the form required by the Scotch law.

DAVID LAING *again called, and examined by* Mr Parke

Mr. Laing, you say the marriage was in the ordinary form—the marriage ceremony was performed in the ordinary form?—Yes, the old form of Scotland

How was that done—was a prayer-book produced?—No, there was not

Mr. Brougham.—Don't tell him what he is to say.

It was done in the old ordinary form of the church of Scotland, was it ?—Yes.

Cross-examined by Mr. Brougham.

What do you mean by the ordinary form of the church of Scotland, when it had nothing to do with the church ?—That is the way it has been done for centuries.

Are you a Scotch clergyman ?—No, I am not

What are you—are you any trade at all ?—Nothing at all.

Do you mean to say you never were an ostler ? —Me an ostler ! No.

How long have you been engaged in this traffic of making this sort of certificates ?—Eight and forty years.

How old are you ?—I am beyond seventy-five.

Well, before the last eight and forty years what did you do to get your livelihood,—that is my question ?—Why, I was a gentleman—sometimes poor and sometimes rich.

Well, when you was poor, what did you do to get your bread—what occupation did you follow ?—I followed many occupations.

Let me hear one of them ?—I was a merchant

What do you mean by a merchant—a travelling merchant—a pedlar ?—Yes

What else were you—were you any thing else ? —Never

Well, now I come back to what you call the marriage What do you mean by this being the common form of the church of Scotland—do you mean to say that nobody is ever married in Scotland by ministers?—Yes, they are.

Is not that the general way?—No, not the general way altogether If you go before a person and own yourself to be man and wife, that is the way to marry in Scotland, in general

Mind you are swearing upon your oath—do you mean now to represent on your oath, that the common way of marrying people in Scotland is not to go before a clergyman at all—do you mean to represent that?—Some go before a clergyman, but there is many a one that don't go before a clergyman.

But is not the common and regular mode of marrying in Scotland, to go before a clergyman?—They are not in the habit, altogether, of going after a clergyman

Do you mean to swear, sir, upon your oath (and recollect there are people here who hear you)—do you mean to swear, upon your oath, that the regular mode of being married in Scotland is not to go before a clergyman?—I did not say that

Then what is the regular mode? I am asking you about the regular mode

Mr. Baron Hullock —And attend to the question

Mr Brougham —Or you may not find it so easy to get back to Scotland

Mr Baron Hullock —The regular mode, as I understand him to say, is to be married before a clergyman in Scotland, in the church.

Mr Scarlett.—To declare they are man and wife

The Witness —The marriages in Scotland are not always done in the churches

I know that as well as you do, because it sometimes takes place in clergymen's private houses?—Or before a depute

What depute?—There are many deputes—the justices of the peace

Re-examined by Mr Scarlett

What is the irregular mode of marrying in Scotland? Was this the irregular mode?—No, not the *unregular* mode it may be *unregular*, but it is right, still

You married these in the regular mode, did you?—I married them as many a hundred has been married before, and I have been in the courts, both in Edinburgh and in the city of Dublin, and my marriages have always been held good

Well, the marriages that have been made by you have been held good, have they?—Yes, they have

What form of words do you use?—Well, you come before me and say——

No, I don't want to be married, but suppose any body did, I want to know what form of words are used. Do you make any declaration between the parties?—I ask them whether they take one another for man and wife, before myself and two witnesses that is the mode in Scotland.

Well, you asked them if they took one another to be man and wife, in your presence and that of the witnesses?—Yes.

Well, what answer did they give?—They said they did

Well then, when they say that, do you make any declaration, or what do you do?—Why they embrace one another, and *so and so*

Tell us what the " *so and so* " is I don't want to be married, but some of my friends here do, and they want to know the ceremony. What is the " *so and so?* "—what do you say?—After they take one another by the hand, I say " Now I declare you *so and so* "

What is it you declare? What are the words you use? You declare them what?—I declare them to be man and wife before the witnesses, and *so and so* that is the Scotch rule

Mr Baron Hullock (to Mr Scarlett).—Is this the whole of the evidence you have of the marriage? because I shall expect some person to tell me this is a good marriage, according to the law of Scotland I thought you were going to call some witness to prove that ; you must show that, or you do nothing

Mr. Scarlett —I am going very soon to call that gentleman I am going to show their departure from this place first

Mr. Baron Hullock —Are you going to carry these parties from this place to Calais ?

Mr Scarlett —Not all the way, my lord

Mr. Baron Hullock —You must know, perfectly well, that it is quite useless in this proceeding, and really, I must rely upon you to exercise your discretion in the use of the time of the court, in going through evidence of this description

Mr Scarlett —I understand it is a corroboration of such a marriage, that the parties are afterwards appearing to be hanging on each other as man and wife

Mr Baron Hullock —Be it so

Mr. Scarlett. —And, therefore, I am going to give that evidence before I call the gentleman to prove the validity of the marriage

M QUILLAC *sworn, and examined in part through the medium of an interpreter, by* Mr Scarlett

Be so good as ask him if he keeps the hotel that goes by his name at Calais ?—Yes.

Mr Scarlett (to the witness) —Can you speak English?

The Witness —Very little

Mr Scarlett.—But you can speak enough, I think, to be understood.

You keep the hotel at Calais, that goes by your name?—Yes

Do you know Mr Edward Wakefield, who sits here (*pointing to him*)?—Yes

Have you known him some years?—Yes

Do you remember his coming with a lady, in the month of March last, to your hotel?—Yes

Did he introduce her to you?—Yes.

In what way did he introduce her?—As his wife.

Did she hear that?—I suppose she did, she was quite close.

Mr. Scarlett (to the interpreter).—You had better ask him the questions in French

Did they remain some days at his hotel?—Five or six days

Did they pass as man and wife there? Did she go by his name?—As Madame Wakefield

As far as he observed, did they appear to treat each other as man and wife?—All the while

Did she go out with him a good deal?—Very often.

Did she go to the play with him?—She did

And to the different shops in the town ?—Yes

Cross-examined by Mr Williams

Please to ask him the question, whether or not, they did not sleep in separate chambers?—They rented a saloon and two chambers, with each a bed.

Re-examined by the Attorney-general.

Did those bed-rooms communicate with each other ?—Yes

Are they apartments that married people often have at his house ?—Very often

Did the apartments both open to the saloon, and also to each other ?—They did, they communicated all one in another

Is that the plan of the rooms *(handing it to the witness)* ?—It is, sir

> *(The plan was shown to the jury, and the situation of the saloon and the two bed-rooms pointed out to them There was an outer door into each of the three rooms, out of the passage or lobby, an inner door between the two bed-rooms, and an inner door between one of the bed-rooms and the saloon, but, with the exception of the inner doors of communication, they formed three distinct rooms out of the passage)*

DUNCAN M'NEIL, Esq *sworn. Examined by*
          Mr. Coltman

Mr. M'Neil, how long have you been in the
profession of the law?—I have been at the bar
for about eleven years, and I went through an
apprenticeship with a writer to the signet, before
I came to the bar

I believe you are sheriff-depute of Perthshire?
—I am.

I presume you are perfectly well acquainted
with the Scotch law, as it relates to the contract
of marriage?—I think I am.

I believe you have been in court, and heard the
examination of the witnesses in this cause?—I
have

According to the Scotch law, sir, taking the
facts, as they have been spoken to by the witnesses to be accurate, was that a valid marriage
between the parties?—I think that the proceeding
that has been stated to have taken place at
Gretna, is all that was necessary to constitute a
marriage, if it stood by itself without other evidence; and I have not heard any thing that takes
away, in my opinion, from the valid effect of that
ceremony so performed

By Mr Baron Hullock —You have heard
nothing to invalidate it?—I think not, I was

going to say, taking into consideration the evidence that was given by Miss Turner, if she is Miss Turner?

Cross-examined by Mr Brougham.

You mean to say, that you, as a Scotch lawyer, give it as your opinion, first, that what is stated to have happened at Gretna, standing by itself, would constitute a Scotch marriage, and secondly, that having heard all the rest of the evidence, you can find nothing in that to alter that opinion? —Yes

How long have you been at the bar?—About eleven years

During that time, have you answered many cases on questions respecting the validity of marriages?—Not many I have answered some—not many, as many, I suppose, as persons of my standing at the bar

Gentlemen come, as we know, at the Scotch bar slowly into practice?—That is a comparative question I don't know how they come into practice at the English bar, and therefore I cannot compare it

Mr Baron Hullock —It is the same here.

The Witness —It is a comparative question.

And those gentlemen who have been eleven years at the bar, have not answered many cases on questions of Scotch marriage, generally speaking?—Many cases will depend on the number of cases that we have in Scotland

What do you call many cases—how many in the course of a year?—Why, I suppose that there are not a great many cases in the consistorial courts, I fancy, perhaps about three in the course of a year

Then you may have answered, in the course of eleven years, three in the course of a year?—I don't think more

You don't mean to say that you have answered altogether thirty-three, but that you have not answered more than three in the course of a year?—I don't think I have answered altogether more than that

I am talking of questions on marriage?—On the validity of marriages

Now, do you mean to represent that the Scotch law upon the subject of marriage (I am now upon the first point)—do you mean to represent that the matter which is said to have passed at Gretna-Green, would constitute a marriage in Scotland, if you are merely to take that into account?—Yes, taking into consideration the evidence of Miss Turner

Oh! but I am merely speaking of what passed at Gretna?—The proceeding at Gretna constitutes a marriage, certainly, in my opinion

Do you mean to represent that, on the subject of marriage, the law of Scotland is perfectly clear, and without doubt?—I think it now is—I know the matter was a good deal controverted some time ago, but I think now it is settled

Don't you know, sir, that three of the present judges now on the bench in Scotland, have sworn that, in their opinion, a mere consent *per verba de præsenti* does not constitute a marriage?—don't you know that?—I know that they have, and that several of the judges now on the bench have sworn it does constitute a marriage, and that in the case referred to, it was decided to be a marriage

Not in Scotland?—But by a decision which was held to be law in Scotland.

Don't you know that there is a very great difference of opinion between the Scotch lawyers on the subject? and have they not imported an English decision to help them to what the Scotch law on the point is?—Do you mean the case I have now alluded to?

Yes —I know that that is considered an important case.

Don't you know that it is now considered as settled law, and that ever since that case, it has been so settled, but not before '—I did not say it was not the law, I said it was controverted, but

R

not since the case of Dalrymple and Dalrymple, and M'Adam and Walker.

But since the case of Dalrymple and Dalrymple you consider it more settled than it was before?—Yes, I do.

Not by a Scotch decision, but since that English decision?—Yes.

So I understand you, by the decision of an English judge—and that three of the present Scotch judges swore to a directly different state of the law, from that which you now swear to be the law—is it not so?—I don't think it is exactly so, but nearly so—I don't think the proceedings in the case of Dalrymple and Dalrymple were precisely the same as are sworn to have taken place at Gretna, but I don't think there is any material difference in the law.

Now, I want to ask you this question again: when the Scotch courts find, on certain questions touching marriages, that the English judges have held a different opinion unanimously (the whole of the twelve judges), do you not know that the Scotch courts have been in the practice of adhering to their own opinion in deciding subsequent cases, notwithstanding the unanimous decision of the English judges?—Don't you know that?—What sort of a question do you allude to? I don't think that the Scotch judges on questions of Scotch law have been influenced by the decision of English judges on questions of English law

No, but on questions of Scotch law, I am asking, because Sir William Scott's judgment was in a case of Scotch law?—I am not aware of the case to which your observation applies

My question applies to the effect of the dissolution of a marriage in Scotland?—Yes, I believe the opinion of English judges is adverse to the opinion of Scotch judges, that is, that the Scotch judges retain their own opinions

We have now been talking, supposing the facts that are said to have happened at Gretna Green stood alone without any extraneous circumstances—do you mean to represent there has ever been a case decided in Scotland, in which the facts resembled at all those you have heard given in evidence to-day?—I mean the facts out of Scotland—I mean the facts that happened before the marriage?—No, I do not know of any case where the facts were similar to these

Don't you know that there never has been a case decided in Scotland where the facts were at all similar to these?—I don't think there is any reported case.

Has there ever been an unreported case—any case at all?—I have said already, I am not aware of any case, and I think I can go further, and say I don't think there is a case

In which the facts at all resemble those that have been given in evidence to-day?—No

Is not the Civil Law of high authority in the Scotch law of marriage? and does not the Scotch law import into the law of marriage the principle of the Roman law, *consensus non concubitus facit nuptias?*—It does. and we long used to go by the Civil Law, but we now think we have cases on which we can proceed

But the Civil Law principles are of high authority as respects the Scotch law of marriage?—Certainly

Mr. Baron Hullock—The Civil Law is the principle on which they proceeded, *consensus non concubitus facit nuptias?*

The witness—I understand we did proceed on the principle of the Civil Law, but we now have cases on which we can proceed without going to the Civil Law

Mr Brougham—You, of course, have passed your examination as a civil lawyer?—I have, but I cannot pretend to be very versant in it

Are you not aware it is a principle in the Civil Law, that a contract is void "*cui dolus dat locum;*" that there is a principle in the Civil Law which voids a contract of that sort?—There is such a general principle.

Are you not aware that there is also a Prætorian Edict very well known in the Civil Law, "*Pacta conventa quæ neque dolo malo, neque adversus leges, neque quo fraus cui earum fiat, facta erunt servabo?*"—I don't recollect the particular dictum, but I think there is a dictum to that effect

Are you not aware that by the Civil Law—by one of the Novels of Justinian, a person by fraud taking away a young woman, and by fraud marrying her, is guilty of a capital offence?—I believe he is, but I don't recollect.

But you believe there is such a law of Justinian, which is parcel of the Civil Law?—Yes.

Is there in the law of Scotland any statute or is it at common law, an offence to inveigle and take away an heiress for the purpose of marrying her—was it ever punished as a capital offence, for instance?—The forcibly taking her away, has been.

But I mean inveigling her by fraud?—I don't know of any case—certainly there has not been one for centuries I should say no capital offence

But is it an offence to inveigle and take her away?—I don't know of any case being prosecuted in a criminal court.

Suppose now (I am going to put a case), suppose that it were an offence of a high nature, pu-

nishable by transportation for life, and that it had
only within three years ceased to be a capital offence by the law of Scotland to inveigle away a
person for the purpose of contracting a marriage
with her,—suppose that was the law of Scotland, should you conceive that the marriage, in
such circumstances, solemnized by the law of Scotland, would be a valid marriage?—It is very difficult to form an opinion upon that   I should say
by the law of Scotland, if a person inveigled away
another for the purpose of contracting marriage,
if that person afterwards freely gave her consent
to be married, and was married, that the marriage is a valid marriage, and I am so taking it in
your qualification of its being a capital offence to
inveigle her away

And that yet the same law would support the
marriage of the person so inveigled as valid,
which made it punishable with death to inveigle
her away, and marry her?—I cannot conceive
such a state of matter

Can you conceive such to be the civil law of
Scotland, if such was the criminal law of Scotland.   Can you in your imagination conceive they
could, by the law of Scotland, make that marriage good, the contracting which was, by the same
law, a capital offence?—If the law of Scotland
was very different from what it is; but that sup-
poses a law that I never heard of in Scotland.

Mr. Baron Hullock.—You are only to ask him to this particular case

Mr. Brougham —My lord, he says he never knew such a case as this.

Mr. Baron Hullock —I should just ask him, whether he ever knew where a person inveigled away under false pretences, by misrepresentation, afterwards consented to marry, whether that would be a good marriage?

Did you ever know an instance of a person inveigled away, and told it was necessary to marry A B, in order to save her father from the sheriff's officers, and a marriage, under those circumstances, takes place, that the marriage was held to be a valid marriage?—I never knew a case in its circumstances at all similar to this, but I know of no doctrine in our law which lays down that any deception short of a mistake in the identity of the person invalidates the marriage

Mr. Sergeant Cross.—My lord, I object to what this gentleman has read as the law on the subject, because the law of Scotland, as well as every other law, must be proved by what the law is

Mr. Scarlett.—I beg he may be allowed to state what the law is.

Mr. Baron Hullock.—He tells you he never knew an instance of the sort.

Mr. Scarlett.—It is almost impossible that two

cases should have happened where the circumstances are precisely the same. It is very possible, that the very next cause which your lordship tries may not be in its circumstances exactly like this, and yet you may have no difficulty on the law nevertheless, and that is the very reason why he is giving a reference to other cases, and to show that the circumstances of this case are such as to make this a good marriage

Mr. Baron Hullock.—There can be no objection to his doing that, but he must state something like a fact

The Witness —I believe—

Mr Scarlett.—It is a question of law

Mr Brougham (to the witness)—You were going to say something

The Witness —I believe there is no case in the books of a marriage having been set aside on the ground of deception and misstatement to induce the consent to marry   I believe there is no such case, I know of no case in which the marriage has been challenged, and I can state further that the doctrine, as I find it of our law, and as I understand in practice in Scotland, is, that there is no case to be found in which deception goes to invalidate a marriage, except a mistake as to the identity of the person.

Now, you say you know of no such case in

which the marriage has been set aside or challenged?—I do not know of any.

Do you know of any case in which a marriage under such circumstances has been affirmed—has been set up?—It is impossible, if none has been challenged

There is no case either way then I understand you to say it never has arisen?—I know of none where there was any deception, or any state of facts similar to the present. The only recent case of deception that I know of at all is the case of Jolly

And that is now under appeal, is it not—Yes, It is, in which the statement on the part of the lady was, that she had been deceived into the marriage by the husband saying he had obtained her father's consent

And what became of that?—And there did not appear, as far as I could discover from the evidence, any evidence of the consummation of that marriage In the course of a month after, the lady was married to a gentleman who had been a suitor of her's before The first husband was present at this marriage, and was in the habit of visiting them, and when the old gentleman, the father, died, leaving a considerable fortune to the lady, the first husband claimed her as his wife, and they held he was the husband. There were children born of the second marriage.

In that case there was a difference of opinion between the judges ?—There was one dissenting judge

And how many the other way ?—I think three.

And that is now under appeal ?—That is now under appeal

Now, Mr. M'Neil, are you acquainted with the case which certainly comes nearest to the present of any that I know, Harford and Morris, in which a marriage under such circumstances was set aside —a marriage obtained by fraud ?—I don't think that is a Scotch case.

No, not a Scotch case, I don't mean so to represent it ?—I am not acquainted with it.

Now, supposing that a marriage had taken place in a country where the law of marriage was substantially the same as the Scotch, would not that case, decided in England, be citable by a lawyer in support of an argument on the present question in the Scotch courts ?—Which case ?

A case decided by the Delegates in England ?—You mean the case of Harford and Morris ?

Supposing in a country where the law of marriage is the same as the law of marriage in Scotland—understand me—I say, suppose a case had

arisen of inveigling and taking away a young girl
from the care of her guardians, or inveigling her
and taking her away from a boarding-school, and
marrying her in a country (in fraud of the English
marriage act) where the law is the same as the
law of Scotland, do you not consider the authority of the Court of Delegates (the highest consistorial court in England) an authority of weight
in the Scotch courts?—I do not consider it of
authority, in illustration, it would be of weight,
but I don't think the judges would hold it a decision to guide them

Don't the Scotch judges allow the opinion of
individual practitioners to be read in court?—If
a question relative to the law of England arises
in the course of a Scotch case, and that case is
sent for the opinion of English counsel, that is
allowed to be read. That is on a point of English
law.

But upon a case where the law is common to
England and Scotland, for instance, the mercantile
law, don't they every day read opinions of counsel
as authorities?—I don't think our judges are
at all bound by English decisions.

Are they at all bound by their own decisions?—
I think they are, where they are in a uniform series

Mr. Baron Hullock —In that very case you
allude to, Sir William Scott's opinion was read.

The Witness.—Sir William Scott interposed the discrepancy, that is—what I say—the opinion of an English lawyer is read on a question of English law, when it arises in a Scotch case, but not on a question of Scotch law

Re-examined by Mr Scarlett

Though you know of no case where the circumstances are precisely like the present, I beg to ask if there are circumstances that involve the principle in your judgment sufficient to decide the present case, allow me to suggest a case to you suppose that a woman—

Mr Sergeant Cross—You had better let the witness state his own case

Mr Baron Hullock—What evidence can that be? I cannot take his opinion That is a question that is to be decided hereafter, whether there are any cases which furnish the principle for the decision of this. I want to know what the law is, not what might have been decided by this gentleman

Mr Scarlett—But still I apprehend I have a right to ask him what his opinion is, if the gentlemen on the other side choose to investigate whether his opinion is accurate or not, that is another question

Mr Baron Hullock.—The result of the exami-

nation by Mr Brougham is this, that taking the
facts to be true as to that which occurred at
Gretna, in his judgment, that constituted a valid
marriage according to the law of Scotland Then
another question is put, whether, if a person had
been carried away by fraud under circumstances
such as are in evidence in this case, for the sake of
argument, whether or no there is any case in the
Scotch law which states in what way that marriage would be decided , whether a good or a bad
one ? Then if I understand you, you want to
know whether there is not a particular Scotch
law which may be applicable to another case   I
cannot take his opinion as applicable to any question of Scotch law

Mr. Scarlett —Then I will ask him, whether
by the Scotch law, any deception short of identity, is sufficient to invalidate the marriage ?

The Witness —I don't think it is, and I don't
find it stated in any of the authorities , some of
our authorities doubt even that identity is sufficient   Mr. Wallace, a most eminent writer,
doubts it

Mr. Scarlett —I should not doubt that myself,
I own

Suppose a woman of abandoned character
makes a man believe she is perfectly modest and
chaste, and a marriage takes place under those

circumstances, would not that marriage be a valid
marriage ?—That case was expressly put by my
Lord Stowers, and he said it would be a valid
marriage

Mr Baron Hullock.—Is there any decision to
that effect ?

Has such a case ever been questioned ?—No, I
am not aware that it has   Lord Stowers, who is
held to be the best authority, and the authority
of other writers, all concur in that respect with
the exception of Lord Benington, and there is no
doubt the judges would be bound by that.

Mr Scarlett.—I have Sir William Scott's
judgment here.

Mr. Baron Hullock.—In what case is that judgment ?

Mr Scarlett.—Sullivan and Sullivan. I believe there is no case in which a marriage that
has taken place by consent, has been set aside
on the ground of its having been effected by a
conspiracy. Suppose a person conspires to in-
toxicate another, and impose upon him in that
way—

Mr Sergeant Cross.—Does he say that is a
legal marriage ?

Mr Scarlett.—No, he says it is not.

Mr. Baron Hullock.—I know of no case holding that.

The Witness —That case of intoxication is the same in Scotland, as the case of no consent.

Then I wish to know whether the law of Scotland is this, that if there is an actual consent to the marriage by a party understanding what she is about, that is sufficient?—Certainly, I have no doubt of it at all

Although that consent may have been procured by false representations?—Certainly, I have no doubt of it.

Now, let me put another case to you?—

Mr. Sergeant Cross.—I beg my learned friend will not put other cases but this case, the question is on this case, and on no other. And I object to my friends' putting any other

Mr Scarlett—Mr Brougham put cases, and therefore, why should not I?

Now, let me put this case to you, suppose the case of a lady going a long journey in apparent contentment?

Mr Sergeant Cross —This is a speech of my learned friend's, and not evidence.

Mr Baron Hullock.—It is like a question, if he could put it more shortly

Suppose the case of a lady who has originally been obtained by fraud and deception—suppose that—but is proved to have gone a long journey in apparent contentment, pleasure, satisfaction

and joy, without the least restraint, and freely
and openly consenting to a marriage, have you
any doubt that would be a good marriage ?—If
there is open and full consent to the marriage, it
is a good marriage

By Mr Brougham —You have heard a certificate read of this being a marriage according to
the forms of the church of Scotland,—is there the
slightest pretence for saying this was a marriage
according to the forms of the church of Scotland?
A marriage by a drunken pedlar ! Is there any
pretence for saying that a marriage witnessed by
a drunken pedlar at an alehouse, before a post-
boy, is a marriage according to the service of the
church of Scotland ?—Is it not an offence according to the church of Scotland, and would not a
clergyman be censurable for committing such an
illegal act ?—Yes, he would, but the marriage is
still legal

Mr Scarlett —Will your lordship allow me to
state a case which occurred before Mr Justice
Holroyd ? It was a case of this nature, where a
gentleman who had taken a lady into Scotland in
a steam-boat, took out a book and declared she
was his wife, and that was held to be a good marriage, but Mr Justice Holroyd held that the
witness was competent to give his opinion on the
subject without showing it was in a case where

the facts were precisely the same ; and I venture
to say, if an English advocate gave his opinion in
Scotland on a question of law, if he was not able
to cite a case where it had been so really decided,
that he might still give an opinion.

Mr Baron Hullock.—Yes he may, there is no
doubt about that

By Mr Baron Hullock —Do you know of
any case in which the question that arises in this
case, under the circumstances that have been
stated, ever arose in Scotland ?—Under the circumstances of this case, certainly not I never
knew a case where the circumstances were the
same as these. I never heard of a case where the
circumstances were the same

Mr Baron Hullock —I am prepared now to
give an opinion with respect to the admissibility
of Miss Turner's evidence I should think myself bound to admit Miss Turner's evidence,
although I should be satisfied in my own mind
(which I am not) that this is a legal marriage I
think that all the cases to which reference has
been made with respect to the relation between
husband and wife, are quite foreign to the present question I take it, it is quite clear now,
that a wife is a competent witness against her
husband in respect of any charge which affects
her liberty or her person That was long doubted.

S

It was first decided in a very great case, which is known to every one it was afterwards, however, doubted for a considerable time, but by a series of decisions down to the present day almost, cases have been referred to in which the evidence of the wife has been received against the husband in cases of personal tort She may file articles of the peace against her husband, she may prosecute him for a misdemeanour, as was done in the case of Jagger at York, before Mr. Justice Lawrence, which was the case of an attempt by the husband to poison his wife. It was done in the case of Lady Strathmore against Mr Bowes and others, and in various other cases that have occurred since that time I think it would be a strange incongruity in the law of the country with respect to the practice of the admissibility of evidence, if it was to shut out the evidence of the only individual who was competent to speak to the facts of the case It should seem that she is a witness *ex necessitate*, because if she was not a witness, injuries might be committed with impunity, the law of the land might, in fact, be violated with the greatest possible ease, with impunity. the husband would be allowed to commit the grossest acts of violence without punishment, if the wife was not allowed to be a witness to prove them. Supposing after this marriage—this gentleman

(assuming that the marriage was a legal marriage)
had committed any force or restraint on her person, I apprehend it would be open to her to apply
to the Court of King's Bench for redress, or she
might have exhibited articles of the peace against
him   Then is it to be said, that because that
which was done to her took place prior to that
act of which he himself was the author,—that
therefore she is not a witness, and that he is to
shelter himself under his own wrong? and preclude her from giving that testimony which she
might, as I conceive, in point of law, have been
permitted to give, if the transaction had occurred
subsequent to the marriage? I think myself
bound, therefore, to give that opinion, assuming
for the moment that the marriage is good, though
I think that that is doubtful,—but I am not called
on to decide that question   I have no right to
decide the question of marriage in this case; but
the validity of this marriage has by no means
been proved to my satisfaction by the only witness that has been called, certainly a most respectable individual, from the Scotch bar   His evidence by no means reaches the case   He says
distinctly, he knows of no case like the present,
he knows of no case in which judgment has been
given, affirming a marriage contract under these
circumstances   And, therefore, if the marriage

S 2

be wrong, she is admissible, and if it be right, I think still, in point of law, she is, under all the circumstances of this case, a competent witness And therefore, *quácunque vâ data,* I am disposed to say her evidence ought to be received

Mr Scarlett —I feel it my duty to say, with respect to Mrs Wakefield, that I really do not think it necessary to offer your lordship any evidence I think so conscientiously, otherwise I should not say so I have witnesses, but it does not appear to me to be necessary to trouble your lordship with them

Mr Baron Hullock —I don't want to put you out of any line of defence that you may think proper to take, you must exercise your own discretion, but I have a very strong impression upon my mind, with respect to the effect of the evidence you have given. I have no hesitation in saying that upon it

Mr Scarlett —My lord, I am quite satisfied —Then that will be my case —*(The learned counsel then left the court)*

Mr Serjeant Cross then addressed the court and jury on the part of the prosecution, in reply, as follows .—

May it please your lordship,—Gentlemen of the jury,—

My learned friend, who has conducted this defence, feeling that he had a desperate case to deal with in the outset, treated you with a political proposition, which it is not my intention to dispute with him, but I think it was this,—that there were no honest or wise men at the bar that did not belong to a political party, and that the party to which he belonged, has a monopoly of all the talents and integrity of the kingdom I congratulate my learned friend on his having the honour of belonging to such a party, and I hope my learned friends, and the rising generation of the bar, will take the hint of my learned friend, and take care to enlist themselves under his banners Depend on it, without they do that, they will never get any reputation for talent at all, or for any skill in the exercise of their profession

Gentlemen, you have for the last five hours, I think, been totally carried away from the real question in this cause, let me, therefore, take the liberty to remind you what it is The indictment now before you charges that the three defendants, Mrs Wakefield, Edward Gibbon Wakefield, and William Wakefield, did conspire, confederate, and agree together, in the first place, to carry away a young female from the custody of her instructors, without the consent of those instructors, or of her parents, with intent to marry her to one of the cul-

prits—that is the first charge. Did they so conspire,
and when was the crime of conspiracy, if committed, completed and brought to its final termination ? When that letter was delivered at Liverpool, and the young lady conveyed away in the
carriage,—then was the crime that is now before
you committed,—then had that crime attained
its full consummation, but this case has been de-
fended to-day, with a degree of hardihood and
folly, that I never witnessed in the whole course
of my experience. We charge these defendants
with a conspiracy to commit an atrocious crime,
and their defence is this —true it is that we committed it, we set about it, and we completed it—
that is the defence, and there is no other defence
offered to you on the other side, but that the
crime which we charge these defendants to have
conspired to commit, they have, in fact, perpe-
trated under circumstances of singular atrocity—
that is the defence But, gentlemen, this atrocious
offence is aggravated by a circumstance which I
could not believe that any man of human feeling
could have pressed into this case Notwithstanding the confidential letter which one of these defendants wrote to his confederate, asserting, what
is the fact, that there had been no violation
of the person of this much-injured young lady,
yet have they the audacity to come here, in the

face of the public, and to insinuate that she has
been defiled   Merciful God! God forbid, I say,
that I, in the exercise of my profession, should
lend myself, for a moment, to so atrocious an insinuation!—What! have they not dared to cross-
examine the witnesses, to know what happened in
the beds at Penrith? and why, but to stain, for
ever, the injured lady who has been the victim of
this crime, and to wound for ever the feelings of
the afflicted family! to belie that which one of
these defendants recorded in his confidential letter
to the other —that he had never lived with this
young lady, but as a brother with a sister, you
have had under his own hand solemnly declared!
Does not all the evidence confirm that? Were
there not separate beds at Penrith on the night of
this pretended marriage? Were there not separate beds all the time at Calais?   And is there any
pretence for that horrible and audacious insinuation which, whatever may be your verdict, I
trust will never be forgotten by the court which
is to pass judgment on these delinquents? and I
trust it will largely recoil on them when they are
brought up to receive that judgment

Gentlemen, I shall not trouble you with a single
observation on the question, whether the two
Wakefields have or not committed this crime, but
I will just make one remark on the nature of the

evidence which they have brought before you, the object of which is to show, that during the whole time that these deceptions were practised upon this young lady, she was in good spirits, and to leave no doubt that she believed them   Twenty, or thirty, or forty, witnesses are called to prove that —Does any man deny it ?   Has she denied it, that she was deluded and imposed upon—that she believed she was going for the preservation of her whole family ? and that, when she had gone through this foolish ceremony of a marriage, she had accomplished that preservation ?   Was there not some reason for her being cheerful ?   But was it not the object of these defendants to keep up a continual talking and laughing and jocularity ?   They contend that you never did, in the whole course of your lives, hear of such a merry party, according to their evidence , and one of their witnesses, whom they have called before you, to-day,—a man of the name of Wilson, a waiter at Manchester, has been brought here to say this — he was present at the first interview between Edward Wakefield and Miss Turner , that the moment he entered the room, the lady went up to him and shook him cordially by the hand !   Do you believe that man ?   Is it possible ?   You have seen the young lady, and you have heard all the circumstances of the case.   Can you have any doubt that that is a detestable and utter falsehood? But by whom is that witness brought here before you to give such testimony? I own I did expect a great deal of false testimony—a great deal! for I did not think there would be any difficulty in persons who could demean themselves as the defendants are proved to have done, who have committed a forgery, and by that means, have got possession of the person of the young lady, in a way in which, if they had obtained a bale of goods by the same means, they would long ago have been transported as swindlers!—That such witnesses should be brought forward by persons who had begun their career with a forgery, and who had followed it up by a series of abominable falsehoods, invented hour after hour for several successive days, that persons so acting and so conducting themselves, should be able to procure a few witnesses to serve their purposes, I never entertained the smallest doubt but I should do them, perhaps, some injustice, if I did not acknowledge that it is probable enough that there has been only one false witness on the part of the defence, although the rest, I have no doubt, have been very much encouraged to swell the statements that they have made

Gentlemen, I shall confine what remains for me to address to you in support of the prosecution, to the facts which relate to Mrs Wakefield, because I conceive, from what has passed in this cause, that it is impossible you can entertain the smallest doubt as to the guilt of the other two defendants, and I do assure you it is a painful duty which I am proceeding to perform, when I reflect that a lady is the subject of the observations which it is my duty to make I am sorry that I cannot but collect from the evidence that has been adduced before you, as far as respects that lady, that she is proved to have been (what I stated her at the outset to be) the suggester, and the contriver of all this plot, and that I am thoroughly convinced that it never would have been carried into execution without her assistance —Now how stands the matter, gentlemen? First of all, Miss Davies lives at Macclesfield in the neighbourhood of Mr. Turner's family; the other two defendants reside at Paris, and never knew there was such a person in existence as either Mr Turner or Miss Turner Miss Davies visits them at Paris she marries their father, and conceals that marriage for three years, and during all that time has been, I am sorry to say, practising duplicity towards her father, and her friends, and acquaintances, until that marriage was discovered She must from that course of life have been pretty well practised in the habits of dissimulation: she goes to Paris, and she suggests——

Mr. Coltman —This is a very improper course which the learned Sergeant is taking, to be stating facts which are not supported by the evidence in the cause

Mr Baron Hullock —I know, Mr Coltman, there is no evidence in the cause of that assertion —you are right—none whatever There is no evidence, brother Cross, that she was married under the circumstances you now repeat

Mr Sergeant Cross.—I understood Mrs Brocklehurst to state she told her she had been married in the way I have stated

Mr. Baron Hullock.—It is new to me if she did I don't mean to say she did not, but if she did not, it is improper to be stating it

Mr Sergeant Cross.—Gentlemen, I pass over that, I will not detain you to recall the witness in order to clear up that point, but let us see how Mrs Wakefield has acted in this particular transaction She did, in fact, go to Paris at Christmas she did, in fact, as soon as she came back, call on Mrs Brocklehurst and express a wish to get introduced to the Turner family, she did, in point of fact, shortly afterwards get an introduction through Mrs Brocklehurst In the next place, having got that introduction, she gets the other two defendants into her father's house there they remain riding up and down the country

about a week   during that time she calls upon
Mr Grimsditch, gives them a personal view of
Mr. Grimsditch, and affords them the opportunity of pretending to the young lady they are well
acquainted with Mr Grimsditch, and know his
person   she conducts them all about the grounds
at Shrigley to endeavour to get an opportunity
of seeing Mr Turner and the rest of the family,
if they could not get introduced to them, but she
gives them an opportunity of seeing the whole
estate, and being enabled to talk to the young
lady about it, as if they had been perfectly well
acquainted with the family   In the next place,
she meets Mr Grimsditch in the street—has a
long conversation with him about Mrs Turner's
health, and about Mr Turner's journey to London   she learns from Mr. Grimsditch that Mrs
Turner has had an attack, which he, Mr Grimsditch, calls by the name of paralysis, and she, and
she alone, learns from Mr Grimsditch that Mr
Turner is going to London on the Monday evening
—All those communications, therefore, must have
come from her   In the next place, when her two
confederates are about to depart on this expedition, she raises the money, one hundred and fifty
pounds she obtains from the banker   does she
state to him the truth? either she stated to him a
falsehood in the first instance, or in the second

Her pretence to the banker on the Sunday was, in the first instance, a very pressing and urgent necessity—that a cousin of her's was in gaol, and she wanted the money immediately, for his liberation

Mr Baron Hullock.—No, not in gaol, but she wanted the money

Mr Sergeant Cross —Wanted it for him

Mr Baron Hullock —For Doctor John

Mr. Sergeant Cross —The next time that she sees this gentleman on the subject, when she hears the advancing that money is to become a matter of inquiry here at the assizes, oh! she did not then want it for her cousin, but she wanted it to change some French bills which these persons had, and which they could not get changed!—Had she told her father of the transaction? No, she never mentioned it to him! Why, then, can you have any doubt she advanced that money to the two other defendants for some sinister purpose, which they understood perfectly well between themselves, but which was not explained to Mr Bagshaw, the gentleman who furnished the money?

Then, in the next place, remember what happens on the Monday evening. On the Sunday the two Wakefields and the Frenchman leave Doctor Davies's house In the course of that evening they get on to Manchester, and on the following morning, the Monday, they sent the man back express, in a post-chaise, to Doctor Davies's house.   He remains——

Mr Parke —There is no evidence of that at all

Mr. Sergeant Cross —My learned friend interrupts me by saying there is no evidence that he went to Doctor Davies's house. You will judge whether he went there, or not   The witness said this —he inquired for the way to Mr Ryle's house it was pointed out to him, and, instead of going to Mr Ryle's, he went the direct way to Doctor Davies's house, where we knew he had been all the preceding week and there he remained half an hour, and then got into the chaise, and insisted on the horses being brought out, and he arrived at Manchester after midnight Whatever communications he made on that occasion, or what communications he received from Miss Davies, we don't know,—but those we must collect from the circumstances in the cause,—she being on the spot could know that Mr Turner had gone on that same Monday evening to London What is the subject of the forged letter ? Mr Turner's departure to London ! And Mrs Turner's paralysis, which Miss Davies had from Mr Grimsditch ! These are circumstances which leave but little room, I think, to doubt that she knew perfectly well they were going to carry away this young lady clan-

destinely —Let me ask you this do you believe
that at that time she expected they were going to
pay their addresses, either of them, to the young
lady, and to be received as suitors, and that that
was all she was lending herself to—that one of
these gentlemen might get an introduction to Miss
Daulby, and through her be introduced to the
young lady, and that that was all Miss Davies intended ?—Remember this (for that is the only
way that her conduct is consistent with innocence
in this case)—that she knew nothing at all of the
matter—that she knew nothing of the means by
which she expected they would get possession of the
young lady's person —Now how does she conduct
herself on the Sunday following—the Sunday
after the parties had been at Gretna Green ?
The matter was then fully known at Macclesfield,
it had appeared in the newspapers. William
Wakefield, it would seem from this letter, had
been himself at Macclesfield in the interval, somewhere about the day, or day but one, following
the transaction in Scotland Now see whether
this letter is consistent with Miss Davies's innocence, and her ignorance of the fact of the young
lady being clandestinely carried away, either
against her will, or against the will of the go-
verness of the school ?—You will recollect Miss
Daulby's evidence in this,—that she, never sus-

pecting anything at all, thought nothing more of
the matter till she received a letter from Shrigley
on the Sunday morning following   She immediately went over there, but she did not arrive at
the house at Shrigley until the Monday morning.
Now I beg you to attend to this letter, which will
show what Miss Davies was doing —

" Sunday morning —Dear William,—Mr Turner did not come down the night you left—[still
corresponding about Mr Turner, you see, and
his movements] it was a mistake —My father saw
Mrs. Critchley yesterday, who seems very kindly
disposed, but she did not know what her brother's
feelings would be—perhaps Edward or Madame
ought to write to her *touching tender chords*
The old uncles have been written to by her wish
—Miss Daulby has not yet written to Shrigley—
[Why, how was Miss Daulby to write to Shrigley?
What had Miss Daulby to write about, unless
this lady, when she wrote her letter, knew that the
young lady had been improperly taken out of the
custody of Miss Daulby?] But Miss Turner (the
niece) wrote to her yesterday. This is all Mr
Critchley's information to my father "

Now, gentlemen, supposing this lady was perfectly innocent, how would she have expressed
herself when she knew what had happened ?
What would have been her conduct ? would not

she have expressed, and, by her conduct too, have shown, if she had been perfectly innocent, to all her neighbours and acquaintances, a feeling of disgust and abhorrence of the transaction that had occurred ? What would she have said ? would not she have said, you have made a pretty tool of me in this business, you have brought disgrace and reproach upon me ; you have carried off this young lady from school by stealth, and I will have nothing more to do with you, or to say to you ? But instead of that, she is corresponding secretly on this very subject, with two of her confederates, after the final commission of the crime, several days ! And when they themselves knew perfectly well that a forged letter to Miss Daulby had obtained the possession of the young lady, and when nobody else at Macclesfield knew anything at all of the matter.

Well, gentlemen, she does not stop there, but she writes a letter to Mr Randall in these terms Mr. Randall seems to be a person in London, in some way or other connected with her husband " Dear Sir, I am greatly obliged by your kindness in sending the paper, I will thank you to send me a line, directed ' P. O. Buxton,' to-morrow, where I shall be I wish to know whether William is in England. I heard yesterday there would be a warrant for him, and also a hint that

T

a search would be made in Pall Mall for papers,
&c   I know it would have been awkward to you
to have any which were committed to your care,
brought forward, as it might implicate you.   If
you received a communication which might surprise you, you will now know the reason.   I feel
many obligations to you "

Gentlemen, I would ask you, is that the act of
a confederate, or the act of a person who had
been an innocent instrument of a great and alarm-
ing crime?   Do you believe that, if this lady had
not been privy to the criminal design of these
parties, she would have still gone on corresponding in this clandestine manner? and suggesting
to Mr. Randall, in London, the suppression of
papers that might afford some evidence of guilt?
Well then, the next   The other letter I won't
trouble you with at all.

Now, gentlemen, with regard to these letters
It is again, I must say, my painful duty to submit
to your consideration, whether you can reconcile
it to your oaths to say that she was not a guilty
participator in this crime?   Was she not a guilty
perpetrator in assisting in the first suggestion of
the crime, in the completion of it, in obtaining
information, and important information too, and
furnishing it to the other defendants? In furnishing them with the means, by money, of carrying
on their enterprise, money which is distinctly

proved to have been uttered and paid away by the two other defendants on their journey, and in the purchase of a carriage   She furnished them, among other things, with a bank post bill for 60*l.* How was that disposed of? It was disposed of in the purchase of a carriage at Manchester.   She furnished them with a 50*l.* bill, and how was that disposed of? it was paid away at Penrith, and change obtained for the purpose of raising further supplies for this journey   Now, I own it seems to me not to be possible to draw any other conclusion from this body of evidence, than that Mrs. Wakefield was a guilty perpetrator of this crime.   But that question, gentlemen, I leave in your hands.   I am sure, for one, I shall not lament if, in the discharge of your conscientious duty, a different result should occur from that which I feel it to be my duty to anticipate.   But having myself a strong impression that the evidence does irresistibly lead to the conclusion of her guilty participation, it is on that ground I submit it for your consideration

Gentlemen, the case of all the three defendants is now in your hands.   I have said already, I humbly conceive it is impossible to entertain a doubt with regard to two, the only doubtful question will be with regard to the third; but it is for you to decide.

Mr Baron Hullock then addressed the jury.

Gentlemen of the Jury,

This is an indictment against the three defendants, four in fact, but three only are upon their trial, namely, the two Wakefields, Mr Edward Gibbon Wakefield and Mr William Wakefield, and Mrs. Frances Wakefield

Gentlemen, it certainly will be important for you to see how far it appears that the facts laid before you establish the charge against the two individuals, Edward and William Wakefield, and how far, in your judgment, they clearly establish a case of the same character and description against the three   In a case of this description— in a transaction of this sort, so disgraceful to themselves, and, probably, most highly painful in its consequences, if you entertain a fair and reasonable doubt in your minds with regard to the guilt of any of the three, it will be your duty to acquit the person with respect to whom you entertain that doubt   you may find some guilty, and acquit others, or you may find them all guilty, according as you may think that the evidence bears on the case   The evidence, as it affects Edward Gibbon Wakefield and William Wakefield, is of a character so clear and so decisive as it should seem to leave but little doubt on the mind of any one person who has attended

to that evidence, but you will have the goodness
to recollect that Mis Fiances Wakefield was not
in any other manner engaged in this tiansaction,
than in the way which I shall by-and-by call youi
attention to, which was at the time of the beginning of these pioceedings It is not necessaiy,
for the purpose of making hei a conspiiatoi, and
theiefoie to subject hei to a conviction, that she
should be with these peisons at the pi ecise time
when Miss Tuinei was taken from Manchestei.
It might be sufficient to wairant her conviction,
if you shall be of opinion that before the time at
which the thing ai rived at that state of matuiity,
she borrowed the money to enable the othei defendants to prosecute this enteiprise, foi no
doubt can be enteitained on the evidence that a
portion of that money, viz, the 60*l* bill, found
its way into the possession of the othei two defendants, and was applied by them for the purpose of accomplishing their object It is not
necessaiy that she should be present thioughout
every stage of the pioceeding, that is, present at
Manchester, oi present at any inteivening place
between the time oi their leaving Manchestei,
and thei aiival at Gietna Gieen The only
point you have to considei with refeience to her
is, has she oi not by her conduct satisfied youi
minds that she was one of the peisons who was

privy to this transaction, and who co-operated, as
far as she could, in the manner in which it has
been stated by the witnesses she did, for the purpose of accomplishing it? Or did she not do
those things, or might she not have done all
those things under a total ignorance that this
enterpi ise was about to be undertaken by these
two men? It is said that she was at this time,
(and probably she was,) although known by the
name of Miss Davies, the wife of the father
of the two defendants, the two Wakefields
Therefoie, when she found that these proceedings
had taken place, it is not unnatural to suppose
that a degree of indignation might be excited in
hei mind on the subject; and it is not unnatural
that she should have adopted those steps which
she did take, either to apprise them of certain
facts, or to endeavour to give, as far as she could
do, her information and advice and assistance with
respect to one of them.   The question for your
consideiation is, did the two Wakefields and Miss
Davies (Mrs. Wakefield that now is) conspire
togethei for the purpose of taking Miss Turner
from the boarding-school at Liveipool, for the
purpose of having her married, or getting her
maiiied, to Edward Gibbon Wakefield? It is
for you to say, gentlemen, on the evidence which
has been laid before you, what object these per-

sons could have in view in taking away a young
lady under sixteen years of age—an heiress, the
sole daughter and heiress to a large fortune.
What purpose they could have, I say, in taking
her away against the knowledge, against the will
of the person under whose charge she was, or
rather, I should say, with the consent and knowledge of that person obtained through the medium of a false and forged letter,—what earthly
object they could have in view but that which is
imputed in this indictment? What object do they
themselves affect to set up? what does Edward
Wakefield state at Calais? why, that having
heard she was a fine girl, and an heiress to a large
fortune, he determined at all hazards, and at all
events, to possess himself of her. Is not that a
declaration to the full extent of the charge made
against him? When you consider the evidence of
Miss Turner, (if you are not prepared to lay out
of your consideration that evidence,) how does
her evidence affect William Wakefield? Why, in
going from Carlisle, he states to his brother, in
her hearing, that he had something important to
communicate, and that important communication
was, that the father was in a back room at the
Bush Inn, at Carlisle, along with his professional
adviser, Mr Grimsditch, surrounded by sheriffs'
officers, who were in pursuit of, and in search for

him at that time ; and that unless she consents
to become the wife of Edward Wakefield, her
father must be utterly and inevitably ruined.
What does she say? for fear of that, and for the
purpose of obviating that calamity, she consented,
as she stated, to be his wife.   A ceremony was
gone through at Gretna Green, and the parties
went from thence to Calais, and there staid in the
manner you have heard described, and they were
apparently on a good footing, according to the
evidence, not of the witness who was called from
the hotel, and the other persons who saw them, but
according to the evidence of Miss Turner herself

Gentlemen, that being the outline of the case,
I will now call your attention to one or two circumstances with respect to Mrs. Frances Wakefield   The first time she is implicated in this
transaction is by the evidence of Mr. Grimsditch—
no, I think it is by the evidence of Mr. Brocklehurst, and she states, that she resides in the neighbourhood of Macclesfield, and that she has been
acquainted with Miss Davies some time   She says,
that she knew that Miss Davies was at Paris, I
think, in the Christmas of 1826, she was not
there herself, but she entrusted her with a commission to purchase something for her there, which
she did   After that, she called on Mrs Brocklehurst, and she talked a good deal about the family

of Mr Turner. At that time it should seem it was known in that part of the country, or surmised, that Mr. Turner was about to become high-sheriff of Cheshire, and he did, in fact, become so And it was stated by Mr. Grimsditch, I think, that the former high-sheriff (which is not at all unusual in many counties) had given a public breakfast before he set off to Chester, and whether it was any knowledge of that sort, or what it was that induced her to wish for an introduction to Mr Turner's family, I know not. they would have you believe that Mrs Wakefield wished for an introduction to Mr. Turner's family with a view to facilitate this enterprise; but, gentlemen, I think, without some facts to warrant more than a mere inference, you will hardly be disposed to find a person guilty of the crime of conspiracy. She states, that after Miss Davies returned, which was after the expiration of her father's vacation, (her father being a schoolmaster at Macclesfield,) she called upon her. she says she don't know which it was that first mentioned the subject of Mr. Turner's family, but it was spoken of in general conversation She said, "I was induced to believe from what she said, (that is, from the turn of her conversation and from her expressions, probably,) that she wished for an introduction to Mrs Turner I proposed to accompany her, if it was agreeable to her,

to introduce her to Shrigley Hall. She said
she never had called, and regretted never having
done so." It appears Mr Turner had resided in
that neighbourhood about seven or eight years,
and Miss Davies regretted that she had not made
an earlier call, and therefore, in her judgment,
it was necessary to have an introduction to the
family. She states that she proposed to take her
there, and accordingly a day was fixed, which was
shortly after the time when she called upon her
A short time after that, she continued, " We went
together to Shrigley We saw Mrs Turner, and
Mrs Critchley, Mr Turner's sister " Then she
states, that Miss Davies inquired after Miss Turner, and nothing was so natural as to make such
an inquiry. There is nothing very unnatural or
unusual in that course of proceeding—at any rate,
there is nothing so unnatural or so unusual as to
raise an unavoidable inference, that that inquiry
was made for some sinister and improper purpose.
I think her expression was, she inquired particularly after Miss Turner she regretted that she
had not then an opportunity of seeing her ; it was
mentioned that she had returned to school She
says, on cross-examination, that she had been acquainted with Mr Turner's family several years ;
it was known some time before that, that Mr.
Turner was to be the high-sheriff. " I was not,"

she says, " on terms of very great intimacy with Miss Davies, she often called on me, though I did not often call upon her " She stated that she was sufficiently intimate with her to take the liberty of requesting her to get something for her at Paris.

Then Mr Grimsditch says, that he knows Miss Davies, and that he saw her on the 1st or 2d of March, in the last year. He says, " In consequence of a message which I received, I went into the street to speak to her, she was on horseback, and the two Mr Wakefields were also on horseback with her " Now, according to the testimony of this gentleman, it appears that she wanted to see him to ask him if they might ride round Adlington grounds However, it is said that was not the object for which she wanted him, but the object for which she wanted him was to give the two other defendants, Edward Wakefield and William Wakefield, an opportunity of seeing Mr. Grimsditch It does not appear that, subsequent to that time, they had any knowledge of this gentleman, Mr Grimsditch, of which they could avail themselves. It does not appear that Mr. Grimsditch ever afterwards came in contact with them throughout the whole of the proceeding, except when they finally encountered one another at Calais. He says, " I never saw either of the

Wakefields to my knowledge before the time I had that conversation with Miss Davies she asked me whether they might ride through Adlington grounds, for they were going to Shrigley and round by Lyme." It appeared after that, that Adlington was under his care, that he was the agent, or had something to do with the place, and he was authorised to grant the privilege she asked   That is all that took place then. " On the Saturday following," he says, " I saw Miss Davies again," she did not go to him on the Saturday, but he says " I met her by accident in the street   I was walking up the street where Dr. Davies lives, and when I had passed his house about a hundred yards, Miss Davies met me ; and she told me, that she and her two friends had been to Shrigley and Lyme, and had rode into the grounds at Adlington, but had not seen me there." It seems Mr Grimsditch had told her he was going to that place that day, and he would tell the housekeeper to let them see the house. " Then," he says, " she began to speak of Mr. Turner's appointment as high-sheriff, and said, she supposed he was from home, as they had not seen him in their ride to Shrigley, or any of his family. I told her, that Mr Turner had been very much from home of late, in consequence of the death of his eldest brother, at Blackburn , but that he had

returned home the night before, when I had had
a conference with him. Upon that she said ' I
believe Mrs Turner is very ill.' I told her that
she was very ill, and she asked me what was the
nature of her complaint," and he told her that, in
his judgment, it was something of a paralytic
affection, and that he had made that remark to
Mr Turner, who did not accede to that—he was
of a different opinion.

"Now that is all, I think, that passed that
time. No Then she began to talk about the preparations for Mr. Turner's going to the assizes as
sheriff; I told her I had heard but little about
that, as Mr. Turner had been so much from home
This was on the Saturday She then said, ' You
are a great deal in London; are you going with
Mr. Turner?' I told her I was going to London, but not with Mr Turner" Then, on cross-
examination, he says, " Adlington Park is under
my care I told her they might ride through
the park, and that I expected to be there about
one o'clock, and if I was, I should desire the
housekeeper to let them see the house. I was
there that day, but was too early" Then he
mentions the distance from Macclesfield to Shrigley is five miles, and Lyme seven miles and a half,
so that they are those short distances which a
party would be enabled in a morning's ride to go.

Those are the circumstances which he detailed to you as having occurred on the Saturday, and it is for you to say how far those circumstances fairly and justly warrant a conclusion so injurious to this person (Frances Wakefield), as to induce you to believe she was at that time a party to that enterprise which afterwards took place. Because she was at Paris, because she was married before, and (of which you have no evidence) concealed that marriage; because she came home; because these young men came to her father's house, and because she had this conversation with Mr. Grimsditch, it does not appear to me that, because all these things did occur, that that would justify you in coming to the conclusion, that she was a party to the criminal proceedings of the character and description that is the subject of this inquiry.

The main evidence that implicates her, is that of Robert Bagshaw, and you will have the goodness to attend to his evidence, for there certainly is a part of his evidence which goes to implicate her, she not giving always the same account of the purpose for which she procured that money; because you will find that, on one occasion, she stated her object was to enable her to give some assistance or relief, no matter what, to Doctor John, a cousin of hers, and that, upon another occasion,

when the transaction began to develope itself, and
began to be disclosed and known in the neighbourhood, she stated she obtained the money for the
purpose of changing some French bills, which
Edward and William Wakefield had brought from
France, and which, of course, therefore, were not
a convenient currency in this country, but no bills
of that sort have been produced or shown to you.
Now the statement of Mr Bagshaw is, that he is
a banker at Macclesfield, and that, on the Sunday,
he was sent for by Miss Davies, that he went to
her father's house, and saw her, and she said she
wanted a little business done; she wanted a little
money, if I could conveniently assist her with it.
I said I could, and wished to know what kind of
money she wanted. She told me two 50*l* notes,
and the rest in fives and tens, to the amount of
150*l* in the whole She said she wanted it to
pay on Doctor John's account.—Doctor John, it
appears, was her cousin. She did not state he
was in gaol, or any circumstances of that sort, but
she said she wanted it to pay for him Then he
says, " I went and got the notes," and he stated
the numbers and amounts; and, I think, but little
doubt can be entertained that the 60*l* bill found
its way into the possession of Edward Wakefield,
and was by him used in his progress towards
Liverpool, in the purchase of a green-bodied car-

riage, which he bought of the coach-maker at Manchester.

Gentlemen, this evidence is for your consideration. you will take all the circumstances into your consideration before you arrive at a conclusion unfavourable to Frances Wakefield. The only part of this evidence which appears to me to bear against Frances Wakefield, is that afterwards she gave a different account of the purpose for which she obtained this money He says, " I gave her the notes, and was about to write an order upon the Manchester saving-bank, in which she had some money, a little more than 150*l*, for the purpose of getting it from that place," and then he says, " two gentlemen came in, I believe they were the two Wakefields, Edward Gibbon Wakefield is one, and I believe the other is the other (on looking at the two prisoners, he said " I am sure Edward Gibbon Wakefield was one, and I believe the other was the other"). It is quite clear that they were at Macclesfield Mr Grimsditch had seen them there, on horseback, before, with Miss Davies, therefore, it is quite clear they were there, independent of this gentleman's testimony, if there was any doubt about it Then, he says, " I handed the order to Miss Davies to sign, and then Mr Edward Gibbon Wakefield asked her if she was signing her will " Then, he says, when he was

afterwards served with a subpœna, he went to inform Miss Davies, which was not an unnatural
step, he knowing nothing of the transaction, but
that which resulted from the interview with her
in which the money transaction occurred, he went
to her, and he says he told her he did not know
anything about the business, but the money transaction.—Then what did she say? Did she adhere
to the story she told him in the first instance, when
she obtained the money, of the purpose for which
she wanted it? No, she did not · she said she did
not deny advancing some of the money to the
Wakefields, because they had some French bills
which they could not part with there—that is, part
with at Macclesfield. Now, certainly, that is in-
consistent—that does not tally—does not corre-
spond with that which she stated at the time when
this money was procured from Mr. Bagshaw. It
is for you to say whether that circumstance alone,
that discrepancy between the professed and declared purpose of appropriating the money at the
outset, and that which she stated afterwards,
whether that alone, and I confess it appears to me,
that independent, of course, of the letters to which I
shall by and by call your attention, that that is
the only evidence that seems to warrant a suspicion
at this period of the case, at least, a suspicion of
any knowledge she might have on the subject. He

U

says, " I asked her if she had informed her father of
the transaction?" she said she had not —" I recommended her to do so, and she said she would."—
Then he was asked whether there was any thing
said about French bills, when the money was first
obtained, and he said there was not —Then, he
says, she did not bank with him —That is quite
unimportant with respect to this part of the case.
—He was willing to accommodate her. These are
the circumstances he details with respect to that
part of the proceeding; and, certainly, as far as
you can rely on this conversation arising out of
a proceeding of this kind, after a considerable
lapse of time, he states, indisputably, that she
said she did not deny having given the money—
some of the money to them, but that was for the
purpose of enabling them to get rid of some French
bills

This, gentlemen, I think, is the only evidence
which relates to Frances Wakefield, with the exception of one or two letters which have been put
in upon the subject: at least, at present, I don't
call to my mind any other part of the case that is
calculated, I think, to implicate her.

Mr. Sergeant Cross.—There is no other, my
lord

Mr Baron Hullock.—Then, gentlemen, there
wereseveral letters put in which dont appear to

have dates, I think. I don't know whether I have got the letters

Mr. Cross —Yes, my lord, I handed them up

Mr. Parke —There is the post-mark, my lord

Mr. Baron Hullock —Here is a letter without any date of the month —" Sunday morning—Dear William—Mr Turner did not come down the night you left; it was a mistake. My father saw Mrs. Critchley yesterday, who seems very kindly disposed, but she did not know what her brother's feelings would be Perhaps Edward or Madame ought to write to her, touching tender chords." (She suggests a subject that certainly was calculated to affect the feelings of the father, under the circumstances which had taken place This is quite obvious, that this letter must have been written subsequent to the time when she must have known what had taken place—there is no direction The direction is, unfortunately, torn off, but this must have been subsequent to that time, because it is quite clear that some steps must have been taken by her, or somebody, since she had obtained intelligence on the subject, but there is nothing in this letter which shows any previous concert, or any thing to implicate her in any criminal proceeding. It was very natural, as the step-mother of these individuals, that she should be applied to

U 2

for her advice and assistance, under circumstances
of this sort. The question is, whether this letter
is calculated to satisfy your minds,—to warrant
you in inferring that, from its contents, she, at
that time, had been privy to what had taken place,
and accessory to the facts that had taken place at
Manchester, and subsequent to that time) She
says, "the old uncles have been written to by her
wish. Miss Daulby has not yet written to Shrigley, but Miss Turner (the niece) wrote to her
yesterday —This is all Mrs. Critchley's information to *your* father" Why then a letter had
been written by Mis Critchley " to *his* father?"

Mr. Grimsditch —" To *my* father"

Mr. Baron Hullock.—" To *my* father," is it?

Mr Grimsditch.—Yes, my lord

Mr Baron Hullock —That is, to her father,
Doctor Davies Then there is a postscript. " you
must not let a foolish account of the affair get
in the paper It would much annoy Turner, I am
sure "—That is the letter which she writes on the
Sunday Then there is another letter or two

Mr Sergeant Cross —One other, my lord —
The other, I conceive, on a closer examination, is
not applicable. There is a letter to Mr. Randall,
my lord

Mr Baron Hullock.—Oh, here it is—Mr. Randall, 34, Pall Mall, London.

Mr Sergeant Cross —There are two letters to Mr Randall, my lord, and they are both so directed. If your lordship will permit us, for one moment, to see them, we will withdraw one, and only trouble your lordship with the other.

Mr Coltman —They were both read in evidence.

Mr Sergeant Cross —My learned friend wishes them both to be read, and therefore I have not the least objection.

Mr Baron Hullock —Then, gentlemen, there is another letter of Mrs Wakefield, and that is addressed to " Mr Randall, 34, Pall Mall

" Dear Sir —I am greatly obliged by your kindness in sending the paper —I will thank you to send me a line, directed P O Buxton, to-morrow, where I shall be —I wish to know whether William is in England (that of course is William Wakefield) I heard, yesterday, there would be a warrant for him, and also a hint that a search would be made in Pall Mall, for papers, &c. I know it would have been awkward to you to have any which were committed to your care, brought forward, as it might implicate you If you received a communication which might surprise you, you will now know the reason I feel many obligations to you "

Gentlemen, that is the letter—it is for you to

say whether, in the latter case, with the evidence
to which I have already called your attention,
with respect to the conduct of Mrs Wakefield,
how far this letter is incapable of being explained, looking to whom it is addressed   It is
for you to say how far that letter, or the other, to
which I have called your attention, is of so decisive a character and description, as to warrant
you in finding this lady had implicated herself so
far in this transaction, as to make her a conspirator
in the general object of the parties.

Mr Coltman.—I believe the date appears to be
the 20th of March, by the post-mark.

Mr Baron Hullock.—Where does it appear ?
There is no post-mark on this, that I see

Mr Sergeant Cross.—There is on one, not the
other.

Mr. Baron Hullock —Gentlemen, those are the
facts with reference to Frances Wakefield.

With reference to the other two persons, it is
for you to say how far you can entertain any doubt
upon the subject, because it appears to me, if you
believe the evidence of Mr Grimsditch, and the
other gentleman, Mr. Critchley, as to the conversation which took place at Calais,—it appears to
me that the whole of this charge is distinctly and
unequivocally acknowledged by Edward Gibbon
Wakefield.   The evidence of Mr. Turner shows

that his daughter was at a boarding-school with
his consent, put there for the purpose of education, and where she had been four or five
years Miss Daulby states that she had no
intimation that any thing had occurred in the
family, until she received the letter which has been
put in, which was not proved to be the hand-
writing of any individual, but which is proved,
certainly, to have been a gross and palpable forgery, and that, in consequence of receiving that
letter, she permitted this young lady, Miss Turner,
to leave her house You are to say whether, under
the circumstances in which her abduction was obtained, any doubt can be entertained but that the
object that these parties had in view, at the time
they went to Manchester, was, as Edward Wakefield distinctly avowed at Calais, namely, that
having heard she was a fine girl, and a girl of
considerable property, he had resolved to possess
himself of her , and that, therefore, this plan was
devised for the purpose of accomplishing that
object. It appears to me, I confess, under the
circumstances of the case, difficult to entertain a
doubt on the subject. You, however, are to decide the question for yourselves

Now, the first letter which was produced runs
in this form " Shrigley, Monday night, half past
twelve, March 6th.—Madam," (this letter you see,

is directed to Mrs Daulby)—" Madam,—I write
to you by the desire of Mrs Turner of Shrigley,
who has been seized with a sudden and dangerous
attack of paralysis   Mr Turner is unfortunately
from home, but has been sent for, and Mrs Turner
wishes to see her daughter immediately " (What
could be so well calculated to lull the suspicion
of the mistress of any seminary whatever, as a letter written like this, brought by a servant in a
private carriage, alleged to belong to the physician who professes to sign this document, but
who never had any existence, but in the imagination of the person who wrote it?)   Then he says,
" a steady servant will take this letter and my
carriage to you, to fetch Miss Turner, and I beg
no time may be lost in her departure, as, though I
do not think Mrs Turner is in immediate danger,
it is probable she may soon become incapable of
recognizing any one " Then it says, " Mrs. Turner particularly wishes that her daughter should
not be informed of the extent of her danger, as,
without this precaution, Miss Turner might be
very anxious on the journey, and this house is so
crowded, and in such confusion and alarm, that
Mrs Turner does not wish any one to accompany
her daughter "   That is, in order to preclude any
servant, or any person going along with her , for
if any servant had accompanied her, it is quite

clear the object which the parties had in view
would have been frustrated, or at least might
have been——

The Foreman of the jury.—My lord, the jury
think it is not necessary to go further

Mr Baron Hullock.—Then, gentlemen, you
will take into your consideration the circumstances
of the case, as far as it relates to the different
parties, Edward Gibbon Wakefield, William
Wakefield, and Frances Wakefield, and you
will say, gentlemen, whether they are, or are not
guilty.

Mr Coltman.—My lord, the third count is peculiar—perhaps your lordship will think there is
no evidence on that count

Mr Baron Hullock.—I really do not know
what to say upon that.

Mr Coltman—That count charges a conspiracy
to do the thing by force entirely

Mr Baron Hullock.—I think there is no evidence on that count, brother Cross—the third

Mr Williams.—There is no force alleged in
any other

Mr Sergeant Cross.—The charge is, to do it
feloniously, and against the statute

Mr Baron Hullock.—I think, Brother Cross,
there is no evidence that warrants a conclusion of
that sort—no evidence.

Mr. Sergeant Cross.—It is not worth troubling your lordship with it at all.

Mr. Baron Hullock.—Not at all

The Prothonotary.—Gentlemen of the jury, on the third count you find for the defendants, and on the other counts you say——

One of the jury.—We have not made up our minds exactly yet

After the jury had consulted a few minutes in the box, they expressed a wish to retire.

Mr. Baron Hullock.—Do you want to retire with respect to the whole of the defendants, or only with reference to one?

The Foreman.—Only with reference to one, my lord

The jury retired at half-past seven, and after an absence of three-quarters of an hour, returned with a verdict of GUILTY AGAINST THE THREE DEFENDANTS, EDWARD GIBBON WAKE-FIELD, WILLIAM WAKEFIELD, AND FRANCES WAKEFIELD

Mr. Baron Hullock.—Now, what do you do with the other indictment?

Mr Sergeant Cross, after consulting with his juniors, said—We cannot decide very well to-night. It is the same jury, my lord

Mr. Baron Hullock.—Oh, the same jury is it?

Mr Sergeant Cross —The same jury, my lord Perhaps there will be no objection to letting it stand till to morrow morning

Mr. Baron Hullock.—None at all, that I know of.

———

Lancaster-Castle, 24th March, 1827

The KING, on the prosecution of WILLIAM TURNER, Esq., *against*

EDWARD GIBBON WAKEFIELD, *and* WILLIAM WAKEFIELD,

FOR ABDUCTION

Before Mr Baron Hullock, *and the same Special Jury*

———

AFTER this case had been called on, and the jury sworn,

Mr Coltman said, My lord, in this case we consent to a verdict on the fifth count, and my learned friend does not propose to offer any evidence on the other counts

Mr Sergeant Cross.——We don't call for a verdict on the other counts.

Mr Starkie stated the fifth count of the indictment as follows ——Gentlemen of the jury,

" The defendants, Edward Gibbon Wakefield and William Wakefield, stand indicted, for that they, on the 7th day of March, in last year, at Manchester, in this county, did unlawfully, injuriously, and knowingly take and convey, and cause and procure to be taken and conveyed, one Ellen Turner, then being a maid, unmarried, and within the age of sixteen years, out of and from the possession, and against the will, of Margaret Daulby, Phœbe Daulby, Elizabeth Daulby, Ann Daulby, and Catharine Daulby, they having, by lawful means, that is to say, by the consent, direction, and appointment of William Turner, the father of the said Ellen Turner, the order, keeping, education, and governance of the said Ellen Turner, against the form of the statute in such case made and provided, and against the peace of our lord the king, his crown and dignity"

(Here Mr Scarlett came into court)

The Prothonotary —Gentlemen, you find the defendants guilty on the fifth count, and not guilty on the other counts. It is arranged between the parties

Mr Sergt. Cross.—No, don't say it is arranged ; the defendants submit to a verdict on the fifth count.

Mr Scarlett.—No, there has been no arrangement, certainly. It is not for me to question the right of the prosecutor to proceed by two different methods for the same offence , I am afraid the law is so, and I can make no resistance.

Mr Cross.—The defendants submit to be found guilty on the fifth count

By Mr Baron Hullock —And no evidence is offered on the other counts.

Mr Scarlett —Gentlemen of the jury, after what passed yesterday, it would not become me to resist a conviction, for you must hear exactly the same evidence, although it might be put in some different form, but we certainly should resist a conviction on any other count but the fifth, as matter of law, which is open to us. As the law allows them to prosecute for the conspiracy, as well as the abduction, so long as that law lasts, which I think is a great reproach to the law of England, we must submit to it.

The jury then, under his lordship's direction, returned a verdict of GUILTY AGAINST BOTH THE DEFENDANTS

Mr Sergeant Cross—I believe, my lord, it is of course that the two defendants should stand committed

By Mr Baron Hullock—If you make the application, they must stand committed—Let them stand committed

The two defendants then left the court in custody of Mr. Higgin

---

X

APPENDIX.

THE KING

VERSUS

EDWARD GIBBON WAKEFIELD AND WILLIAM WAKEFIELD

Judgment delivered in the Court of King's Bench, Monday, 14th May, 1827

Lord Chief Justice —Brother Cross, do you move anything

Mr Serjeant Cross —I am to pray your lordship's judgment against Edward Gibbon Wakefield and William Wakefield, who were convicted at the last assizes for the County of Lancaster, of a conspiracy, by a forged letter, to carry away a young lady, an heiress, under the age of sixteen years, from the protection of her parents, and afterwards, by fraud and intimidation, to force her to marry one of the defen dants—who now stand before the court for judgment

Mr. Brougham —I have just seen the Attorney general, he is counsel for one of the defendants, he will be here immediately

Lord Chief Justice.—This matter was appointed to

X 2

come on the first thing this morning it is twenty minutes past ten—we cannot wait

The Attorney-general immediately after came into court

Lord Chief Justice —There were two indictments

Mr Sergeant Cross —Yes, my lord

Lord Chief Justice —Upon which do you pray the judgment

Mr Sergeant Cross —Upon that for the conspiracy the court are furnished with a copy of the indictment

Lord Chief Justice —Do you pray the judgment of the court upon that only

Mr. Sergeant Cross —Upon that for the conspiracy, if your lordship pleases

> *Mr Justice Littledale read Mr Baron Hullock's Report of the trial*

Lord Chief Justice —Now read the affidavits

> *The affidavit of Edward Gibbon Wakefield was read*
> *The affidavit of William Wakefield was read*
> *Another affidavit of William Wakefield was read*

Mr Attorney-general —My lords, I appear before your lordships as counsel for William Wakefield exclusively Edward Gibbon Wakefield appears on his own behalf From what has appeared in the course of these proceedings, I am sure your lordships will feel that it would be quite impossible I could say anything in justification or even in palliation of the offence now brought before your lordships for consideration at the same time, there are shades of difference existing in the cases of the two defendants, which it will be my

duty to bring under your lordships' notice My lords,
the person I now represent is a very young man, and
he has stated in his affidavit the affection existing between himself and his elder brother, and the control
which he exercised over him your lordships know that
relationship often produces the highest degree of control, and a young man may find some degree of palliation for misconduct in the affection that a younger
brother feels for an elder These topics lie so much
upon the surface, that I think it hardly necessary to do
anything more than suggest them I hope your lordships will see that the motives under which he acted at
the time, are not unmixed with some of the most
amiable feelings of the human mind,—that of attachment to a brother

There is another circumstance I wish to draw your
lordships' attention to, which is, that at the assizes
held in August last year, his trial might upon one of
these indictments have taken place, but he absconded,
and, to a certain degree, may have frustrated the objects
of the prosecutor I need not assure your lordships
that those who appeared as William Wakefield's counsel were wholly ignorant of his design at the same
time, I must say, that I certainly myself laboured
under the impression that at that particular moment
for him to have taken his trial without his brother
would have been disadvantageous to the interests of
both I very probably expressed that opinion, but
without the least idea that it would have produced any
effect of that kind, for I had had no communication

with either of the defendants, I had not seen them nor had any of their counsel, I believe but it was a moment of great anxiety to all the parties, that he should be brought forward upon his trial upon one of the indictments, and that the whole case should be anticipated upon his trial, and at the same time that the party (the principal) should have his trial postponed to the next assizes, without expecting or believing either the counsel or the solicitor could have been a party to any idea entertained by that gentleman, of quitting Lancaster, I think it right to say, that I think it very probable that that opinion, expressed without any intention of influencing his conduct, might have found its way to him at the moment he left Lancaster At the moment he left, no communication was made to me, I heard of it afterwards, and was much surprised at it but, under the very peculiar circumstances under which he was placed, I think there were circumstances that might have operated upon his mind at the time, and made him incur all the odium of having absconded, though he entertained the intention of returning I am persuaded he acted on that occasion with the same spirit of affection towards his brother, which unhappily led him to the commission of this offence With these observations I conclude I hope your lordships will see a considerable difference between the cases, and that, in respect of William Wakefield, you will be disposed, in the exercise of your discretion, which is always exercised with a due regard to the feelings of parties, to look at his conduct with some degree of favour upon this occasion, he is a young man, lately married just before this unhappy transaction took place, which has involved not only himself, but others in the deepest misery ever since

Mr Coltman —My lords, I have only to draw your lordships' attention to one circumstance in the affidavits My lords, it appears from the affidavits, both of the one and the other defendant, that William Wakefield went upon entirely different grounds to Macclesfield, and without any communication with his brother, he knew nothing of his intention until that moment

Mr Parke —I am on the same side, but it is unnecessary for me to trouble your lordships with any remarks.

Lord Chief Justice —Now, Edward Gibbon Wakefield, will you say anything?

Edward Gibbon Wakefield (from a paper in his hand) —My lords, appearing here convicted of a very grave offence, I hardly dare to beg for your lordships' indulgence, whilst I address you in mitigation of the sentence you are about to pass upon me immediately and, though I am aware that it is highly presumptuous in me to undertake the conduct of my own cause on this occasion, when I might have confided it to one of the ablest advocates of the present day, though I feel that in almost every case a person who is inexperienced in courts of justice and becomes his own advocate, deserves the usual fatal consequences of such extreme folly,—still, my lords, I am not sufficiently presumptuous to detain your lordships with an explanation of the peculiar reasons which have induced me to adopt so dangerous a course

Perhaps, however, I may, without indiscretion, inform the court, that, though my recognizances in the sum of 10,000*l* to appear and receive your lordships' judgment, are still in existence, I have been confined at Lancaster since my trial, and, as I arrived here but yesterday (Sunday) I have been precluded from consulting efficiently with any professional adviser. Perhaps, also, I ought to state that I have received no assistance whatever in preparing the observations with which I am about to trouble the court

My lords, I am desirous to confine myself to such remarks as may tend to a mitigation of punishment, or may, in some degree, anticipate the observations and arguments in aggravation which I have reason to expect from the prosecutor's counsel, indeed, I may say that it is not my intention to urge any thing in mitigation of such sentence as has been usually pronounced for offences similar to that of which I have been found guilty, my only object is to obtain a sentence according with the conviction, and to prevent the counsel engaged against me from too far succeeding in the attempt (which I well know they will make) to obtain a sentence unusually severe, and founded, not upon the conviction, but upon other circumstances

In this endeavour I shall proceed with confidence, because I know that this court, which dispenses justice and not vengeance, will give me a patient hearing

My lords, I cannot but feel that in using the words "unusually severe," I invite the counsel for the prosecution to say that my offence is unusually heinous, and that it merits an unusual punishment. In expectation of this remark from them, I hasten to acknowledge (though for any other purpose it were needless to assert so plain a truth) that the offence of which I am convicted is a grave offence, and one that deserves a corresponding punishment. But I must venture to deny that it can deserve a punishment unusually severe, as compared with sentences passed by this court in similar cases. I am now brought to feel the great difficulty and positive suffering of being my own advocate, for it now behoves me to call your lordships' attention to a sentence passed by this court upon certain defendants, and to admit, of course, that as their case bears immediately upon the subject before the court, there is a certain resemblance between their atrocious offence, and that of which I stand convicted; I allude to the case of *The King* versus *Bouditch and others*, in that case eight or nine defendants were convicted of a conspiracy to carry away a young lady of the age of sixteen, by force, and to procure her marriage with one of them against her will. It appeared on the trial that she was a person of good condition, and entitled to a large fortune, in her own right; that the principal defendant, to whom she was to have been married, was a labourer in husbandry; that she was a total stranger to him and his family, until, for a change of air, after an illness, she was sent to his mother's farm-house;

that, whilst lodging there, she and the principal defendant never exchanged words, but that some of the other defendants, including her own maid, led her to believe that he would certainly murder her unless she consented to marry him , that, shortly afterwards, she returned home, she was forced from her bed half naked, in the middle of the night, by several of the defendants, and was compelled, by threats, to swallow a stupifying potion , and that she was conveyed, in a state of insensibility caused by that potion, to some place where the marriage ceremony was to have been performed against her will

It matters not that in this case the evidence on which the defendants were convicted turned out to be strongly tainted with perjury they were convicted by a special jury , and so clear did their guilt appear, that the jury declined hearing the presiding judge sum up the evidence, and they received sentence in this court long before the perjury upon which they were convicted was brought to light I humbly beg of your lordships to remark this, because those defendants were sentenced when this court must have believed them guilty of a conspiracy to commit a capital offence under circumstances of peculiar aggravation, and there is in one of the indictments against me a count charging a similar conspiracy , on which count, however, not only have I been acquitted, but the learned judge who tried these indictments would not even submit that count to the jury, on the ground distinctly stated by him, that there was no evidence to sustain the charge contained in it When, therefore, I presume to deprecate an unusually severe sentence, I use the word "unusually" not in a general sense, but specially with reference to this other case, which came under your lordships' immediate notice, and between which and my own there is a certain resemblance—a resemblance, however, that is accompanied by the difference between conviction and acquittal

Spite of that vital difference, I have a good reason to believe that your lordships will be urged to pass sentence upon me, as if the two cases were exactly similar in their degrees of criminality —and I come now to the main object of this intrusion upon your lordship's patience

The learned Sergeant who conducts this prosecution, through ignorance, I am bound to suppose, of the law and of the facts, was pleased to say, during the trial, that if the offence with which I was charged had been completed in England,—that is, if my marriage had taken place in England instead of Scotland,—I should have suffered death by the hands of the common executioner: I do but repeat the learned Sergeant's words, " by the hands of the common executioner on the walls of Lancaster Castle "

The learned Sergeant has been engaged in this prosecution for nearly a year, and was, if I am not mistaken, consulted by the prosecutor, when I was a prisoner on a charge of felony In spite of this circumstance, I am willing to suppose that, even up to the period of the last assizes, he had not discovered that

the statute which inflicted a capital punishment had
been repealed, for, my lords, did I suppose otherwise, I
must conclude (what, of course, I cannot even suspect)
that the learned Sergeant condescended to make a wil-
ful mis-statement, for the purpose of distracting, without any conceivable object, the harassed feelings of a
man who had already enough to bear Be this as it
may, the learned Sergeant did indulge in that observation, and, if he were ignorant of the law and of the
facts, he was, in my humble opinion, perfectly justified
in making it, I say, that in that case, but not otherwise, he was perfectly justified in making the observation, because one of the indictments against me
charges an intention to use force, now, the intention
could, of course, only be gathered from subsequent
acts

Now, my lords, a mass of evidence was adduced
on the part of the prosecution, for the purpose of establishing that force was used, yet, before any witnesses
had been called on my behalf, the learned judge who
presided at the trial of these indictments expressed an
opinion that the evidence for the prosecution did not
establish a case of force So distinctly and decidedly
was that opinion expressed, that it became needless,
indeed it would have been affronting to the court, to
call witnesses for the purpose of disproving the charge
of force, consequently, no witnesses were called for
that purpose but the jury, adopting the suggestion of
the learned judge, acquitted me on the count wherein
force is charged I call your lordships' attention to

this circumstance, because I have the best reason to
expect that the counsel for the prosecution will pre
sently repeat an argument which has been much used
by them, and on which I know that they are still in-
clined to lay considerable stress The argument is
this, my lords That nothing but a defect in the law of
venue—nothing but a want of jurisdiction, has enabled
me to escape from a conviction for felony Your
lordships will perceive that, by indicting for a conspiracy to take away and marry feloniously, the prosecutor has, in fact, found a remedy for the defect, if any
there be, in the law of venue, and has brought the
question of force to a fair trial Having been fairly
tried and fully acquitted on the charge of force, I should
be indiscreet to detain your lordships with another observation upon that subject

I must now advert to another charge against me—
indeed, it is the main charge—I mean the charge of
fraud upon my wife, which is specifically made in some
of the counts of the second indictment My lords, I
have been acquitted of that charge on all those counts
Perhaps, I ought to stop here, and rest upon the acquittal but, my lords, it is not my intention to pursue that course I hasten to admit that, if the evidence
for the prosecution had completely established the
charge of fraud upon my wife, I must still have been
acquitted of it The reason is clear—the charge is
made in counts technically untenable , the merits of
those counts could never be tried—an acquittal was
certain when the indictment was drawn I do not say,

therefore, that I have been fairly tried and fairly acquitted of the charge of the fraud upon my wife. My lords, instead of asserting that, I have to impress upon your lordships that I have not been fairly tried on that charge. Further, my lords, I have to complain that the charge has been brought in such a manner, that I have had no opportunity to repel it, nay more, in such a manner that I have been precluded from meeting it— not by the learned judge—not by any disinclination to meet it—not by any accident—not by any difficulties arising out of the facts—no, but by the careful management of those who made the charge. Of this I trust to be able to satisfy your lordships' minds by a very brief reference to the proceedings against me.

Some months before these indictments were preferred, I surrendered myself to meet a charge of felony. I was committed to prison to take my trial for that offence. Was any indictment for felony preferred against me?—No, because the learned Sergeant would say, "Because your offence was not completed in England, and therefore we could not hang you on the walls of Lancaster Castle." I will admit that the principal reason why no indictment for felony was preferred against me, may have been that my marriage took place in Scotland. There may have been other reasons—the result of the charge of force contained in these indictments, shows that there were other and very conclusive reasons, but with those other reasons I have nothing to do just now. I will take the only reason given by the learned Sergeant, as in truth the

only reason   At all events, it became clear, and must
have been impressed upon the minds of the prosecutor's
advisers before these indictments were preferred, that
the want of jurisdiction was a fatal objection to the fair
trial of any charge technically connected with events in
Scotland   Yet what did they do ?—Why, they so
framed the charge of fraud upon my wife specifically,
my lords, in the second count in the second indictment, so that it never could be brought to issue, for
the very reason that made the charge of felony untenable , that is, they technically connected it with events
in Scotland, though the circumstances on which is
founded the charge of fraud upon my wife (I mean that
specific charge at Carlisle) are alleged to have occurred
in England, at Carlisle , and though nothing could
have been more easy than to have brought that charge
to a fair trial, by its insertion in a count for a conspiracy, free from technical objections, not only is it made
in counts having fatal technical objections, but it is
confined—yes, specially confined—to those counts   I
intreat your lordships to remark this circumstance.
Could that circumstance, after my absolution from the
charge of felony, have arisen from a mere oversight ?
Hardly, I should suppose,—at least when I remember
this is the main accusation against me

Then, my lords, if one cannot attribute that remarkable circumstance to ignorance or forgetfulness,
it must have occurred through some design   If that
design had not been twice made apparent, when, on
two several occasions, I have been sent back from

Lancaster unheard, and a host of witnesses, who were taken there solely to repel the charge in question,—it will be clearly exposed to day, when the counsel for the prosecution, who will refer your lordships to the evidence, and will indignantly call for an extraordinary sentence upon me, because—yes, this will be their reason—because, though I have been technically acquitted on the charge of fraud upon my wife, still that that charge is morally established, and that I have failed to repel it   Yes, my lords, I have failed to repe that charge—those who prepared the indictments against me took special care of that—they had a special object in the manœuvre   I venture to say, my lords, that that object was to close the mouths of my witnesses, most of whom have been closely examined by the prosecutor's attorney, and with whose evidence, therefore, he is intimately acquainted   That object has been effected for a time

It may, and probably will, be asserted, that the charge of force having been tried, I had, through the means of that charge, an opportunity of calling all my witnesses   I must again, my lords, refer you to what passed at the trial   On that occasion, Mr Baron Hullock said — (I am about to read from a report made of the trial, by Mr Gurney, which I have no doubt is perfectly correct)—upon that occasion Mr Baron Hullock said, " I consider that the offence stated on this record is to be satisfactorily proved to the jury," &c (*reading the paragraph from Mr Baron Hullock's observations in the progress of the cause*)

My lords, in consequence of this very decided intimation from the learned judge, that it was needless for me to produce evidence of what occurred after Manchester, and as I had not a single witness to speak to anything that occurred before Manchester, it would, as I have said before, have been almost affronting to the court to produce any witnesses at all, and not one of my witnesses would have been heard, but that a collateral question was raised as to my wife's admissibility as a witness. To prove that she was inadmissible, some witnesses were examined, but I can safely say that the most important of my witnesses were never heard at all

I deny, therefore, that the trial of the charge of force gave me an opportunity to examine the witnesses by whose testimony I propose to repel the charge of fraud upon my wife

My lords, I have been compelled to refer thus minutely to the proceedings, in order to show that the prosecutor's advisers have, of all people in the world, the least right to urge, as matter of aggravation, the fact that I have not repelled the charge which they carefully prevented me from repelling If they had adopted a more straightforward course, if they had wished to try fairly this main accusation against me, if they had not taken pains to prevent its being tried, if they had only given it a chance of being tried, if they had not carefully avoided the easy, simple, self-evident means of bringing that charge to a fair trial, then, my lords, I should have been placed here to-day,

fairly convicted or fairly acquitted of the fraud upon
my wife, I should have had an opportunity of producing the mass of evidence by which I proposed to
meet that charge, and your lordships would have been
spared the trouble of listening to this address, because
I should not have had to contend that I ought to be
punished only for the offence of which I am guilty, and
not for one of which I declare myself innocent   If I
have succeeded in convincing your lordships that I
wished to bring the question of fraud upon my wife to
a fair issue, and that I was prevented from so doing
by the form of the indictment, the prosecutor's counsel
are driven from their main position

Doubtless they will take up another   I expect to
hear them say, presently, "the defendant comes here to
read a cut-and-dried speech, which, in the calm retirement of a gaol, he has had plenty of time to prepare;
and, instead of defending himself, he makes accusations
against others   If his assertions are true, if he grieves
to have been hitherto deprived of an opportunity to
repel the main charge against him, why does he not
give some answer to the evidence by which that charge
is, as we alledge, made out? Why does he not produce
affidavits from the host of witnesses about whom he
talks? Why does he not explain his own confidential
letter to his brother?   Why has he not on his affidavit
denied the charge in question?"   My lords, I feel that
it is incumbent upon me to anticipate those questions,
which, even if they were not asked by the prosecutor's
counsel, must exist in the mind of the court   First,

as to the witnesses —On two several occasions, those witnesses have been conveyed to Lancaster from Scotland, all parts of England, and from France, and, after all, it has been decided that their evidence is irrelevant Can it be matter of surprise that I should hesitate to bring for a third time into court evidence so characterised, particularly when I state that the time of the court would have been occupied several hours only in hearing that evidence read? Still, my lords, my anxiety to meet in some way the most serious parts of the evidence for the prosecution would have impelled me to press on your lordships' attention matter of questionable relevancy, did I believe that this is the last or the best opportunity of establishing my innocence—innocence, I mean, of the crime alledged to have been committed between Manchester and Gretna I am informed, my lords, indeed I know, that the prosecutor will leave this court, to petition the House of Lords to pass a bill of pains and penalties against me, on the ground of that very crime 1 shall be the last person to question so extraordinary a measure, because that measure will surely afford me an opportunity of which I have hitherto been deprived,—which I ardently desire,—an opportunity of bringing the charge of fraud against my wife to a fair trial In the House of Lords that charge will not be inserted in a count technically untenable, and there (which would not be the case here) my witnesses will be cross-examined, and their evidence will not be open to the suspicion which evi-

dence upon affidavit often obtains and deserves   The
cost of three defences—one against a charge of felony,
another against these indictments, and a third against
a prosecution in the House of Lords—may also afford
some excuse (as it is a weighty reason) for my not
making here (perhaps irrelevantly, certainly under
great disadvantages) a sort of fourth defence

   Having, on these grounds, decided to abstain from
producing in this court affidavits on the merits, it
appeared to follow, as a matter of course, that I
ought also to abstain from mentioning the subject in
my own affidavit   Had I said one word upon the
subject, I must necessarily have given a detailed
account of all the circumstances of the case, and such
a course seemed open to nearly all the objections
which have deterred me from producing a mass of
affidavits from other persons   besides, even were it
not open to those objections, I could not expect that
the smallest weight would be given to my unsupported
assertions, particularly when accompanied by the declaration I have just made, that I can support them
when I please

   I must now call your lordships' attention to another
subject, which is immediately connected with the question of punishment   I am legally convicted on two
indictments, and this court will be called upon to
punish me as if I had been guilty of two separate and
independent offences, not merely in law but in fact,
whereas, my lords, I venture (with all humility that

befits my ignorance of law and my present situation)
to submit that, in point of fact, and in justice, there is
but one offence

The law undoubtedly subjects offenders to be prosecuted for an offence, and concurrently, for a conspiracy to commit it, but your lordships best know
whether it is the intention of the legislature, in main-
taining this state of the law, to inflict two punishments
for one offence does it not rather appear that, as cases
often occur where it is difficult to prove the offence itself, the legislature, for the ends of justice, gives to a
prosecutor a choice of proceeding either for the offence,
or for a conspiracy to commit it Were it otherwise,
many parts of the same offence would often become
subjects of separate indictments, and accumulated
punishments Indeed, this is just what has occurred
to me Permit me to remind your lordships that I
have been already punished on a charge of feloniously
taking away, that I have been fully acquitted of that
offence, and that I am brought here by those who expect me to receive, first, a sentence for conspiring to
take away, and, secondly, a sentence for taking away

It would be presumptuous in me to say more on this
merely legal subject, and I am well aware that I have
done quite enough in calling your lordships' attention
to it

But there is another point immediately connected
with this unusual course of two prosecutions for the
same offence, which absolutely requires some remark
The court is, I imagine, aware that I submitted to a

verdict of guilty as to one of the indictments, and that
no evidence was heard on that indictment.   Undoubtedly, my lords, I was somewhat surprised to hear the
learned Sergeant—immediately after I had submitted to
a verdict of guilty, on the express condition that the
prosecutor would never call for a sentence upon Mrs
Wakefield, my co-defendant—declare, in emphatic and
solemn terms, that such submission on my part was
wholly unconditional, and that no arrangement whatever had been made between the parties   But, upon
reflection, I rejoiced to hear that statement by the prosecutor's counsel, because my only object in submitting
to a verdict of guilty, was evidently to serve Mrs.
Wakefield, and I conceived that after the learned
judge's very decided intimation respecting her, she
would be virtually acquitted by an unconditional release from sentence   I was, indeed, grateful to the
learned Sergeant for the strong and unqualified way in
which he denied that any bargain had been made   I
cannot doubt that his assertion was induced by a senti-
ment of justice and honour, I am sure that he wished
to perform the bargain faithfully, as well in the spirit
as in the letter, and I ask his permission to say that I
acquit him of all share in the subsequent proceeding
by which I was cheated of the promised consideration
for my submission to a verdict of guilty

I must, in a few words, describe that proceeding to
the court   The attorney for this prosecution is also
the proprietor of a newspaper, which newspaper is
published in the town where Mrs Wakefield has al-

ways resided   Within one week after the time when he was a witness—or rather, I should say, a party—to the prosecutor's undertaking with me that the proceedings against Mrs Wakefield should cease, on the condition of my submission to a verdict of guilty, he inserted in his own newspaper the following paragraphs——

Lord Chief Justice —This court cannot attend to facts without they are verified by affidavit , now, perhaps, you are not aware that the prosecutor has entered a *nolle prosequi* against Mrs Wakefield, and she cannot now be brought up here for judgment

Edward Gibbon Wakefield —I am quite aware of that, my lord

Lord Chief Justice —We cannot hear any facts unless upon affidavit   You had better pass over that part

Edward Gibbon Wakefield —There is another subject to which I must advert, though I do so with hesitation and extreme repugnance   The learned Sergeant in his reply at the trial, threatened to urge upon your lordships, as a reason for the most aggravated punishment, a circumstance that occurred then, and as to which I shall joyfully avoid any further allusion if the counsel for the prosecution will intimate that he does not intend to put his threats in execution   *(Mr Gorton, the defendant's solicitor, pointed out to Mr Serjeant Cross a passage in the report of the trial, but the learned Sergeant refused to hold any communication with him upon it)*

(After a short time)

Lord Chief Justice —Go on.

Edward Gibbon Wakefield —An earnest appeal similar to that I have just made to the learned Sergeant (I should have made it more earnestly, but that its object would have been defeated by giving it an air of too much importance) was urged upon him by Mr Attorney-general as my counsel on the trial   On that occasion, just before my wife was sworn, Mr Attorney-general, addressing himself to the learned Sergeant, said " If you insist upon calling her, you must take all the consequences " The learned Sergeant's answer was, " We will—we will " My lords, one of the consequences that resulted from this exercise of the learned Sergeant's discretion was, that principally by the cross-examination of one of the witnesses afterwards called in support of the marriage, circumstances were elicited tending (though in so slight a degree that it would have remained unnoticed but for the loud threats of the learned Sergeant's reply,)—but tending in a very slight degree to contradict an assurance which I voluntarily—eagerly, I may say—delivered, in writing, to my wife's uncle, when we were separated at Calais

My lords, was I to blame for this unfortunate result ? Was it necessary, in order to procure the only conviction of which there was a chance, to examine my wife at all ? (I beg to impress this question upon your lordships' notice) If it were not necessary, to use the words of Mr Baron Hullock, ' it was of no use whatever to state what occurred after leaving Manchester." if supported by Mr Baron Hullock's opinion, I can boldly say it was of no use whatever to force my wife into the witness-box, spite of my earnest endeavour to prevent it —then I ask, was it I who needlessly exposed her to the stare of the multitude, and brought into discussion subjects which every man of delicacy considers sacred? Did I not, on the contrary, abstain from asking her any questions beyond what were absolutely necessary to prove that she was inadmissible as a witness? Yes, and I called only such witnesses as were necessary to establish the marriage, and thereby, as I fondly hoped, to spare all discussion and all question on this subject, which the prosecutor's counsel will have discussed The counsel for the prosecution thought proper to cross-examine those witnesses, and afterwards to ring the changes on what they had elicited from them To-day they will try to throw all the blame of their cruel indiscretion upon me. My lords, instead of acknowledging myself guilty of having conducted my defence, so that to use the learned Sergeant's words, "it ought to recoil with tenfold vengeance on my head," I claim credit for my forbearance, nay, for my solicitude to render harmless towards my wife the Sergeant's rashness in producing her as a witness without necessity My lords, I should be ashamed to claim merit for conduct which the habitual feelings of a gentleman imperiously dictate, but, as the learned Sergeant has before now, and probably will to-day, apostrophize me as a wretch, for pursuing a totally different line of conduct, I have thought it absolutely necessary to mention what I did do, and to draw this comparison between my consideration and that of the prosecutor's advisers for the feelings of the unhappy person whom, whilst they professed to seek her advantage, they have sacrificed, for the present at least, to a blind pursuit of vengeance upon me

I must now just mention some other circumstances which, I trust, may be considered reasons for a mitigated sentence. First, my lords, I was abroad with my family when the charge of felony was first preferred against me A messenger came to me from London with the unrepealed Act of Henry VII, and an account of several executions under that Act I was urgently requested to escape to America I came at once to England, and (I must mention this to show that if the facts of the case had given cause for alarm, there were not wanting other circumstances to excite it) I travelled from Dover to London by the side of my brother, who was in the custody of the prosecutor's attorney, and a Bow-street officer I left London and surrendered myself to Mr Newton, a Cheshire magistrate, in the immediate neighbourhood of Mr. Turner's house, and I was by that gentleman committed to prison on a charge of felony though no indictment for felony was preferred, I incurred all the anxiety and expense of a defence against that charge, just as if it had been persevered in My expenses, my lords, on the first occasion, amounted, as I have stated, to above three thousand pounds In order to provide that sum, I was compelled to raise money on a life-interest, and in consequence of my being a prisoner on a charge of

felony, the only security I could offer was considered
so bad, that I was obliged to effect the loan upon terms
ruinously extravagant. In order to meet the new
charges of conspiracy and misdemeanour, without de-
priving my two infant children of a maintenance and
education according with their past habits and reversionary fortunes, I have since been compelled to sell a
reversionary life-interest of fifteen hundred pounds a
year, for less than two years' purchase My lords, I
do not urge this last consideration upon your lordships
in charity to my children, because I am prepared to
bear anything rather than encroach upon their comforts, or neglect their education, but I mean to say
that, circumstanced as I am, and feeling as I do with
respect to them, if your lordship should impose a heavy
fine upon me, your sentence will amount to perpetual
imprisonment

My lords, I must just mention one circumstance
which is rather in aggravation, than in mitigation of
punishment, if I thought it really an aggravation, I
should not mention it I allude to the affidavit in
which I state that whatever share my brother may
have had in this transaction, his conduct was pursued
by my suggestion, request, and direction I shall re-
joice, my lords, if this aggravation of my offence should,
as I imagine it does, furnish a reason consistent with
the ends of justice, for increasing my punishment, and
diminishing my brother's in an equal ratio

My lords, I must conclude by expressing a hope
that I have not in this address exceeded the bounds of
discretion, or failed in respect to the court If I have

been betrayed into the use of any unguarded expressions with reference to the counsel for the prosecution, I take this opportunity to apologise for it I have no right to complain of his anxiety to punish me I have attempted to avoid that which appeared to me insidious and unjustifiable in my address and I conclude with asking permission to apologize to the court for this attack upon their patience, for, though I know I must be punished, I know I have already been severely punished, and I know that in the minds of the court that will have its proper influence, and I know that this court will act calmly and impartially, and give to my remarks whatever weight may belong to them.

Mr Sergeant Cross —My lords, I did hope, when I brought this case under the consideration of the court, that it might pass without any observation at all from either side My learned friend, the Attorney-general, concluded his short address to your lordships by saying, that his client, one of the defendants, is plunged into the deepest affliction I am afraid he is not the only party that has been plunged into the deepest affliction by the proceedings now before the court I represent those who also, from the first moment that this crime was known to them down to the present hour, have suffered nothing but the deepest affliction My lords, it has been said that these defendants have also suffered considerably from the great expense that they have incurred in their defence—that they were put to the expense of appearing twice to take their trial at the assizes, but it has not been stated to your lordships that this was purely at the option of

the defendants themselves, one of whom had the right
by law to traverse, and of his right he availed himself
the other had no such right by law, as circumstances
then stood, and he absconded from public justice, and
therefore not only the defendants were put to the expense of appearing twice at the assizes, but the prosecutor was, by their contrivance, put twice to the expense and twice to the pain of following them thither

My lords, it has been urged, that the defendants being acquitted of the most aggravated charge in the indictment, it is a case of great extenuation   There is
one count in the indictment that charges a conspiracy
to commit this offence by force, and it appears by the
evidence of the principal witness that her sole reason
for consenting to the contract of marriage was *fear*
Now, fear, I conceive, is intimidation, and, if I recollect right, the learned judge upon the trial stated that
proof of intimidation would be proof of force   But we
are not now discussing whether the defendants were
rightly, or not, acquitted upon that third count of the
indictment, at the same time, I cannot suffer it to go
forth that it was by the consent of the prosecutor's
counsel they were so acquitted   I did feel it my duty
to insist then, as I shall upon every occasion when it is
necessary, that this was a case of marriage by force,
because it was a marriage obtained by intimidation,
combined with fraud

My lords, it would ill become me, standing here as I
do as counsel on the part of the public conducting this
prosecution, to enter into any thing like a controversy

with the party who now awaits the judgment of the court, in the allusions that have been made to what passed at the trial One circumstance that has been represented as arising either from ignorance or mistake, your lordships will, perhaps, allow me to explain It was stated, undoubtedly, that if this crime had been completed in England it would have been a capital offence That was an erroneous statement, but he who made that erroneous statement, before he concluded his address to the jury, had been corrected by his learned friends, and he corrected himself, by stating that he had made a mistake in representing that it would have been a capital offence, for, by a very recent act of parliament of his present Majesty's reign, the capital punishment (whether rightly or wrongly we will not now discuss) is abolished I was not aware of that, for these changes in the ancient law of the country are occurring every year, and many of us at the bar, and perhaps in higher places of the profession, do not always happen to be apprized of them

My lords, it has been stated that certain evidence has been kept back even yet, that would have gone not only to the acquittal of one of the defendants, but would now tell greatly in extenuation of his crime, but that it is kept back because the prosecutor is proceeding to obtain a bill of pains and penalties How such a notion could get into the head of the party making the statement, I cannot guess, but that there is no foundation for it in fact, every person acquainted with the law of the country must be perfectly aware

There is only one other circumstance which has been alluded to, which, I think, does deserve your lordships' attention. An observation has been insidiously deprecated—we have been threatened by the party accused that, if a certain topic should be touched upon, he can bring forth statements from which the feelings of a gentleman would induce him to abstain. Your lordships perceive, from the evidence that has been read, that the parents of this young lady have, at least, had the consolation of believing that their innocent child was restored to them free from contamination—they have had the solemn pledge of one of these defendants to that effect, the only human being, save one, who could give it—they had the satisfaction of finding that statement repeated in perfect confidence, in a letter written by the principal defendant to his own brother, his confederate—they were perfectly satisfied of the purity of their child. but when we came to trial at the assizes, I own I was petrified with horror to find that the defence was to consist of proof of the young lady's contamination. And, my lords, it is now falsely stated that we forced from them that course of defence. Never did we imagine that such a defence would be attempted in a court of justice. Our witnesses who were called to prove merely their proceedings on the journey, were carefully cross-examined, in order to extract from them circumstances from which the public might suspect a violation of her person. But, not content with that—not content with trying what they could extract from the prosecutor's witnesses, they actually brought over and examined the keeper of the hotel at Calais, for the sole purpose of proving that there was a facility of access that gave the opportunity for communication, and to fortify that evidence still more, they put themselves to the expense of having a plan of the house prepared, in order to show the relative situation of the rooms, for no other purpose that ingenuity can suggest, but to brand a stigma upon the honour of this young lady, that may remain with her for life, and to inflict a deadly wound upon the feelings of her afflicted parents My lords, I will not say another word upon the subject—I will not advert to what is pressed on behalf of the other defendant he is at your lordships' mercy I own I felt strongly the cruelty and depravity of the defence resorted to at the trial, and again basely insinuated to-day—I felt it then, and I feel it still, and I trust your lordships will not forget it

Mr John Williams —My lords, although it was not originally my intention to obtrude myself upon the court, by saying any thing in aggravation of punishment, yet, I do conceive there is, in the singularity of this case—in the novelty of the address that has just been heard, as well as in its public importance, abundant reason to justify me in departing from that purpose The defendant, however, need not suppose that I am now obeying instructions, as he is pleased to term it, or that, from " the anxiety of the prosecutor for punishment," (to use his own phrase,) I stand up to address the court Far from it That Mr Turner has no such feeling is tolerably apparent from the fact, that one of the defendants convicted is not now upon the floor to receive the judgment of the court It arises from my own solemn impression of the nature and quality of the case Not that Mr Wakefield need fear that I shall insult his present situation, by the adoption of language unfit for " a gentleman" (to use his own phrase twice repeated)—unfit for "a gentleman" to hear—I may add, unfit for your lordships to hear, and for " a gentleman" to use But those feelings, of which he speaks, where he himself is concerned, so fluently, and of which he seems to have such an adequate idea in his own individual case, I will thus far, at least, respect, and will endeavour to speak, at least, in the language of " a gentleman ' But to that extent only does Mr Wakefield owe me any obligation, for it shall not be my fault, if he does not exhibit an example for those who are to come after him, adequate, if possible, to the extent and enormity of his guilt

How could I feel otherwise ?—Suppose an unfortunate person in the lower ranks of life, uninformed by education, with none of the feelings of " a gentleman" (to use the language of Mr Wakefield)—unconfirmed by those habits which are sometimes said, I know not with what truth, to belong exclusively to the upper parts of society, and with the excuse, I will not say, but with the palliation of want, had purloined from Mr Turner, to the amount of a few pounds, or a few shillings, property which those pounds or those shil-

Z

lings might replace ,—that man might be driven from the country to make some reparation and atonement to its offended laws. Supposing that to be the case, what are we to say, where in an indictment, (as to which he complains of "a manœuvre" practised in drawing that indictment, which, so far as I can understand the defendant, chiefly consists in this, that it is made to meet his case) in which it is distinctly charged that for the sake of getting possession of the large and ample possessions of Mr Turner, he practised "sundry stratagems and artifices, and false pretences" to carry that object into effect, and that it was his object to get the whole of those extensive possessions, and further to take from them the support and ornament—the comfort and delight of the declining age of her parents,—the daughter herself?—how is it that I can feel otherwise than strongly in this case, and be reminded, when pressing for punishment against such an offender, of a celebrated declaration of a great orator of antiquity,—" *Hoc in negotio illa me res consolatur, Judices, quod hæc quæ videtur esse accusatio mea, non tàm accusatio, quàm defensio est existimanda*" ? I say, then, that your lordships have before you the case of a person who, upon that indictment, is distinctly charged with the purpose of getting possession of this lady, for the sake of the ample property of her father , and when we come to put into contrast this case with one of the ordinary delinquents who suffer judgment at the place to which the defendant has more than once alluded, I

am astonished that he should be so anxious to invite
the consideration of the court to the difference between
his case and that of the other

My lords, there is another point to which he has
called particular attention My learned friend the Sergeant, has, with great propriety, abstained from com-
menting upon a large portion of that long and able,
though, as it struck me, somewhat technical address
that has been read by the defendant to your lordships;
but he has given us a species of threat (whether it was
that he was conscious that we could not by any forgetfulness of duty have forgotten the circumstance, I know
not)—but he has given us a threat, that to-day we
might not again, in the exercise of our accustomed indiscretion, bring before the court a topic which, as he
says, the feelings of every gentleman would have kept
in the back-ground I am surprised that the defendant, upon the deliberation which it appears that paper
has been prepared with, could have forgotten that nothing could be more frivolous (I beg pardon for using
even so strong a phrase as that),—that nothing can be
more unfounded than the statement of the defendant,
wherein he would have your lordships believe that it
was introduced by the prosecutor's counsel Your
lordships will find that upon the *cross-examination on
the part of the defendant*, of Hamilton, who was called
as a witness for the prosecution, the facts to which I
allude, which took place at Penrith, were extracted,—I
mean as to the selection of a chamber for Miss Turner,
in which the defendant himself took a share; and I

will not repeat that which was so forcibly stated by
my learned friend, as to the introduction by the defendant of the testimony from Calais —But the defendant
voluntarily, in writing—deliberately to his brother, the
other defendant (of whom I say nothing, I almost forget he is here)—I say, in writing to the other defendant,
and also in a formal declaration, as proved by Mr
Grimsditch and Mr Critchley, at Calais,—he twice,
with all truth, I do not doubt, with every species of
consideration, emphatically and distinctly discarded
any such supposition It is, therefore, reserved for to-
day, as one of the greatest aggravations which I should
be deficient in the feeling of an advocate, I will not
say, but of a man, if I did not present to your lordships, that after he had studiously and deliberately to
his loving brother abandoned the insinuation, he again
brings it forward at the trial, and now, in a dubious
and hardly intelligible manner, but clear enough for
the object I am now imputing to him—he again intro-
duces it, as if it was for the purpose of showing that
whereas, luckily, he has been prevented from destroying,
his very last effort shall be to injure, this unfortunate,
this unhappy young lady

My lords, take any view of the subject Suppose he
had been successful, and had married Miss Turner,
whom now he holds forth to the country and to your
lordships as his wife (which she undoubtedly is not)
—with all this study, the term " wife" has been introduced as often as the subject could allow —supposing
it to have been so, supposing for life she had been

consigned to the possession of Mr Wakefield He must excuse me, if I say, that when the indictment charges, when the evidence sustains, and when the conviction the jury pronounced authoritatively upon the subject confirms, that his object was the money and not the possession of Miss Turner, what but misery could have been expected from an association with such a man, actuated by such a purpose? If, on the other hand, as has fortunately happened, justice has interposed to prevent him, what is the other consequence? By this prosecution, and this defence, this unfortunate young lady, for the very purposes of justice, is dragged from the retirement befitting her age and sex, to be made the subject of gaze to anxious but unfeeling curiosity In whatever way it is considered, that is her case And with regard to the parents, it is stated truly, that, from the beginning to the end, it has been a tissue of anxiety and of affliction,—it is one continued subject of heart rending to both those parents, from which (and there are further proceedings still pending, though not of the nature to which the defendant has alluded), until their termination, it appears that they never can be delivered

My lords, it appears to me that you have a case that is naked and bare of every circumstance of mitigation, that you have a case of a man, not young—himself a parent (and I give him credit for the possession of paternal feelings in his own case,)—you have a defendant who, at the trial, abandoned the only ground of mitigation he ever could have adopted, and, by insinuation, again reverted to the most severe of all injuries, by which insinuation he chooses to abide to-day My lords, it seems to me that this is a case in which, notwithstanding what Mr Wakefield may have said about the anxiety of the prosecutor, which does not exist, I, for myself, from my own feelings, from no instructions whatever, do say that, by timely interposition of fear, your lordships should endeavour—not with reference to him, but for the sake of example—to put a stop hereafter to the exercise of such monstrous and unbounded cupidity, and (since the defendant has chosen that these transactions should not be known in these realms alone, but in other countries) I will add, in concluding, that an example does seem to be necessary for the sake of the honour and public justice of the country.

Mr Brougham —My lords, I am discharged from the necessity of performing my duty towards this prosecutor not so much, though that would have been a sufficient release, by the addresses which have just been delivered, as by the situation in which, were I to address your lordships, I should feel myself placed, it would be, to speak in aggravation of the punishment by which the demands of justice are to be satisfied, but, beside the addresses of my learned friends who have spoken with that view, there has been delivered an address by the principal criminal himself, which has done what, before I heard it, I should have deemed impracticable,—aggravated the malignity of this most unprecedented misdemeanour—an address, not dictated by the feelings of the moment, but sedulously prepared —elaborated in the retirement of a prison,—with the same crafty spirit which has pervaded his conduct to the end—with the same sordid inclinations in which that crime was originally hatched—with the same malignant, cold-blooded disregard of the feelings of others—the same mighty contempt of the law, and the same utter disregard of all the facts, but I am also restrained by the instructions of him whom I represent—by those " habitual feelings of a gentleman," which have throughout regulated his conduct—which teem fruitfully in the address of the defendant—and on which his whole conduct is a grievous, a scandalous outrage!

I am told that this man wanted to spare *her* feelings whom, in utter contempt of fact as well as of the law of the country, he slanders with the name of " his wife " I am told that while *he* wished to suppress a something which he dares not now more than darkly insinuate against her honour, the indiscretion of the counsel for the prosecution cross-examined into light at the trial. Was it the cross-examination which produced the defendant's evidence? Was it the indiscretion of counsel which brought forth what the defendant intended to conceal? Did the indiscretion of counsel bring witnesses across the channel? Did the indiscretion of counsel indeed produce, by magic, a plan of the chambers on the other side of that channel? Did the indiscretion of counsel collect and produce the evidence, parol and documentary, at Lancaster? or dictate the scandalous, unheard-of, and incredible address that has been uttered upon the floor to-day? That man had forgotten the letter he wrote to his brother, or, if he recollected it, he little believed it was in the prosecutor's keeping If his own denial, under his hand, when a purpose might be served, should have been no evidence—(and I grant that anything the belief of which could serve him, though affirmed how solemnly soever by himself, would rest upon a light proof indeed)—after the delusions, and falsehoods, and false pretences, and forgeries, which he has acknowledged himself to be guilty of for the most sordid, the most profligate purpose that ever yet a human heart was known to harbour, yet that letter to his brother was penned for no such purpose—that document, meant for his private and confidential ear, was above all suspicion, and what is there found, that will I believe —even though it comes from that man I will believe it, because he had then no purpose of his own to serve for once, and the only time in the whole course of his conduct, I have here, before me, laid bare the workings of the heart—of that heart to which, with a prophetic spirit, an author, who knew human nature well, but viewed it as, till this day, I had thought harshly, at least uncharitably, when he said " that the Deity had reserved for no eye but his own that prodigious deformity—a naked human heart."

My lords, Miss Turner's honour stands utterly untainted—this secret letter demonstrates it—all the facts brought forward at the trial confirm it —This is a high, and it is the only, consolation which her venerable parents carry away with them from your presence, except that which you are now about to administer as the consummation of their disinterested labours and painful efforts, not for themselves, but for other parents, and for their country—the signal vindication of her outraged laws!

Mr Starkie—My lords, I am on the same side with my learned friends who have preceded me, and as I cannot add anything to the able addresses that have been made to your lordships, I shall say nothing further than merely show what the defendant's own opinion is of the extent and nature of the injury committed, and I will state that from the evidence of Mr Grimsditch, who speaks of an interview between himself and Edward Gibbon Wakefield —" I said he had struck a blow," &c *(reading the passage from the evidence of Mr Grimsditch)* Your lordships are now to pass your judgment upon a man whose feelings are so acute in his own case, but who does not hesitate to destroy the peace and happiness of others

Mr Justice Bayley—Edward Gibbon Wakefield and William Wakefield You are to receive the sentence of this court after having been convicted upon an indictment, which charges that you, for the sake of lucre and gain, did conspire and combine to take away Ellen Turner, a maid, unmarried, and within the age of sixteen years, out of the possession and from the care of a lady of the name of Daulby, and with conspiring also, unlawfully, to cause her, so being such maid, to contract the most sacred obligation that can be contracted,—that of matrimony, with Edward Gibbon Wakefield, unknowing of, and without the consent of her father, who must, of necessity, feel interested in the welfare of his child, and who ought to be consulted before that child was disposed of in marriage

A design of more aggravated description, and originating in baser motives, I can hardly conceive to have entered into the mind of man; a child between the age of fifteen and sixteen, incapable of judging for herself, is placed by her father under the care and tuition of persons who may form her morals, and who may qualify her to be a comfort to her parents, and to be properly associated for life with a man, not of cunning, of art, of intrigue, but with a man of probity and honesty,—with a man who has a regard to truth,—with a man who will not be guilty of fraud,—with a man of whom, probably, the father may be proud,—whom he may not be ashamed of introducing to his own connexions and friends, and this conspiracy is entered into, not upon any of those honourable principles or honourable feelings upon which a man may be drawn in hastily to contract a marriage, but to induce her to contract a marriage with a man who previously had no acquaintance with her,—who previously had never seen her.

Now, by what means is this effected, and what is the description of man who hopes to be able to call that child his wife for the remainder of her life,—a man who has been guilty of the practices detailed and proved in evidence in this case? It begins by a forged letter sent to Mrs Daulby, a letter well written, and a letter artfully conceived, a letter calculated to impose,

and not to excite suspicion   The first act of the man
who is to be this lady's husband for life, is an act of
forgery, not merely a falsehood, but an act of plain
and direct forgery, intimating that the letter came from
a Dr Ainsworth, who never had written it, and intimating a detail of certain facts, which facts were, from
beginning to end, without foundation The transaction
of falsehood does not stop there, but the man who is
the agent, the man who is to carry that letter to that
place, goes with a carriage purporting to be the carriage of Dr Ainsworth, and he has on him the livery
of Mr Turner he goes there, with a falsehood in his
mouth, to impose upon this lady who had the care of
Miss Turner there is, therefore, not only falsehood in
the letter, but there is subornation of falsehood in the
conduct of the individual employed as an instrument
in the transaction   Pause for a moment, and consider
whether a man who can so have conducted himself,—
who can so far have forgotten the principles of honour,
the principles of rectitude, and the principles of truth,
as to practise falsehood and forgery to that extent—
and not to that extent only,—was he a person to be
introduced into respectable families? Is he a person
to be associated with an innocent, artless, unoffend-
ing young woman, as her companion for life? The
very outset of the transaction shows the malignity of
the conspiracy

A lady of years is imposed upon, the child is sent
away in that carriage She is sent under the expectation that she should meet her father, whom she is told

she shall meet at Manchester —does she? is there any
deception there?—is there any fraud there?—is there
any repetition of falsehood there? She is met by the
two defendants, who are now to receive the sentence of
the court Then a new fabrication is announced to
her, that her father is not there, that he is under the
necessity of leaving his home, that he has been under
the necessity of absconding, that he will be found at
Halifax,—and then this young woman, who has been
harassed by journies from Liverpool to Manchester, is
to find her way to Halifax, where a letter has been
sent Was there any expectation of a letter being
there? That is an additional falsehood —If not there,
it was to be at Kendal, then she is hurried on, and
travelling all night, she arrives at Kendal, and then
there is a pretence that there was a letter there, and that
her father had gone forward, and they must follow him,
then a declaration is made to her, still conducted with
great art, calculated to impose upon an ingenuous
mind, likely to operate upon the good and kind feelings of a good and affectionate daughter She is told
that her father is greatly embarrassed by the failure of
a bank, and she is induced to suppose that the person
in the carriage with her is the nephew of a kind-
hearted man,—a man who has stepped forward and
lent to her father, in his embarrassed circumstances,
no smaller a sum than 60,000*l* Is not that calculated
to make her look upon the person with whom she is
at that time in company as if he was a person who,
from having been kind to her father, was entitled to

kindness and respect from her? Then there is an insinuation that Mr Grimsditch, the solicitor, whether a
relation or not I do not know, who was in the confidence of the father, had suggested as an expedient
that she should become the wife of that person who at
that time was in the carriage with her She is pressed
for an answer over and over again She hesitated, as
well she might do, to consent to marry a man who,
until that interval, she had never seen, and of whose
disposition she could not be aware, who might be a
man of great art, of great talent, of great attraction,
but who might be a man without that which is likely
to make life happy,—without principle, without regard
to truth, regardless of honour, would any woman be
drawn in at once hastily to give her assent under circumstances of that description? They reach Carlisle,
the stage before you reach the borders of Scotland
Does falsehood stop there? A communication is made
to her that her father is there,—that he must not be
seen, that Mr Grimsditch is there, but she must not
see him, that they are bailiffs who are round the
carriage, who are waiting for her father, that he had
made two attempts to cross the borders and get into
Scotland, that there would be no hope of his being
safe but by the consummation of the marriage, which
was stated to her as being the recommendation of Mr
Grimsditch That is the character of the transaction
till the period at which they reach Gretna.

It has been insinuated that, although she might remain perfectly virtuous and perfectly untouched so long

as she remained within the confines of this kingdom—there has been an insinuation as if that did not continue to be the case after she had crossed the water Now, let us see for one moment—supposing that to be the case—whether that does or does not recommend the individual who now claims from the court, on that ground, a mitigation of punishment I have already said that a regard to truth is one of the most important features in every man's character and conduct, and that no woman, with any degree of prudence, would associate herself with a man who is regardless of it No father would consent that a child would be associated with a man upon whom truth is not deeply impressed Now, to meet that insinuation, we will see whether there be or be not any additional circumstances that aggravate the case, or show the impropriety of the individual becoming the husband, and she becoming the wife of the party [*The learned judge then read from the report of the trial as follows* —"Mr Grimsditch, I assure you, upon my honour, that Miss Turner is the same Miss Turner that she was when I took her away—there has been no consummation of the marriage"] Now, that is true or false If true, my observation does not apply There is an insinuation as if it was not true, then the conspiracy is to associate her for life to a man who will declare, upon his honour, that one thing is true, when he knows that that is not the case There is also the letter to the brother, in which the same thing is stated I find there a solemn declaration, that " she and I have been as brother and sister." If that be true, then the observation fails, but if it be false, why what an aggravation would it have been that there should have been a conspiracy to associate her with a man who would give a solemn declaration, in words and in writing, to that which was not founded in truth !

There are two defendants upon the floor, one of them, William Wakefield, is younger than the other no doubt, but of an age in which, though, however attached he might be to his brother—however under the influence of his brother he might be—he was yet of an age in which he could not but know that what his brother was practising was calculated to bring disgrace upon his brother, and disgrace upon his family, and that it was calculated to destroy the comforts and ruin the prospects of those individuals who were the objects of this attempt. Though he was younger, yet he ought not to have lent himself a willing instrument,—ought he not at once to have made a communication to his friends, and to have taken care to have obstructed the completion of that which must involve his own family in a very considerable degree of degradation, and which was calculated to produce upon Miss Turner, and upon her parents, the greatest and bitterest distress, if she were to become the wife of an individual who had conducted himself in the way in which this individual has conducted himself. It was not merely that a child had married, of an age in which she could not judge for herself—that she was married without the knowledge and without the consent of her parents— but that she was married to a man who, from his conduct in this transaction, never could be looked upon with an eye of respect, and scarcely could expect to be looked upon with an eye of affection

The court has carefully considered the circumstances of this case—it recollects there has already been inflicted upon one of the individuals some period of punishment That individual has, in the address he has made here to us, contrasted this case with an earlier case before the court, but a case not of this malignity—a case in which it is true there was a conspiracy to bring about a marriage, but in which the circumstances did not amount to anything like the malignity that has been shown here, and in which the aggravation, of the parties being in a higher situation in life, did not occur This is a case in which one of the defendants is a person not young, but acquainted with what ought to be expected from a husband, and what may be expected from a wife many years below his own age

The court has carefully considered the circumstances of this case, and it doth order and adjudge that, for this offence, you Edward Gibbon Wakefield, be imprisoned in his Majesty's gaol of Newgate for the term of THREE YEARS, and that you, William Wakefield, be imprisoned in his Majesty's castle at Lancaster for THE SAME PERIOD.

LONDON
Printed by W Clowes, Stamford-street